Rise above it, Darling

DATE DUE

GAYLORD			PRINTED IN U.S.A.

THE STORY OF JOAN WHITE

Actor, Director, Producer, Teacher and (sometimes) Mother

TOLD BY HER DAUGHTER

Judy White Staber

In memory of
my late mother, Joan White
and for all the hardworking members of the Theatrical
Profession, past and present, who enrich our lives

"The story that is uncomfortable to tell is the one you should tell!"

Toni Morrison

"This above all to thine own self be true." (Hamlet)

William Shakespeare

Joan White in 1956

Chapters of Her Life

Prologue

JANUARY, 1947

Imagine being just shy of four years old and left on the doorstep of a house bigger than any you had ever seen before: a giant's house! an ogre's castle!

My earliest memory of Silverlands, the Actors' Orphanage, is arriving in a black taxi from Chertsey Station in Surrey with my sister Susannah, then aged seven, and being handed over to a forbidding man called Commander Aggitter on that doorstep by our actress mother, Joan White. I can recall no tears shed, no hugs or kisses goodbye, just the feeling of being dwarfed by the huge front entryway, the high ceilings and the very large people. Perhaps there's a remembered whiff of Je Reviens perfume as our Mother walked down the six stone steps and into the waiting taxi without a backward glance. We watched it disappear down the oh-so-long driveway. An older boy was summoned to take our small belongings upstairs to a room on the first floor.

My memories of those early years are spotty. I do remember beatings and other punishments. Corporal punishment was an accepted norm in British boarding schools and Silverlands was effectively a boarding school, despite being called The Actors Orphanage. In hindsight, most punishments were unnecessarily harsh until 1952, when there was a clean sweep of the staff and change was in the wind.

Founded in 1896, by concerned members of the theatrical profession, for the children of those less fortunate: actors who spent their lives acting in small theatres throughout England, where the wages were low and the lodgings even lower. Their children were dragged from town to town, poorly educated, poorly clothed, and ill-fed. Some were often orphaned or simply deserted by their parents. In 1896, a building was found and staff hired and, for the first thirty or forty years, the children were given a home and a rudimentary education. The charity was run by a committee of well-meaning, well-known theatre people, unaware of how poorly the children were cared for. In 1934, Noel Coward became president and remained so until 1956. He took a deep and continuing interest in the children. Little by little, he and others made it a better place.

In 1938, they purchased Silverlands, a 27-room neo-Georgian mansion that had fallen on hard times. It sat on 42 acres of land outside Chertsey. After the War broke out, Coward arranged for the children to be evacuated to America. Most returned in 1946, when Sue and I and other younger children were admitted. Until 1958, the house was home to about fifty children like myself, who weren't really orphans but, as the letterhead said "for children made destitute by the profession."

That letterhead listed the names of the theatrical luminaries on the Committee: Laurence Olivier, Richard Attenborough, Trevor Howard, Edith Evans and on and on and, most importantly, Noel Coward who, as President, spent a great deal of his time raising money to feed and clothe us. They visited on special days. But it was Dickie Attenborough, joining the Committee in 1951, who came regularly, chatted with each of us, and helped to turn our lives around.

But why did our mother leave us there?
We were neither destitute nor orphans.

Matey Irvine was Matron when we arrived and I remember her being firm but kindly; literally pouring salt on any wound, and dispensing cod liver oil as a cure for any illness. She and the Aggitters left in 1949, when I was six or seven. Until I was nine, staff members came and went. I don't remember their names. Punishments continued, but were never as harsh as the Aggitters.

In those early days, the older boys and girls could be pretty rough, too. The boys initiated new children in the Den of Death, and they had the Sneak's Chair. The older girls made us drink pee, do jobs for them, and put dead frogs and mice in our beds.

In 1951, Miss Berry and then Mr. Gordon arrived; our lives would never be the same again. Standing in the courtyard barefoot for talking after lights out; eating your left-over supper cold for breakfast; bread and water for a week for any infraction – those were Miss Berry's specialties. And she was complicit with Gordon. David Victor Gordon was a sadistic brute. He tortured one little boy to show the others he was boss. He made us run up to the house from the football field after games on Saturdays, saying, " last one up gets a beating" which pretty much guaranteed it would be a small girl. One day Brian, one of the older boys, deliberately came in last. Gordon was furious. He and Brian had a brutal fight in front of us all.

You might wonder if we told our parents. We didn't, because when Brian reported him, he was singled out for punishment. We learned to be stoic. Eventually, the head office heard about Gordon and Berry, and they were fired. They were only there for a year, but damage was done.

In retrospect, our lot wasn't always bad. We gave as good as we got and while often the punishment didn't fit the crime, sometimes it did. Many of the staff members were not unkind — bad apples are always the ones remembered. I'm sure that the labor pool, available to the Actors' Orphanage Fund after the War, had pretty slim pickings. It probably listed many ex-army officers. We became their next boot camp.

Early food was unmemorable. We said Grace at every meal, went to church on Sundays, and went to local schools. We had chores too, the boys mostly outdoors, raking and moving coal; the girls indoors, dusting, sweeping and helping in the kitchen. When second-hand clothes arrived, the older girls helped Matron sort them into piles by size and type. You didn't get clothes you liked, you got clothes that fit. Later, when we went to better schools, we wore uniforms.

After chores were done, we were free to amuse ourselves. The big bell rang summoning us indoors. The gong told us to wash our hands for meals. We had so many games: Kick the Can, Conkers, Murder in the Dark, oh! I could go on. We climbed trees and fell out of them. We had secret camps where we learned the facts of life. We made hobby horses out of sticks and string. Any piece of junk became a toy. And we read donated books. I spent hours up a favorite Chestnut tree with a book. We were inventive and resilient.

After Gordon and Berry, Mr. Fraser came. He taught us to grow vegetables and introduced us to chickens. With fresh eggs and vegetables, and a new cook, food improved. We also had "Chibby" nights, roasting chestnuts around a fire and singing.

Rationing ended and in 1954 Mr. Fraser left and David and Kirsten Slater were hired. For my last five years, they gave me a sense of worth and security which enabled me to pass my "O" levels and make something of myself. They also introduced us to new clothes and thicker mattresses. Liz, Janet, Sarah and I went with Kirsten Slater to Marks & Spencer's in Staines. I remember my pale blue twin-set, a grey wool skirt and three pairs of brand-new white cotton knickers (underpants).

We held a reunion in 2000 in Chertsey. About eighty former inmates came. I was standing with Liz, my oldest friend (who now lives near Kingston, NY) when Pam King saw us and said, "I used to bathe you." Pam, one of the big girls when we first went there in 1947 as little ones, recognized us after fifty years.

Silverlands was my home for twelve years and, mostly, I was happy there. You make your family where you find it and many of my "siblings" have become lifelong friends. I have survived, thrived and am living happily ever after because, as Liz says, "We'll be alright, Judibugs. We can survive anything. We went to Silverlands."

* * *

After leaving us at Silverlands, Mother was free to follow her life-long passion: the theatre. Susannah would stay under the care of the Actors Orphanage until 1954: first at Silverlands until 1950 and at the London Hostel until that closed in 1954. She soon joined Mother in Canada. I remained at Silverlands for twelve and a half years until 1959 and Silverlands closed. I flew to America never to return. Our mother continued acting and added directing, producing and teaching to her life's work until 1995, four years before she died.

People ask me how my mother felt leaving us there. I don't know.

This is not about my childhood. I have already written about that time: *Silverlands Growing Up at the Actors Orphanage.* (The Troy Book Makers ISBN 978-1-935534-846). This is about my mother, Joan White, and trying to understand her. She was a single mother in war-torn London with little money. She needed to earn a living the only way she knew how – acting. She heard about the Actors' Orphanage and Silverlands reopening. As a member of the profession in need, she qualified. I suspect, after a while, she got used to us being there. She came down on Visiting Sundays and we seemed well. We visited her at her Repertory engagements from time to time, and we spent holidays with our grandparents. Mother was a self-centered person, not unkind just totally absorbed in her life.

Now she was gone, I wanted to know her better and understand her.

* * *

Some years after she died in 1999, I began researching my mother's life. I first used the scrapbooks and photos my sister and I had inherited. I learned a lot from the long, page-filling obituaries in the major British newspapers. I went to the Mander and Mitchenson Theatre Collections and gathered reviews and stories about her and about my father A.P. Moore. I went on-line to the British Newspaper Archives, The Lincoln Center Theatre Collection and The New York Times archives, which have proved invaluable. I went through the records of her five years at The Berkshire Playhouse in Stockbridge, Massachusetts.

I then searched for, and received, information about her various repertory engagements, teaching engagements and life in the theatre in both North America and Great Britain. I wrote and received e-mails and letters from those who had known her and known of her.

I concluded she had had a busier, fuller and more varied life in the theatre than I had imagined. She had known and acted with many great and good actors and directors. She had taught hundreds of students. Into her eighties, she was still acting, as well as producing plays in churches and town halls all over England. She NEVER stopped working. Rarely did she make time for either of her three husbands or her daughters.

I obviously didn't know her very well and the more I gleaned, the more I came to appreciate her as a woman of the theatre: now that she was gone and I couldn't talk to her.

I did try when she was alive, so did my sister, but she would brush us off. If we asked about our father, she would get very emotional and would close down and say no more. In my research I found out why!

She wrote and performed a monologue, *Alive to Tell the Tale*, about her life. She had also written a deliberately incomplete remembrance of it all, before she retired to Denville Hall, the Actors' Retirement Home outside London. In her writing, she mentioned only briefly Susannah and me. Her three husbands get short shrift, too. Although incomplete, these remembrances have been useful, especially for the stories of her long-ago childhood and schooldays: memories Susannah and I never knew about. Her childhood was alluring and colorful; she spent all of World War I in neutral Portugal where her father was a chief engineer of the Eastern Telegraph Company.

I decided to write about her life because I believe her story gives a true picture of her commitment to the theatre in the 20th century. She influenced and inspired many people over many years, both as an actress, teacher and director. She gave back to her profession through her English Theatre School and The Next Stage Company.

Inevitably, once Sue and I were grown, our lives meshed with hers somewhat. And I have included those times. Both of us experienced theatre life. We both married and became mothers, with very different results.

I realize this biography has a different slant, with her life uncovered and discovered by her daughter rather than "as told to…" This is not a memoir, except where I, the author, am directly involved. This is a biography of a woman who happened to be my mother. A woman who was fully immersed in her profession, often to the detriment of her daughters. When I began, I was only dimly aware of the depth and breadth of her achievements.

Most people only remember the names of a few outstanding and well-publicized stars. Yet it is the work of talented and dedicated performers like my mother, working constantly in major and minor roles, and as mentors and teachers, who support a vibrant theatre world.

Unlike most mothers and wives of her day, she knew little of the life of childrearing and housekeeping, beginning with her unusual childhood. She was a force unto herself and any regrets she may have had, she kept to herself.

Hers was a fascinating life, especially to anyone wanting to know about the life of a strong-willed woman who was hard-working in both the British and North American worlds of theatre, for sixty-five years.

Here it is.

Judy White Staber
Old Chatham, New York

Chapter One

CHILDHOOD AND A MIXED EDUCATION
1909 – 1929

*"Believe it or not, I am an Egyptian. Having come from a long
line of hard-drinking English lawyers, clerics and soldiers on
my father's side and on my mother's, a healthy middle-class trade
family, I naturally assumed I was British to my very short back-
bone. But in 1956, American Immigration told me,
"Lady, you're an Egyptian!"*

So begins my mother Joan White's monologue about her life in the theatre, "Alive to Tell the Tale." While her adult life was consumed with
acting, and later with directing and teaching, there was more to her story.
She passed away in 1999 after sixty-five years as a woman of the theatre.
This followed a colorful childhood in neutral Portugal during World War
One; as a teenager at an English boarding school; and later studying at
the Royal Academy of Dramatic Art.

At sixteen months my mother Joan, with her mother Kathleen, left
Alexandria aboard a cargo boat to join her father Henry at his next
posting for the Eastern Telegraph Company in Carcavelos, Portugal.
When aboard any ship, Kathleen was often seasick. She always took
to her bunk on the family's many voyages. Young Joan was put in care
of a ship's officer, who probably spoiled her. Joan wrote she could still
remember the boat and the voyage, but she remembered nothing of her
first trip to England.

Joan's first real recollection was of Eastern Telegraph Company
housing in Portugal and of being hoisted up to look at her new baby
sister, Audrey, born November 25th 1912. She remembered *"a frightful*

little thing with jet-black hair sticking through a new lace bonnet." She was annoyed that Audrey wasn't a boy.

A week later, she turned three on December 3rd, but as there had been a recent birth in the family it was not considered proper to have a Children's Party: one more reason to resent the new arrival. As a sop, she was allowed to invite a 'special friend' to tea. His name was Geoffrey Perkins, and he arrived with great excitement bearing a doll's tea set and shouting *"Cups for you!"* After which he asked her to marry him. The first of many proposals!

Joan lived most of her early childhood in Portugal. Henry White, her father, had worked for the Eastern Telegraph Company (now Cable & Wireless) since he was sixteen. From cabin boy, he worked his way up: first working on the ships that laid the great communication cables across the oceans; then postings to remote Atlantic islands to receive the incoming cables or connect outgoing ones. He spent months at a time on St. Helena, Ascension and Tristan da Cunha, in the middle of the Atlantic far from civilization. Finally, at thirty, having wooed Kathleen Mabel Beach when home on leave, he wed her in 1906. As a married man. he now had shore postings and was promoted to engineer. By the outbreak of World War One in 1914, he was Chief Engineer at the Carcavelos Station.

After Audrey's birth, they hired a nursery governess, Jane Jenner, whom they all adored. Miss Jenner soon became part of their lives and was the only employee never to do anything wrong in Kathleen's eyes.

In July 1914, Henry was due for furlough, a decently long leave every two years, and the family sailed for England. The voyage home was aboard a German liner and, while war had not yet been declared, there was plenty of tension aboard ship. The ship's band played the German National anthem, *The Double Eagle*, as it steamed out of Oporto. Joan was four and a half and Audrey, twenty months. It was a dangerous time. War would be declared against Germany by Great Britain on August 4th.

Once aboard, Kathleen had retired to her cabin and Henry spent time wherever men spend their time on liners. Jane Jenner dressed the children in their navy-blue sweaters, long pants, blue reefer coats and sailor hats, and went on deck with them. Shy Audrey stayed with her, while Joan made new friends indiscriminately.

One day, eluding Jane, she became friendly with a kindly German professor and his wife. One day, the professor picked her up and held her out over the sea. She could see the green waves churning beneath her. She lay rigid in his outstretched arms, too frightened to cry. His wife gently begged him not to tease. All her life she disliked being teased, and I'm sure it went back to that professor, as well as a strong dislike of all things German.

It was dark as they steamed past the Isle of Wight. Dawn was just breaking when they reached Southampton. The band again played *The Double Eagle* and Kathleen reappeared. Joan remembered the sunrise over the sea approaching Southampton and later, the unaccustomed green grass seen from the train to Wiltshire.

She later wrote down what she recalled about their stay near Salisbury, where they had rented lodgings close to her grandmother Beach's house.

> *"On Sunday we were taken to a nearby place called "Church." There Audrey and I found ourselves shut in high boxes and we played with toys on the floor while our parents stood above and sang songs. This seemed, at the time, very boring.*
>
> *One day, Father rose excitedly from the breakfast table to show us our first airplane. It looked like two enormous planks of wood with sticks in between. Later, with Jane our governess, we walked up to the main road. I remember holding onto Audrey's high pram and waving to the soldiers going off to the War in open lorries, singing and looking so happy as they drove past. War seemed all fun then, and full of adventure: healthy men singing in the bright August sunshine as their buses sped by in a cloud of dust that would leave the hedgerows a grayish-green along the chalky white roads."*

Somewhere about this time the serenity of the English countryside must have got into Joan's blood.

> *"I was reminded of it, years later, when I looked through the windows of Oliver Messel's lovely set for Christopher Fry's play "The Lady's not for Burning" and saw that same 1914 countryside that I remembered. It has never been quite the same since the Great War came. As Jim Cartwright says in his play "Bed," 'There's no more room anymore for a tra la la...'".*

Grandmother Beach was almost eighty and considered that children should be seen only when she sent for them. They didn't stay at her house on the Wilton Road where she lived with her two maids, Maria and Lucy Ford and her eldest daughter Aunt Mary.

When my grandmother, Kathleen, was a girl, they had lived in a big Georgian house with her three brothers, and her two sisters, Mary and Ethel. A brother had died in childhood before Kathleen was born. Thus, she was the seventh child. Her father William Beach was also a seventh child. As the seventh child of the seventh child she, supposedly, had second sight and was able to predict disasters, storms or... unsuitable companions for her daughters. A broken romance would produce from Kathleen, *"I told you so."* Or *"I knew instinctively this would happen."*

William Beach was a Salisbury cutler who supplied the P & O ocean liners with all their cutlery. After his death, with her children now adults, his wife Amelia Sabina had moved into a little ivy-covered house. Behind the house was a lawn for the children to play on surrounded by a wall topped by white stone cupids, who solemnly supervised their games.

The house was full of large, dark furniture. Most memorable to the children was a high-backed mahogany sort of armchair with tapestry cushions. It stood in an alcove.

Sometimes a red velvet curtain was drawn across. Then the children were shooed away. This was a commode for Grandmother Beach's private use and they were not allowed to use it. When the children had to "go", they used a chamber pot in the side kitchen.

Painted inside this potty was a huge eye and the words, *"I See What You Do!"* At least, that's what Maria, Grandmother's maid, told them.

Much of the furniture was too big for the house, recalling earlier wealthier days. It had a musty smell, not unpleasant but very evocative. Years later, Joan wrote,

> *"I occasionally came across a piece of fabric that held this scent, and I would be transported back to my smocked frock days in August 1914."*

Grandfather Beach's top hat hung in the hall, to imply there was a man in the house.

Each day, Grandmother Beach sat by her dining-room hearth, her Bible beside her on a little mahogany table. She was upright and regal in her black dress, with tucks down to the waist, hung with jet beads and a gold watch chain. She always wore stiff white cuffs and a small stiff white collar turned down over her high black neckband. A silver chatelaine hung from her waist, symbol of her position in life. Her hair was snow white, worn parted in the middle and topped by a white widow's cap with flowing tails.

She had a good sense of humor, but was quite a martinet to her children, especially her daughter Mary.

In 1914, Grandmother Beach was still able to go out for drives. Dismore, her old coachman, would be summoned to drive the family in his horse-drawn landau up to the Salisbury Race Plain. He now had his own motorcar hire service, but he always insisted in driving "the old lady" in the landau. Joan loved these outings. She was allowed to sit up with him on the box and sometimes hold the reins.

A letter from Mary Beach came after their trip home to England:

April 25, 1915

My dear little Joan,

How are you after such a long absence? I expect you enjoy the sea and the sands, and digging castles — it is easier than digging in a garden, isn't it, and cutting off my dead flowers. Do you remember Mr. Wright? He has left us and is no longer the gardener. Do you think he had to join up and fight the war? This summer, without his help, and yours, I shall be very hard worked.

I send you and baby lots of kisses and hugs with love from
Aunt Mary

Aunt Mary was Joan's godmother. She had visited Egypt in 1910 to attend her christening. While there, she became engaged to a charming, consumptive man. Mary and her beau, Sidney Cross, were to remain engaged for nine years. The family suspected that Grandmother Beach insisted on this long engagement to keep Mary at her beck and call. It says much for their devotion that Mary and Sidney Cross stayed faithful all those years even though, it was later learned, Mr. Cross was already married.

My only memory of Aunt Mary was going with Audrey when I was fifteen, to visit her in St. John's Wood, London. Ringing the

bell, a key was thrown down. Upstairs at her flat, Audrey opened the door. There was a strong smell of gas.

"Quick" said Audrey, *"don't light a match."* Audrey dashed into the kitchen and turned off the gas stove and then raced to the windows to open them wide. Aunt Mary sat in her chair, oblivious to the kerfuffle, and said, rather querulously, *"What's all the fuss? Aren't you going to say 'Hallo?'"*

Visits to England always meant two Cathedral cities: Salisbury and Wells. Salisbury Cathedral had a personal connection: Grandfather Beach had been a boy chorister in the Cathedral choir. Strolling by the Cathedral in the evenings, past the houses around the Close, the girls could spy on the rich people at their tea, while picking daisies for daisy chains on the Cathedral lawn. Great walls guarded the Cathedral and its Close. Leading in from the town were Harnham Gate, St. Anne's Gate and the much-used High Street Gate where Grandfather Beach's shop had been. Motor cars, to this day, cannot enter the Close without permission.

Wells Cathedral in Somerset was more interesting to Audrey, who told me about its two wonderful clocks: both, when the hour struck, activated two knights in full armor fighting a duel. A moat surrounded the Bishop's Palace with elegant white swans, who swam to the Great Gateway and with their beaks and tugged at a bell-rope for their food. Every leave, the family went Wells to visit 'the five Aunts'. They were the last of their father's Somerset relations, his deceased father's sisters, and they always expected a visit. Every time the family arrived in Wells to see these venerable ladies, there seemed to be one less than the original five. Their father had been the Magistrate of Williton, Somerset. Joan and Audrey remembered them all fondly.

The mystery was the missing grandmother. They knew that Henry's father had died in 1901, but no one said anything about his mother. There were no pictures of her, and no one mentioned her name. Was she dead? When Joan and Audrey begged a great-aunt to tell them about her, they were firmly informed,

"We don't talk about your grandmother."

It wasn't until Joan was seventeen that her father told her why:

"My father, William White met and married Emma Lee Byron Harril who, I was told, was half Romany — a Gypsy." He went on, *"They were married in St. George's Hanover Square in London. He took her back to the quiet, and rather dull, little town of Williton in Somerset where he practiced law. There she bore him three children: first myself and then my two sisters, Helen and Ethel. My father was a heavy drinker and, after eight years, our mother ran off with a 'hot-headed Irish doctor,' never to be heard from again. That's all I know and what I was told. I don't remember her except she was rather pretty."*

Some of that is true, but thanks to genealogy, we now know the truth.

All our lives, since we were small children, Susannah and I were told that our grandmother, Emma Lee's mother was a Gypsy. When I was growing up, my Grandfather distrusted the Gypsies when they came every spring in their colorful wagons near our grandparent's village, South Moreton. When questions were asked by enquiring small minds, we were told that she had left Grandfather and his sisters when they were 8, 6 and 4, and we should not ask any more questions.

I discovered that Emma Lee was not a Gypsy child, and while she did run off with the Irish doctor, leaving her children to the care of her alcoholic husband and his FIVE spinster sisters, she probably had those six very good reasons.

Joan wrote, *"No wonder he was such a good father to me and Audrey – and so understanding when we suffered broken marriages!"*

Audrey's husband had divorced her in World War Two. She had a long love affair but never married again. Joan was to marry three times. She would voluntarily give up her children, at almost 8 and just 4, to the care of the Actors Orphanage. My grandparents were unhappy about that decision. I think they were embarrassed by it. In all my holidays with them, while they were loving and caring, they never once asked me about life in the Orphanage. Nor did they visit me there.

But I digress.

Back in Portugal in 1914 all was peaceful. Lisbon lay spread out over its hills and down to the quayside, the windows of the houses winking in the evening sun. Belem Tower stood sentinel on the water's edge from where, in 1497, Vasco da Gama had set sail around the Cape of Good Hope to India. The sardine fishing fleet — their pearly sails reflected in the smooth Tagus River basin — seemed quite unconscious of the turmoil brewing in western Europe or the blood about to be spilled on Flanders Field.

On their return from England, the family moved back to Carcavelos, southwest of Lisbon on the road to Estoril. In 1914, the long sandy beach was often deserted. Their new home was called "The Elms" probably because of several straggly elm trees. It was part of "married quarters" and was completely outfitted with Company furnishings. Every cup, plate, fork and spoon bore the Eastern Telegraph Company's monogram. It was woven into the curtains and even carved on the furniture. Joan wondered how she and Audrey had avoided being tattooed with it.

But she wrote that the house itself was good — as far as children were concerned. It had nice long bannisters to slide down, and the bathroom had an inside window for a curious child to peek in. She remembered:

> In the drawing room there was an upright piano, also inlaid with the Company monogram. In those long-ago days, the family and friends sang and made their own entertainment. Father rather fancied himself as a singer of Herman Lohr lyrics with Mother accompanying him in flamboyant style; head flung back, hands bouncing off the keys. She also sang a little. One was a Victorian song called, "Love Was Once a Little Boy," which was quite blameless, but given an indelicate twist, was a great hit for me at parties later on. My parents didn't know how useful their evening soirees were to be for the child hanging over the bannister in my all-in-ones, darting back to the nursery when Miss Jenner came looking for me.
>
> The house had double doors between the dining room and the library. These became a small theatre setting for my first shows, with

a cast made up of Company children. Bluebeard was my most success-
ful production. I persuaded my chubby little sister to play the parson.
In a deep husky voice, Audrey solemnly announced, "Those
whom God hath joined together, let no man put us under." After
which she ripped off her father's reversed collar and fled – never to
grace the boards again. I, of course, played Fatima.
"If you can't play the lead in your own nursery, where can you?"
This was the beginning of my life on the wobbly theatrical ladder.

Outside in the front garden was a large, shady laurel tree. Here the
vegetable *vendedor* would tether his burros to rest in the midday sun. Joan
and Audrey would hoist themselves up and sit like eastern potentates,
their chubby legs stretched out over the panniers laden with fruit and
vegetables. Often the *vendedor* would let them stay on his sleepy burros
while he called at various houses around the village.

Forty years later, when Joan was filming *"The Last of the Mahicans"*
for CBC in Canada, she was required sit on a horse. This burro-
riding experience proved useful when asked if she had ever ridden
a horse, although not altogether accurate.

Audrey grew into a shy and silent child who hated the 'social life' and
went to children's parties under protest. Shortly after arriving at a party,
she retired to a corner to suck her thumb, hoisting up her frock and twid-
dling her knickers button.

Joan wrote, *"I don't know how she managed when elastic came*
into use! 'Inhibitions', 'Problems' and 'Allergies' were unused words
in our family, the prevailing philosophy being 'Faith in God' and
'Common Sense.'"

Audrey became a wonderful and caring woman. I was shy as a child,
too, and like Audrey, that probably came from having two extro-
verts in the family; a mother and an older sister. They were enough
to knock me into a corner and twiddle my metaphorical knickers
button. I think their father hoped that, by teaching his daughters
to 'Come in out of the wet', they wouldn't do too badly in the world.
They would later learn the world was full of rising damp.

However, unlike Audrey, Joan reveled in parties; so much so she got wound up the day before, couldn't sleep, and was over-excited when she got there.

Henry White was a valuable man to the Eastern Telegraph Company. His job was to make sure all communications were sent safely to their correct destinations. During World War I, in neutral Portugal, I can only imagine how very important it was for all that information to quickly reach such far-flung places as New York City, Rio de Janiero, Capetown, and even Darjeeling in India.

The Eastern Telegraph Company cable connections to the rest of the world were centered at Carcavelos. Important, often vital, information was transmitted by British headquarters from a cable station in the tiny village of Porthcurno on the tip of Cornwall, via a deep-sea cable directly to this southernmost corner of Portugal on the Atlantic.

I was watching Penelope Keith's series on *"England's Hidden Villages."* **Devon and Cornwall featured Porthcurno and showed the former tiny cable station, which is now a museum. I was proud to know that my Grandfather had been an important part of all that.**

Attaching an underwater cable was a major undertaking, and a good excuse for a picnic. The routine was always the same. When the new cable was brought ashore to be hitched up to the landlines, the cable ship coming as near to the shore as sea depths permitted. From its stern the cable would be paid out and attached to a compliant team of oxen who, encouraged by the picnickers, would haul it to the little cable house. There it would be connected to outgoing lines. Shortly thereafter someone, somewhere in the world, would get an important message.

My grandparents loved parties and Kathleen enjoyed considerable social success. She was a pretty woman and very athletic, winning trophies for her triumphs on the tennis courts. Joan remembered one gay occasion when her parents were going to a fancy-dress Ball in the Company Mess. Before they left, they paraded in the nursery: Kathleen, immaculate in top hat and tails looking quite svelte as the Music Hall star, Vesta Tilley, and Henry, with his pink round face, dressed up as a baby doll with frilly knickers and a big floppy hat. He won first prize.

Henry was known around his world as 'Pinky' White. Joan always thought it was because of to his pink face. But not so! Years later, when she and Susannah were doing theatre publicity in Manchester, their lunchtime host recognized Henry's name.

"Not Pinky White's daughter?" he asked incredulously.

"Well…yes!" Joan replied cautiously, *"Did you know him?"*

"No, not personally…but in the Eastern Telegraph Company his Pink Gins were legendary."

(Pink Gin is chilled Gin with a dash of Angostura Bitters and a slice of lemon). Henry loved his pink gins. He also loved buns, hence his other nickname 'Bunny'. Nothing to do with rabbits, he consumed lots of Bath Buns when courting Kathleen.

In Portugal, the family had a 'lucky' war. There was some excitement when a torpedoed ship washed up on the coast, but otherwise the children played 'hospital' interminably and all the ladies in the village had Red Cross working parties. Occasionally someone arrived from England with the latest patriotic songs and they sang: "If you were the Only Girl in the World" and "Pack up Your Troubles in your old Kit Bag." Later on, Joan thought that her father felt cheated of active involvement in the war. But the powers-that-be decided that he had far more value to Great Britain dealing with the underwater cables. So, thank goodness for that!

My grandfather was one of the most influential people in my childhood. From him I too learned "to come in out of the wet"; to respect other people's opinions, no matter who they were. And to work hard and be happy at what I did. He used to tell me, *"I'd rather you be a happy dustman, than an unhappy millionaire!"*

In 1916, Jane Jenner decided that she must return to England. Her brothers had been called up, and she wanted to see them before they went to France. The family hoped she would come back, but she never did. She later joined the staff of the National Provincial Bank (one of the first women to do so) and, remaining with them after the War, she rose to quite dizzying heights — for a woman at that time.

In 1918 there were persistent rumors of an Armistice. That autumn, Henry and Joan noticed the Union Jack flying in the breeze with a knotted German flag hanging upside down beneath it.

"Look Jo, look! We must have won!" Henry cried, and he did a little dance. Then more soberly he added,

"Damn decent of the old man to have done that."

"What old man do you mean, Father?" Joan asked, *"and what has he done?"*

"The Boss," he replied, *"He's married to a German woman — she's back in Berlin — nice of him to be British and knot his wife's flag."*

He hurried away to break the news and she followed him back home. The whole thing was beyond her — a knotted flag! What strange things excited a grown-up's mind! Then the neighbors came in and Portuguese Champagne flowed.

In the late spring of 1919, Henry was given a long leave, to make up for the many years of war, and again they set sail for England — this time on a British ship. On arrival, they headed for Shropshire to stay with Kathleen's sister Ethel, her husband Percy Stratton and their small son Macklin.

The two families were together on November 11, 1918, when the Peace was finally signed. Beacons were lit on every hill, as they had been in 1588 when the Spanish Armada was defeated. That night the rains poured down. That did not deter Henry and Uncle Percy, who took the children out of their nice warm beds and dragged or carried them up the sodden hillside to see the flickering tiny lights on far off hills. Shivering in the damp night air, they told Joan, Audrey and Macklin that the lights signified "Peace."

Macklin Stratton became a distinguished Harley Street Ear, Nose and Throat specialist. After my mother left for America, while I was still at Silverlands, Macklin and his wife Joan lived nearby. Their home "Langtons" had a the most wonderful garden. On Visiting Sundays, they would invite me to tea, and there I learned to love gardening.

News now came that they would not be returning to Portugal, but would be proceeding to the Azores via Lisbon and Madeira, home of the eponymous wine. With Americans having joined the war in 1917, a more direct cable connection to New York and Canada, made more sense from the Azores, and Henry White was the man to supervise the job.

Joan was now nine, Audrey was seven, and both quite illiterate. They could read and indeed they read all kinds of books voraciously, and they were both fluent in Portuguese, but their spelling, handwriting and mathematics were sorely deficient. Their father contended that travel and getting acquainted with people of all nationalities was a far, far better education for "Life" than being left to molder in some boarding school in England. I suspect that All Hallows School in Honiton, Devon, where he had been sent after his mother left, was a rather lonely, sad experience.

However, Kathleen insisted that a governess would have to be found. So before leaving England, they went to Bournemouth to find one.

In those days, Bournemouth was a dreary seaside towns, full of pine trees, dogs, and invalids in bath chairs. Many English governesses, who had had good livings in German households, were now unemployed. Kathleen inserted advertisements, and finally a suitable lady was chosen. She was the daughter of a retired colonel of a good, but impecunious, family. The right age – forty: old enough to be reliable. Her credentials from an aristocratic German family were excellent. Her manner was quiet, her talents good, her clothing simple and severe. Her name was Boodle, Miss Boodle.

The children were impressed. She played the piano beautifully; her French and German were better than their Portuguese and English; she was erudite, interesting and tidy. Joan and Audrey became unusually well behaved. Even their parents were noticeably more punctual and more conventional. Audrey, a solemn, silent child who missed nothing, said, *"Humph, it won't last!"*

The weeks went by. Then they boarded the ship. The luggage was in the hold.

There was the hustle and rush of 'casting off.' Joan felt the joy of leaving England and the thrill as the ship pulled away from the quay! Cabins were allotted. Henry shared with another man, also going to Lisbon. Kathleen and Audrey would be together. That left Joan with Miss Boodle.

That first night at sea Joan undressed, washed as much as necessary, and climbed up the ladder to the top bunk, leaving the bottom bunk for Boodle. She switched off the little bunk light and snuggled down. After a while, the cabin door opened softly. Joan sat up. Boodle crept in, impeccably dressed in her good navy-blue suit, hard little hat and gloves.

"Lie down and go to sleep!" she said, *"I'm going to get undressed."*

Joan lay half way down, but kept watch.

"Turn over and don't look!" Miss Boodle repeated sharply.

Joan snuggled down, but didn't turn over. Why shouldn't she look? Her curiosity was aroused. She had often watched her mother undress, there was nothing unusual about it. Her mother just removed garment after garment (usually flinging them on a chair), put on her nightgown, went to the bathroom for her ablutions and finally hopped into bed. So, why couldn't she watch Boodle? She peeked over the edge of the bunk. Boodle was unbuttoning her blouse. She turned and saw Joan peeking,

"Lie down at once!" she commanded, *"it is very rude to watch a person go to bed."*

Joan lay down and wondered. Perhaps Miss Boodle was different from other ladies; perhaps there was something odd about her body. Why else the secrecy? She took another peek. Boodle had her back to Joan and was struggling into a large white tent-like nightgown. She proceeded to wriggle about inside the 'tent', shedding her garments discreetly as she went. This was immensely amusing to Joan, who wondered if she had a hairy chest, or perhaps she unscrewed a false leg at night. Joan eventually fell asleep. She never discovered the hairy chest, but she found out about the wooden leg!

After a five-day voyage, the ship sailed up the River Tagus to Lisbon. They had to disembark onto tugboats which would to take them ashore. They went down the gangway. The tugs were bobbing in the swell. A brawny Portuguese sailor leaned across and lifted them each onto the boat. Joan found all this quite exciting and Henry, carrying Audrey, managed the exercise perfectly. But when Miss Boodle got there, modesty overtook her. She would have none of the sailor's arms. *"Nein, nein!"* she cried, and, attempting to bridge the gap nearly did the splits between the liner and the tug.

Fortunately, the sailor leaped onto the gangway and, clasping Boodle to his massive chest, transferred her safely to the tug. But not before Joan had verified that neither leg was wooden. Miss Boodle stood, pulling down her rumpled clothes and clucking like a flustered hen!

The following day they learned that the boat for the Azores, was not ready. Henry decided to take them all to the Lisbon Zoo.

My mother and Audrey were so lucky. He was such a good father, spending time with his children. I often wished I'd known my own father.

The day was sunny as they sauntered past the animal cages. When they reached the monkey house, Kathleen and Audrey went ahead, while Henry, Miss Boodle and Joan stopped to enjoy a marital argument between a large gorilla and his missus. Suddenly, the male scraped up a handful of muck and flung it at his partner. It missed her, hit the wire of the cage and showered the unfortunate Miss Boodle. Henry sprang immediately to her assistance, wiping her down with his own pocket-handkerchief, and making the sort of noises that grooms make currying horses. From that moment on Mr. Henry White could do no wrong.

The next day they boarded the San Miguel that sailed between the Portuguese islands of the Azores, eight hundred miles west of Lisbon. The first port of call was Funchal on Madeira, not part of the Azores and known for its wine ("Have some Madeira, m'dear" sang Michael Flanders lecherously). They didn't disembark but watched the native boys dive for the coins tossed into the crystal-clear water.

They arrived at last at Sao Miguel, the largest of the nine islands of the Azores and spent the first nine months in a house in Ponta Delgada. Behind the garden was a terraced hill with a fine view of the town and the Atlantic Ocean beyond. Camellia trees, as well as orange, lemon and banana trees, grew on the terraces and there was an intoxicating smell of tobacco plants.

The people of Sao Miguel were mostly Portuguese. Both British and American Consuls were based in Ponta Delgada. An elderly lady, Miss Brown, ran The English Hotel, which catered to travelers changing ships for places north, south, east and west. There were no other English children. Joan and Audrey were left to themselves and Miss Boodle.

Audrey was left-handed. At that time, this was considered socially unacceptable. During her lessons, her left hand was tied behind her back and she was forced to write with her right hand. No wonder she hated school. For the rest of her life, her handwriting was an untidy scrawl. Blame probably could be laid to Boodle and her desire to win approval from their father. He probably didn't care which hand his daughter used.

Boodle was with them in their first home but, within a few months, she succeeded in irritating not only Kathleen, but also her idol, Henry

White. He finally decided that she must go. He had suffered innumerable adoring messages left on his desk, under the guise of thanking him for the loan of a stamp or gift of a cigarette. He was immune to these advances, but finally his temper outgrew his patience, and he requested Miss Boodle's presence in his study in order to give her notice.

Joan and her mother heard Miss Boodle pleading,

"You have always been so kind to me, dear Mister White...I wish I could say the same for..."

Henry cut her short saying *"Miss Boodle, I am sorry to say that I have never disliked anyone as cordially as I dislike you!"*

No more was said. Poor lady! Poor Henry! He must have been shaking. Joan noted in a journal,

> *"Years later, I was reminded of this incident when a small boy of three or so was introduced to me by his gushing mother, "Say hello to Auntie Joan."*
>
> *He looked at me gravely and with dignity said, "I can't like you."*
>
> *I wasn't offended and thought how delightful it would be if everyone could occasionally express themselves so candidly."*

And she often did: to her daughters, her students or some unfortunate actor she was directing. She was often 'Mrs. Candour', when she felt the need.

Shortly after Boodle's departure, the family moved into Miss Brown's hotel and education was postponed until a new governess came from England. Meanwhile, Sao Miguel was full of picnics and surprises. 1920 was the start of the United States Prohibition. When American ships docked in Ponta Delgada, the streets of the town were filled with drunken sailors.

Miss Brown gave a dance for the officers of an American battleship. It was a very smart affair. Joan and Audrey, in their buttoned-up pajamas, managed to worm their way along the passage on their bellies to peek between the legs of the watching servants.

They were spotted and dragged onto the dance-floor, two small girls in pajamas waltzing with large, slightly tipsy, American officers, their parents unable to stop them.

In San Miguel, Henry bought his first car, an open Ford Tourer, christened Maria, after his mother-in-law's servant Maria Ford. It seated six comfortably: three behind and three in front. A picnic was planned. Kathleen invited the American Vice Consul, George Mann, who drove them to the Town Square to pick up Henry at his office.

George went to get Henry, who came out, putting on his gloves, and jumped into the driver's seat. He wore white driving gloves to his dying day, *"so the chap behind me can see my signals,"* he would say. As these were both frequent and erratic, *"the chap behind"* often needed fair warning and quick reflexes.

Gloves on, Henry grasped the steering wheel and trod on the accelerator. With a violent jerk forward, they sped round and round the Square. After circling the Square three times, he managed to find the brake, and brought the poor car to a shuddering halt. Kathleen was exhausted from screaming, *"Stop, Bunny!"* at the top of her voice. George was then urged to take over the driving for the rest of the day.

George, or "Uncle George" as Joan and Audrey called him, was the American Vice Consul on these tiny Atlantic islands and probably had very little to do. He spent a lot of time squiring the lovely Kathleen White around: playing tennis or cards, going for boat rides, visiting such sights as there were and…it was intimated in the family, that there was also intimacy. He does show up a lot in photos and Grandfather was rather busy all the time.

In October of that year, they transferred to another island, Faial; a volcanic island with beaches of black sand. Hedges of blue hydrangeas separated the fields.

In Faial, a replacement for the banished Boodle arrived. She stayed for six months, incapable of teaching and prone to fits of giggling when meeting unmarried staff. After she left, Joan and Audrey were again in the care of their much-loved Portuguese maids.

The sisters were bored with their two-year sojourn in Faial. For some snobbish reason, they never mixed with Portuguese children and were lonely for children of their own age. Joan longed for an English school and enrolled in a Girl Guide correspondence course. Finally, in 1921, they again set sail for England, and this furlough proved much more promising.

All through their childhood, Joan wrote, it was their father who took them to the Zoo, to the theatre or for a drive. He was clearly

the active parent. Their mother, when mentioned by Joan, seemed distant and I wonder how present she was in their young lives. She had maids and governesses to do the child minding, the laundry, cooking and teaching.

In England, they paid their usual visits to Salisbury and Wells. This time, in Salisbury they lodged with Miss Wellington. Her house was so old that it had no plumbing upstairs. Big copper cans of boiling water had to be carried up to the bedrooms for the girls to be bathed in round hipbaths.

Grandmother Beach was now eighty-five. For some years now, she had refused to leave her fireside chair. She welcomed the family fondly, but she preferred to have one child at a time join her for lunch. The girls would toss a coin, and the winner had lunch in the kitchen with Maria.

Joan remembered playing with Grandmother Beach's jewelry while Maria dressed her. Joan watched her being laced into corsets and a flannel petticoat before the black widow's dress and white cap were donned. This came in handy later, when learning 'how-to put-on period costumes'. Across the street there was a lunatic asylum. From an upstairs window, the girls could see wild-looking ladies behaving oddly. All these experiences Joan would take with her for the many roles she was to play. Grandmother Amelia Sabina Beach died after they left that February.

This visit was followed by a brief stay in Wells, but the great-aunts had gradually died off, like withered flowers, and only Aunt Emily remained.

From Wells, the family went to London. From there, Joan would visit possible boarding schools. They had rented a flat on Richmond Hill where they could easily get to Central London.

Joan remembers meeting Corrie and Carrie Slade-Jones, who would become her guardians while her parents were abroad.

"Corrie was a sweet-tempered businessman and his wife, Carrie, became a wonderful influence through my teenage years."

Carrie and Corrie's daughter, Violet, was head girl at St. Helen's School in Northwood, Middlesex. In the autumn of 1922, Joan was almost thirteen, and her parents decided to send her there as a boarder.

Somehow, despite her lack of formal schooling, Joan passed the entrance exam. Soon she would meet girls of her own age at last, and get away from all the "Eastern Telegraph Company" living that she had come to dislike. She was taken to Liberty's in Regent Street to be fitted for a green school tunic, a blazer and other uniform necessaries.

By 1922, the War was long over and Joan boarded at St. Helen's. Once again, the Eastern Telegraph Company transferred Henry White, this time to Gibraltar, and the family moved there with Audrey, almost ten, and another governess. They would remain there for the next nine years. In 1931, Henry retired at fifty-five, after almost forty years with The Eastern Telegraph Company, from cabin boy at sixteen to chief engineer at fifty-five. He would go home to England at last.

I knew and loved my Grandfather when I was growing up. On holiday from the orphanage, I spent many hours with him as he taught me how to fix a puncture and replace a tire on my bicycle and to tie all kinds of knots. He showed me the constellations, told me the names of birds and wildflowers. He would recite many songs and poems. Yet, while he got me first-day covers from St. Helena, Ascencion and Tristan da Cunha for my stamp collection, he never told me about his travels or his work for Eastern Telegraph....but then I never asked.

The school holidays at Christmas and Easter were too brief for Joan to join her family in Gibraltar. She spent them with Aunt Carrie's family or with her Aunt Mary, who with her mother's death was finally able to marry her bigamist, Sidney Cross.

When the summer holidays arrived, those English children who had parents on the Rock of Gibraltar were gathered together on a P & O liner and enjoyed a great time at sea for four or five days — seasickness permitting.

The great Rock itself didn't look like one of the British Empire's most important possessions, but it was. Bristling with guns in its fortified caves, it was one of the strongest garrisons in the world. Gibraltar had belonged to the United Kingdom for more than two hundred years —the two centuries when Britannia truly did rule the waves.

Gibraltar was a wonderful place for eight weeks' summer holidays. But even in Gibraltar in the nineteen twenties, the British were a snobbish lot. There were strong class distinctions: the Army, the Navy and ... the others. If you were a member of the Forces (Officers Only), you were invited to Government House or the Admiralty for parties. Some restaurants and beaches were banned to native Gibraltarians. Notices were put up as shocking as segregation notices in the American South. An English child did not play with the 'native' children. In fact, English children didn't play with other English children until the parents had observed the formalities of calling and card leaving.

The family lived on Europa Road, on the west side of the Rock. To watch the sunrise in the east was a special adventure. Joan, when home on holiday, and Audrey would set the alarm clock for a couple of hours before dawn and dressing hurriedly, quietly leave the house.

They'd make their way through the sleeping town to the path that led up the Rock. Occasionally. they would stop to draw breath and look back at the distant lights of Algeciras across the bay. It was a long climb and they felt very daring, aware that they might come face to face with the Barbary Apes, who roamed free and could be quite vicious.

According to legend, when the apes leave the Rock, Gibraltar would no longer be British. The apes were protected.

Once they reached the summit all danger was forgotten as, replacing the darkness, an opal glow spread across the sky. They sat quietly watching while, pushing itself up over the eastern horizon in the direction of Jerusalem, the sun's great ball of fire would suddenly burst forth. The white houses of Spanish Malaga to their left and to the right, distant Ceuta in Morocco, would seem to catch alight in the sudden blaze. Elated with the beauty (and now ravenous for bacon and eggs) they would turn and make their way back down the dark side of the Rock to the sleeping town.

Glorious sunsets were reserved for the west side of Gibraltar. The house had a large patio that looked across the bay to Andalucía. At sunset, their parents were often joined by a few friends and, sitting quietly over their drinks, they would watch the ships below light up in the direction of Trafalgar Bay. As soon as the sun dipped below the horizon, the Sundown Gun would be fired, and everyone could hear the Last Post being played in town.

Sometimes Joan was required to entertain long-suffering guests with her repertoire of recitations. Audrey had none of these performing chores, but would join Joan in a piano duet called "Happy Together," which, as it always ended up with hair pulling and tears, became a popular attraction with their parents' friends – a sort of cockfight without the bloodshed.

At the end of one summer, days before sailing for England, Joan developed acute appendicitis. Panic set in. What to do? Doctor Gill, the family doctor, refused to allow her to cross "that dangerous Bay of Biscay." As Joan had crossed it eleven times and been seasick almost every time, he had a point. Kathleen said she would not risk the local hospital. She too had a point. Bed bugs were rampant there.

The Company lent their staff Matron as nurse, and F.D. Cairns, a visiting brain surgeon, was engaged to perform the operation. The kitchen table would become the operating table and was moved into her parents' bedroom. Fortunately, Mr. Cairns operated on the correct part of her body. The room now became her hospital ward. Her father rigged the dressing table mirrors so she could see the ships moving in and out of the docks.

She missed the autumn term at St. Helen's. But no matter, for it was now that she really started her life in the Theatre. While recuperating in Gibraltar, she wrote a play called *The Big Bad Baron*, directed the very small cast of four, played the Baron herself, — and had the audacity to charge admission to their dining-room theatre.

By the New Year she was healthy and able to join her friends on the after-Christmas voyage to England. After her unorthodox operation, she became a celebrity for a while, which she loved. She also joined the Girl Guides and became a Patrol Leader. A few years later, in full Girl Guide uniform, Joan was part of the Guard of Honor at the opening of nearby Denville Hall, to be the home for elderly members of the Acting Profession. Ironically, this was where she would live for the last five years of her long life.

Joan loved her schooldays. She progressed fairly well in some subjects but failed lamentably in mathematics. She seized every opportunity to act in all the school plays — both in French or English, and she entered every Public Speaking competition proposed by the speech teacher.

By the beginning of 1927, her last year, Joan knew quite definitely that The Theatre was for her. She told the headmistress this.

"Too short." the headmistress said. *"But then, Lotte Venne was short."*

Joan had never heard of Lotte Venne. Many years later, she learned that Miss Venne was the original Lady Kitty in Somerset Maugham's *The Circle*, a role Joan would play at Salisbury Arts Theatre and again in Manchester.

Her music teacher Kitty Hunt was equally discouraging.

"You need sex appeal to be an actress…but you, Joan dear, have none."

Joan remained determined, even when her father agreed with her teachers and hoped she would stay away from the 'wicked stage'. She was a determined to get her own way.

At St. Helen's, she took piano lessons, as well as weekly elocution lessons with Julie Huntsman, who entered her every year for the progressive Guildhall School and the Royal Academy of Dramatic Art examinations.

Susannah and I knew none of these stories of our mother's school days and successes. I have gleaned them from her notes and short stories. She would probably have said, *"You never asked."*
But then, she was never around to ask!

While she was at St. Helen's, a visiting lecturer was the playwright Ian Hay. She told him about her hopes of becoming an actress. Years later, she would be cast in four of his plays: *A Present from Margate, Admirals All, Housemaster*, which ran for months, and *Little Ladyship*, another box office success. A brilliant writer of comedy, he once told Joan that he liked writing parts for her, because he knew exactly how she would say his lines. To have a good writer's trust is a precious gift to any comedy actress.

Trying out for the Royal Academy, Julie Huntsman helped her plan a one-woman recital to be given in her studio. She performed the last act of Clemence Dane's "William Shakespeare."

The Whites were not a theatrical family and knew no one who could give Joan a leg up. By this time, her father realized he had to help and not hinder. In his address book, he found the name of an actor-friend he had met in South Africa. Henry invited him to attend the Recital, and asked him to give an honest evaluation of Joan's talents.

Charles Vane was an actor of the old school and had understudied Sir Henry Irving. A distinguished, white-haired gentleman with a fine speaking voice, he not only gave Joan encouragement, but also offered to join her in a recital to which the press would be invited. This time it would be the trial scene from The Merchant of Venice. He would be Shylock and Joan would be Portia. This decision, and the press reviews, won Henry over. She auditioned for the Royal Academy of Dramatic Art and — glory of glories — got in.

She left St. Helens winning the Senior Gold Medal of the Poetry Society presented to her by Dame Edith Evans.

At RADA, they were twenty to a class: sixteen women and four men. In Joan's opinion, her best teacher was undoubtedly Alice Gachet, formerly of *The Comédie Francaise*. They did scenes from Racine and Molière, while Madame sat watching and holding hands with her beloved former student, Charles Laughton.

Madame Gachet decided to do Shaw's *Saint Joan* in French. For this she cast Joan as the Man with the Eggs in Scene One. Joan played him, not as an old man but as a half-witted farm boy, anticipating her many future successes in teenage roles.

She learned much from RADA and Madame Gachet.

Chapter Two

CLIMBING THE LADDER TO SUCCESS
1930 – 1935

And so, her life in the theatre began:

Before leaving RADA in the summer of 1930, she applied to The Festival Theatre in Cambridge. This, she had heard, had a good company and a young director, Tyrone Guthrie, who would be responsible for the productions. The actors included Flora Robson, Gillian Scaife and Robert Donat.

The theatre, a converted church on the Newmarket road near Cambridge. Owner Terence Gray, a connoisseur of fine wines, good food and experimental plays, had added an excellent restaurant.

The Cambridge Festival Players was the brainchild of Anmer Hall, a theatrical producer and a wealthy gentleman with money in the Prudential Insurance Company.

Joan wanted to join the company for their second season, but she knew no one who could introduce her. Undaunted, she looked up Anmer Hall's address. He lived in The Albany, Piccadilly. Dressed smartly, she gained entry to the building.

This must have taken some pluck and perhaps some flirting with the doorman as The Albany was, and still is, a most prestigious address. Oscar Wilde has it as Jack Worthing's London home in *The Importance of being Ernest*. Dickens used it for his moneylender in *Our Mutual Friend*.

Summoning up her courage, she rang the bell of his apartment. Mr. Hall's secretary Mary North answered the door and informed her,

"Mr. Hall never sees anyone without an appointment."

"Well," said Joan, *"couldn't I make an appointment to see him now?"*

Perhaps Miss North was impressed by her urgency. She went inside and returned to say that Mr. Hall would see her. He was sitting in his big wingback chair:

"My dear young lady, I can't engage you for my company if I haven't seen you act."

"But you can see me, Mr. Hall, on Tuesday next at RADA." Joan said, *"I am the hysterical maid in Secrets and the girl with the adenoids in Nine 'til Six …Please, please do come!"*

And sure enough, he did. But after that she heard nothing — no letter, no message. What very peculiar behavior she thought, when she had acted her heart out!

She went back to the Albany. Miss North again opened the door,

"Yes, Mr. Hall did like you, dear…Yes, I think he liked you."

She introduced Joan to a very tall man wearing a grey suit, a red tie and sandals with odd socks. He had piercing blue eyes. This was Tyrone Guthrie.

"Yes, Mr. Hall did like you, my dear, but we are fully cast. However, we could offer you an apprenticeship…that means you come with us and work at everything…you don't pay us and we don't pay you."

With the arrogance of youth and only five foot one, Joan looked up at this giant and said,

"Isn't the laborer worthy of his hire."

His eyes twinkled,

"Well, dear, take it or leave it! It's good experience. Hard work and you'll learn a lot."

Luckily, she took it. And he was right, it was a wonderful experience – and very hard work. She persuaded her father to allow her three pounds a week to live on, and moved to Cambridge to join a company that included Hesketh Pearson, David Horne, and Rupert Doone. The apprentices included Isabel Scaife and Robert Eddison, who was to be her life-long friend and ally.

The Cambridge Festival Players did a new production every week with beautifully designed costumes and sets. The apprentices painted scenery and sewed costumes late into the night, played small parts and prompted.

The new plays that season included *Tobias and the Angel* by James Bridie. In this production Joan played the slave Azorah who gets flogged during the play. The Company went on tour. In Glasgow, Joan remembered Bridie's elderly aunts inviting them to a formal tea party in their

Victorian drawing room, with high ceilings and potted palm trees. Everyone was behaving impeccably when an elderly gentleman advanced on Joan, giggling and licking his lips:

"So, you are the one who gets beaten," he said. *"Do you like it?"*

Joan gave a nervous giggle. She was very naïve then.

In her second season, another play with a biblical theme, this time Judas and the Pharisees, was Andreyev's *Betrayal*, which later moved to the Adelphi Theatre in the West End in January 1931, sponsored by Maurice Browne. *Betrayal* gave David Horne a fine leading role opposite Flora Robson who was making her London debut. Robert and Joan were in the supporting cast. Maurice Browne's London company included Catherine Lacey, Margaret Rawlings, Reginald Tate and Alistair Sim. They were now members of Guthrie's company and were required to understudy those 'provincial actors from Cambridge'. This caused considerable tension.

Joan shared a dressing room with Lacey and Rawlings, whose sophisticated talk included explicit descriptions of the joys of sex on a cross-Canada railway journey. She was shocked by such talk. She wrote in her journal, *"For me, love was a private matter."* At the time, she was besotted with David Horne in her first affair of the heart.

Now they were professional salaried London players, digs (lodgings) had to be found for those who didn't live in London. Robert and Joan each took a bed-sitter in a nice house in Pimlico. Each room had its own gas cooker and washbasin. Early one morning Joan was awakened by a lot of squeaking. She switched on the light. Two little mice were running up and down a water pipe. Terrified, she was about to bang on the wall, but was afraid Robert might misunderstand. Finally, the mice were too much for her. She knocked on the wall. Robert quietly opened her door.

"What is it, Miss White, dear?" He asked. Tremulously she explained.

"Oh, dear! Never mind!" he said, *"I'll make you some scrambled eggs."*

He then produced perfectly cooked scrambled eggs.

When the Company had a few days off. Joan, with David Horne, decided to steal away to the south of France. But there was a problem: what to do with letters from her parents who wrote daily? Robert was the only person she felt she could trust. She told him of the predicament and her secret plan.

"Oh, Miss White, dear, do you think you should? Just think of your poor parents!"

But she was determined. She asked Robert to open any mail, and forward anything important, without revealing her whereabouts. He finally agreed, and all went well until one day he opened a small parcel from her mother. Enclosed with it was a letter,

> "Darling Joan, please will you take this little hat back to Bourne and Hollingsworth immediately and ask them to credit me. Bunny says I look awful in it…unless you'd like it for yourself? Please reply at once!"

Poor Robert went into a panic. Holding the horrid little hat, he fussed over what to do. Finally, he wrote:

> "Really Miss White, dear, don't you think you should confess to your whereabouts in the south of France, thank your mother for the little hat and wear it yourself? It's not a bad little hat, and, under the circumstances, cheap at the price."

Robert didn't know that it was the latest millinery fashion called a coal-heaver's hat. Joan reluctantly did as he suggested.

Her idyll over, Joan went to tell the warden of the house in Pimlico that she was back. He greeted her with a wink,

"Your Auntie Mary's here…she's booked room Number One on the ground floor."

Aunt Mary Beach opened her door and flashed Joan a wicked smile.

"On holiday, eh? Personally, I think you've been living in sin. Naughty!

And this from a woman who had married an already married man!!

David Horne was her first love. However, he eventually left the Company and went off to act in New York. There would be many others.

Tyrone Guthrie in his book, *A Life in the Theatre*, describes this next stage of his Cambridge Players' venture into London's West End.

> "The following autumn, 1931, Anmer Hall, our patron at Cambridge, converted a cinema, near Buckingham Palace Mews, into the Westminster Theatre. His idea was to use the nucleus of this Cambridge company as a stock company, which, reinforced by actors of established reputation, should present a series of interesting and serious plays."

The Players were due to open there in the autumn with another James Bridie play, *The Anatomist*. Not a comedy and not from the bible, this was about Dr. Knox and the body snatchers who provided him with corpses for his students' anatomy classes. One critic called it a *"flickeringly atmospheric production."*

> Joan wrote, *"The play starred the golden voiced, matinee idol Henry Ainley as Knox. Those lovely Irish character actors Jimmy O'Rourke and Harry Hutchinson were the body snatchers, Burke and Hare. Flora Robson made her name as the Edinburgh prostitute who is murdered by Burke and Hare for Dr. Knox's experiments. I was cast as her wispy, frightened companion, Janet, with two lines and a scream. The mentions I got in the Press made up for my tiny salary. We apprentices were now elevated to salaries of three pounds a week."*

It was at a pre-season weekend party at Ditton Place, Amner Hall's impressive Edwardian house in Sussex, that Joan first met Henry Ainley. He had recently returned from 'drying out'. Tony Guthrie and his wife Judy were already enjoying a hearty breakfast when Joan entered the big dining room. At a window, looking out over the garden, stood a large man made even larger by loose white tennis clothes. Joan helped herself to breakfast from the sideboard and Guthrie said,

"Joan, I'd like you to meet Mr. Ainley." (He hadn't been knighted yet.)

The large man in white turned around and advanced towards her. He lowered his rather red face to her hand and kissed it, declaiming,

"And I bows and I bows and I bows," relishing every pear-shaped vowel and not meaning a word of it.

Joan remembered feeling acutely embarrassed that such a giant of the theatre would behave so with the least important member of the cast. However, a few months later, she said, *"I came to love and appreciate this kind, warm-hearted human being, who also had a wicked sense of humor."*

> This "kind, warm-hearted human being" was the same man whose two sons, Anthony and Timothy Holmes, born out of wedlock around this time in the early thirties, had been sent to the Actors Orphanage, then at Langley Hall, at the very young ages of three

and four. They were never acknowledged by their rich and famous father. Indeed Anthony, who I remember at Silverlands as Tony Holmes, changed his name to Ainley only after his father had died. As Anthony Ainley, he made his name as The Master in Doctor Who on BBC-TV. Remote and unfriendly at Silverlands, I don't think he ever got over his father's rejection.

Denying one's children is neither kind nor warm-hearted!

From time to time during the 1930s, actors would appear in one-performance-only, "showcase" productions, hoping to be noticed by critics, agents and producers. Joan's first such play was *A Knight Passed By* at The Ambassadors in June, 1931. The cast included Peggy Ashcroft and Nicholas Hannen. *The Stage* wrote the role of Kate "was whimsically and cleverly portrayed by the very promising Miss Joan White." She was on her way.

That season, Anmer Hall revived Bridie's *Tobias and the Angel* with Hermione Baddeley and Henry Ainley. Leading ladies dressed like leading ladies in the 1930s, regardless of inner meanings and motivations of character. Hermione fascinated the younger members of the cast by rehearsing her role in very high heels and spotless white fox furs.

During the run, Ainley had an ongoing feud with the rather intense stage manager. One dull matinee afternoon while waiting in the wings, he nonchalantly struck a resounding chord on the prop harp, which stood beside him. The Stage Manager, spectacles steaming, came tearing around from stage right and hissed *"Shut up, there!"* Despite his rags, Ainley became truly imperious and declaimed,

"Not for you, you lousy bugger!" and strode off to his dressing room.

The next production was Gregorio Martinez Sierra's play, The Kingdom of God. Opening on June 2, 1932, *The Times* said,

> "The Kingdom of God has won, and has deserved to win, an established place in the English theatre. It is not philosophically profound, but it is, as far as it goes, unfailingly just and straightforward in its philosophic attack." It concluded with, "In brief, an uncommonly even and well-balanced performance of the play."

During one performance, prior to opening, playing the hysterical Margarita in Act Two, Joan overdid the emotion and, being inexperienced, became hysterical and continued weeping and wailing into the wings. The stage manager took her firmly by the hand and led her into the back yard. There he doused her with a bucket of cold water.

"Never do that again!" he said, *"Once you lose control, you lose the audience."*
Joan learned from that because the reviewer noted,

> "and Miss Joan White, given the dangerous opportunity of hysteria, uses it for precisely what it is worth, compelling the audience to emotional response but never, by her wildness, driving Sister Gracia from their consciousness."

As Azorah, a dancing slave girl in *Tobias and the Angel*, Joan had worn blue Persian trousers, revealing her bare midriff, and a blonde wig. One day she received a surprise phone call from screenwriter Ben Travers. He wanted her to be tested for a film of his, *Plunder*, to star Tom Walls and Ralph Lynn, famous farceurs of their day. She put on her audition dress, a little black number, rolled her brown hair into a neat bun and reported to Elstree Film Studios. There she faced the camera and heard Tom Walls say *"Roll 'em!"* Afterwards she said, *"Thank you"* and returned to town. A few silent days ensued.

Finally, she rang Ben Travers, who seemed surprised,
"But you never went to Elstree…"
Joan assured him she was there, describing the test and Mr. Walls, who had been most kind.
"Well," he replied, *"they thought they had got the wrong girl."*
Joan suddenly realized that what they had liked was her bare stomach and blonde wig. She didn't get the film.

A well-known agent contacted her. When she walked into his office in her new coal heaver's hat (all the rage in the thirties; hers, courtesy of her mother) and good flat walking shoes, he just roared with laughter and informed her that *'an actress should look like a cross between a lady and a tart'*. He sent her to a good dressmaker and a beautician. He was kind. Unlike Sidney Jay who said,
"You're a pretty little girl, but for Christ's sake don't smile when you meet the director. When you smile, it's awful."

Life for a young actress could be very rough.

After *The Kingdom of God*, they did Guthrie's production of *Love's Labour's Lost* with Anthony Quayle as Ferdinand, Abraham Sofaer as Berowne, and Eugene Leahy as Don Adriano de Armado with Joan (in tights and jerkin) as his page Moth. Joan was prevailed upon by Guthrie to sing "What a Thing is Love" in a high falsetto. She received a brief but laudatory notice in *The Times* July 7, 1932 for "...the liveliness of Miss Joan White's mockery of Mr. Leahy's solemn fantastications."

> **Some thirty years later in 1962, I played Popham the maid in *The Magistrate* Off-Broadway in New York and was prevailed upon by my director, Tom Gruenewald, to sing "The Wine of Love is Music," in a high falsetto. It's all in the genes!**

During the 1932 season Joan made her very first film for Warner Brothers (*The Melody Maker*), as Charles Hawtrey's twin. Hawtrey (no relation to Sir Charles Hawtrey) had told the director that he could drive. He couldn't. So, when the car scene was about to be filmed, Joan had to make a slight bottom-slide into the driver's seat while Hawtrey, having changed places, sat smiling smugly in the passenger seat. He later achieved film comedy stardom in the many "Carry On" movies. Joan would go on to play supporting roles in many films.

During this London Westminster season, Joan moved from Pimlico to share a humble studio in Victoria with Isobel Scaife, for which they paid twenty-seven shillings and sixpence a week. The studio above was occupied by the artist James Proudfoot, who entertained many of his models on a very rickety camp bed — often with noisy results. From this Isobel learned a lot. Joan was already initiated.

> **My sister and I have fond memories of Isobel Scaife. Isobel and Joan remained friends for years, long after Isobel left the theatre world in 1938 to marry Walter Jenke and move to his farm near Blandford Forum in Dorset. As children, Susannah and I visited the large Jenke family for a couple of happy carefree holidays in the late 1940s. Uncle Walter made the most wonderful wooden toys for his children and made Sue a Noah's Ark with many animals. For me, he made a wooden puzzle map with all the coun-**

ties of England and Wales cut out, named and painted in bright colors. I would spend hours putting them back in place. I am sure this started my love of geography. I fondly remember little Rutland, which was bright yellow and often got mislaid. (Rutland has been swallowed up by Milton Keynes, and many other counties have been renamed since my childhood.) The puzzle was left at my Grandparents' house when I went to America and sadly was sold, along with many of my treasured childhood books, after Granny and Granddad made their final move back to Gibraltar in 1963. My mother and American stepfather, Bob Grose, packed up and sold the house and its contents, lock stock and barrel, with little thought or knowledge of any personal items of value to me. How could they have? They never knew what things were precious to me as a child!

The Jenkes' farm was my idea of the perfect home and family when I was small.

The Company opened the Westminster's autumn season with a play by Tyrone Guthrie himself. It was set on the west coast of Ireland and was called *Follow Me!* Sounds like a musical? No, it was a modern version of Saint Matthew's Gospel. Yet another Bible Story!! It previewed at the Alhambra in Glasgow in October and was not well received.

Joan shared 'digs' with three other actresses during the pre-London performance in Glasgow. The landlady (who was far more Cockney than Glaswegian) said the young ladies could invite a friend each to supper. They invited four actors from the cast and were sipping their after-supper coffee sedately, when Mrs. W. put her head around the door and, like a sergeant major, rapped out,

"alf past eleven...Gents must go!"

They all felt guilty and embarrassed suddenly. The men left hastily. Joan and her room-mates, while angry, were left to calm the landlady.

At the Westminster Theatre, *Follow Me!* closed on November 19 after only eleven performances, having been dismally reviewed by nine London newspapers. Unbowed, the Company went into immediate rehearsal for yet another James Bridie biblical comedy, *Jonah and the Whale*, with a lively part for Joan as Jonah's girl-friend Euodias.

One night, Edward Chapman as Jonah while threatening the people of Nineveh with "dragons' fierce jaws" announced, dramatically that *"dragons with dripping drawers will come amongst us!"* — to the great joy of audience and actors alike.

The Spectator summed up the production: *"Jonah and the Whale* is pleasant enough. It was well performed by a large and almost uniformly accomplished cast. But the whale should have a course of lessons in elocution."

The Tatler singled out Joan: "Joan White was witty and personable as Euodias, played in the vein of *What Every Woman Knows.*"

Next was Pirandello's *Six Characters in Search of an Author*, an absurdist play about the relationship among authors, their characters, theatre directors, stage managers and other technicians. Joan played the Assistant Stage Manager.

By the spring of 1933 Joan had left the Westminster Company and was unemployed. On April the First, she met a tall, dark and handsome man of her own age. After a wild all-night party at the Group Theatre, he gallantly walked her home to Victoria. When they reached Grovesnor Gardens at seven in the morning, he sat down on the curb and refused to move until she agreed to marry him.

Little old ladies with prayer books kept scurrying past on their way to early morning service at nearby St. Peter's. They glanced suspiciously at John Vesey Beanes sitting there in his dinner jacket, his hat on the back of his head. Joan found it all a little embarrassing. She walked up Buckingham Palace Road to read *"The Rules for Matrimony"* nailed to the Princes Row Registry Office door. They seemed quite simple. When she got back to Grosvenor Gardens, her suitor was still sitting there, and the devout were multiplying fast. Joan capitulated.

Two weeks later, they returned to the Registry Office with John's mother and Joan's father, who gave her away rather gladly

Under the photo of Joan as "Jonah's little friend Euodias" in *Jonah and the Whale*, the marriage announcement read:

> *"BEANES — WHITE — on 25ᵗʰ April, 1933, very quietly, at Prince's Row Register Office, John Vesey Beanes son of the late Mr. F.E.V. Beanes and Mrs. Beanes of St. Ermin's Westminster to Joan*

White, elder daughter of Mr. and Mrs. H.W.G. White of Huntly Cottage, the Downs, Wimbledon.

Miss Joan White, will keep her stage name under which we hope she will continue to earn the encomiums of press and public alike, as she has already done in the last two or three years."

Kathleen, her mother, would have none of the marriage and took to her bed. She was, after all, the seventh child of a seventh child...they know these things.

And she was right.

The marriage did not last. Sometime during the next two years, Joan fell in love with a gentleman whom she referred to as "the great love of her life." (Another one!) He was the artist, Michael Campbell Ross, and was named as a co-respondent in John Vesey Beanes' petition for divorce in 1935. It was granted. This liaison did not last either, Joan lost contact with him, but in her old age insisted that HE was the love of her life. She went on with her career.

Poor John Vesey Beanes! He wrote a couple of good plays. Joan appeared in one of them, *Our Mutual Father*, with Rex Harrison, before stardom enveloped him.

In 1933 she was in three short-lived plays:

Eve in *The Synthetic Virgin* by W.P. Lipscomb at the Royalty. For the title alone the Lord Chamberlain immediately banned it. *The Times* wrote, "...it might have been an extremely interesting evening." It soon closed.

Vacant Possession at the Fortune Theatre was another poorly reviewed play. *The Times* said, "Mr. Roland Culver's detached study of a degenerate and the child-like sincerity of Miss Joan White as the country sister were the things most worth remembering."

Then came Ian Hay's *A Present from Margate*, a frivolous comedy at The Shaftsbury in December. The play "was not quite up to the mark." according to *The Stage*. It ran for twenty performances. Her school-days mentor wrote several other plays with her in mind.

By 1934, she was Madanika in a lavish musical play, *The Golden Toy*, at the London Coliseum. It was based on an Indian story, but with the exception of the beautiful Indian costumes designed by Rene Hubert, the production was heavily Teutonic with great grey revolving mountains and music by Robert Schumann. Ludwig Berger, the director, had made many silent films with Mary Pickford, and he would often call Joan "Mary."

The cast read like a "1934 Who's Who in the Theatre," among them: Wendy Toye, Nellie Wallace, Lupino 'Nipper' Lane, Peggy Ashcroft, Ernest Thesiger and George Hayes, a large chorus of singers and dancers, and a dancing elephant called Rosie. Despite these stars, the show ran for only four months. Some years later, 'Nipper' Lane visited Rosie in her "Retirement Home" at the Bristol Zoo. He swore that Rosie remembered him and they danced their old *Merry Peasant* routine from *The Golden Toy*.

Immediately after *The Golden Toy* closed, Joan went from the Coliseum, one of London's largest theatres, to its smallest, The Mercury. Ashley Dukes had written a play for one woman and four men called *Charlotte's Progress*, and he wanted Joan to play Charlotte. A typical Twenties girl, seeking the perfect mate, experiments with four different types of men. It was a huge role after her few lines in *The Golden Toy*, and while not overly well received, it had a respectable run.

The Stage critic wrote, "Miss Joan White does such artistic justice to this wayward lady that one wants to slap Charlotte, yet there is a certain human appeal. Miss White's is an interesting performance."

After this run of mediocre scripts, she was 'available' again by Christmas of that year.

> For any actress, the offer of a role in a new play is enticing. The quality of the play itself is overlooked in favor of the role and the chance to perform. From my own experience, I remember the excitement I felt when, in April 1963, I was offered the role of Penelope, an awkward "very British" debutante in *The Saving Grace*. A supposedly satirical comedy about the British upper classes and foxhunting, it missed its mark. The cast and I, individually, received good reviews, but the play was roundly panned and closed after a couple of weeks.

In January of 1935, she joined the cast of *The Barretts of Wimpole Street* as Bella Hadley. It was a revival of the original production and continued to draw good houses.

She followed that with a number of radio plays for the BBC and two films: Ian Hay's *Admirals All* as Wilfred Hyde White's daughter and *The Second Bureau* with Googie Withers.

That summer, she was off to Bexhill to direct Noel Coward's *I'll Leave it to You* and Sutton Vane's *Outward Bound*. It was her first foray into directing and she loved it. She was now twenty-five and working fairly consistently.

Divorced from John Beanes by this time, Joan found a flat at 118 Long Acre, on the top floor. It must have been "between marriages" when she was on her own, because she writes in her journal "*my menfolk would never have put up with anyone so ungainly and so gloriously familiar as my help, Mrs. Herring.*" No other help would have been so loyal as to climb up five flights of stairs each day to work. Mrs. Herring never failed. In a sweltering heat wave or the coldest winter, despite 'me rheumatics' or just plain obesity, she would toil daily up the stars to look after her 'duck', a term of endearment cherished by Joan.

Joan wrote the following essay about Mrs. Herring:

"*She was a little round body of a woman, thick through and sturdy of limb as well as of character. Her hair was sparse and cut too short and what there was of it was tightly permed and stuck out each side above her ears in wiry black bunches. She had small eyes and thick silver-rimmed spectacles, which were never quite straight. They invariably tilted with a list to port or starboard, giving her a slightly rakish look that smart women achieve with Hattie Carnegie hats. Below the glasses was a large nose and below that a generous mouth and good big teeth.*

She favoured grey for pinafores over any old dress, which did nothing for her figure. But the day that she appeared in my first divorce case, she clothed herself in funereal black and managed to look both neat and highly respectable. Though she tripped and fell flat on her face as she entered the witness box, her evidence won glorious freedom for us all.

She had a great sense of humor and the Cockney gift for dramatic story telling. Perhaps this was why she worked so loyally for me. It was the nearest she would ever get to the footlights. My flat at this time was like Waterloo Station for up-and-coming members of the theatrical profession, it being conveniently close to so many stage doors in the area.

Herring would often make coffee for the young Greer Garson when she dropped in on her way to rehearsal. Or she would keep an eye on Val Gielgud (head of BBC Drama and brother of John) while polishing the silver, as his flat backed onto mine and his Siamese cats were often preening themselves in the kitchen window.

But as for the telephone...! She would have nothing to do with that. She completely ignored it. When it rang, she would yell, "It's for you, ducks" and get as far as possible away from it.

Then came the day when I made Collie Knox's column in *The Daily Express*.

About this time, many young women in the public eye were being plagued by anonymous phone calls, and on this particular morning my face had appeared in Collie's column with a nice little mention of a broadcast I had done the night before. Evidently this inspired a gentleman to ring me up and flatter me by saying that he represented a provincial newspaper and would like an interview. "Gullible Gertie" promptly invited him up for coffee in half-an-hour, whereupon the caller used language that would have made a navvy blush and I flung down the receiver with a yell.

"Wot's the matter, ducks?" yelled Herring from the kitchen.

I told her what had happened and she became more protective and far more practical than I knew she could be.

"Phone the police!" She ordered. And I did. "Phone Scotland Yard!" They said, I did.

Scotland Yard promised me a detective who would arrive in ten minutes before the expected rapist, and I promised to admit no one who did not knock three times.

Meanwhile Herring bolted and chained the door and, not trusting to mere ironwork, proceeded to barricade it with the kitchen table and chairs. I would have thought that she, who climbed, puffing and blowing, daily to the fifth floor, would have realized that after that climb no one would have the strength to batter the door down. But I wasn't going to spoil her fun, and I was touched that she thought my chastity so well worth protecting. The detective *arrived, knocked three times and was admitted. Herring gave him coffee and we waited.*

Alas, the caller never showed up. The detective was not surprised, Herring was relieved, but I was sorry. I wanted to see how Herring would have sent him about his business. Would she have dressed him down in her most vindictive Cockney? Or would she have dealt him a swift uppercut to the jaw with that beefy arm of hers? We were never to know."

Come September, in *The Restless Room*, Joan was cast as a girl who is frozen and brought back to life. It was a flop! No surprise there!

In her early years, Joan adopted many theatrical superstitions and was careful with them. I remember years ago, on one of her visits to Silverlands, when she picked a loose thread off my coat, rolled it up between her thumb and forefinger and pocketed it, saying *"That means a future contract."*

Coming home one day, later that September, she heard the phone ringing and rushed up the stairs. It was Charles B. Cochran's office. Was she available and could she play a girl of sixteen? Yes, she was and yes, she could.

She flattened her bosom, put a snood in her hair, and ran to Cochran's offices on Bond Street. There she was offered the role of Connie Windlestraw in James Bridie's new play, *The Black Eye*. It didn't matter that she had no sex appeal or that she was only five foot one, she was in Bridie's latest play and working for London's most prestigious management — C. B. Cochran!

She was about to be on stage and in films non-stop for the next ten years, playing teenagers and winning the hearts of London audiences.

Chapter Three

THE TEENAGE ROLES
1935 – 1939

The Black Eye was to be her fourth Bridie play. James Bridie was the pen name of Osborne Henry Mavor, a Scottish physician, who wrote many plays for the London stage, some successful and some not so. When Joan was cast as Connie Windlestraw in *The Black Eye*, he wrote to her,

> *'It is splendid that you are playing Connie and I am very pleased a) because it is you and b) because it will be very well done.... Ever Yours OH' (Osborne Henry)* And later after it opened, *'This is to say...that last night you made me laugh. Connie was a lovely performance and I'm very grateful to you for it. God Bless You. OH'*

The Black Eye had a decent run and Joan's notices were good. Denys Blakelock and Stephen Haggard played her brothers. Stephen was George, he of the black eye.

I inherited her copy of the little book Haggard had written for his young sons in case he didn't return from World War II. In 1940, in the early days of the war, he was shot down over France. *I'll Go To Bed at Noon* is a slim and special little book, full of fatherly advice about life. She gave me another little book when I became an actress: *The Craft of Comedy*, *the letters between Athene Seyler and Stephen Haggard.* I have long cherished it for the advice it gave me as a young comedienne and because it was rare help from my mother about the art of the theatre.

In her introduction Seyler says, *"There are, it seems to me, technically two kinds of comedy: one that lies in the witty line, and the other that is in the situation or the characters. For the first, only clear delivery of the author's words is necessary — and how lucky is the actor to have such a light task, for the really witty line is a rare thing. For the second means of ensnaring laughter, there is only one essential — namely, truth to one's character. Often these comedic moments are unforeseen by author and player."*

Much of this second kind is physical comedy. Joan White was a mistress of the art.

All Cochran first nights were glamorous and this was no exception. At the Shaftsbury Theatre on October 11, 1935 George Bernard Shaw was there with Elizabeth Bergner, who was casting the film of Shakespeare's *As You Like It* with herself as Rosalind and Laurence Olivier as Orlando. During the scene where Joan, sitting cross-legged on the dining room table, expounds on SEX to her brother George, G.B.S. nudged Bergner and said, "*There's your Phoebe.*" Soon she was under contract.

In a few months, filming would begin, but meanwhile there were other parts to play on the West End Stage. After *The Black Eye* closed, Joan was cast as Claudine in *The Luck of the Devil*, which opened and closed quite quickly at The Arts.

Her next role was Tonie in *Children to Bless You*. Originally produced at The "Q" theatre in February 1936, the producers moved the play three weeks later to the larger Ambassadors Theatre, where it ran to mixed reviews but good houses. Harold Hobson, in *The Christian Science Monitor*, wrote the following:

> *Children to Bless You!* By G. Sheila Donisthorpe.
> "They were not nice children. They treated their widowed mother like long-suffering dirt, and life and each other with extreme modernity." He continued "Our pleasure in these awful examples was due less to their truth to life than to the zest with which the actors projected them." He included "… Miss Joan White was an irresistibly horrid Tonie…"

Joan's reviews in the other papers were also excellent.

The Stage "Joan White makes great success as the noisy selfish youngster Tonie."

The Nottingham Daily "Miss White was quite the best thing in the play,"

James Agate of *The Times* wrote "Joan White dominates the family whims and tantrums with puppyish and amiable impudence."

The aptly named critic, M. Willson Disher said, "…and Miss Joan White as the nasty child, in which she successfully specializes."

But *The Herald* said "…far too much of it was given over to the young people, who all needed spanking."

It transferred, after twenty days, to The Duke of York's Theatre on St. Martin's Lane.

In the West End in those days, successful productions frequently had to relocate due to previous bookings.

> **My father, A.P. Moore was Managing Director of The Duke of York's and it was there that he first met my mother. Given all that was to come later, the title of the play *Children to Bless You* was rather ironic.**
>
> **The following chatty cutting is from a London paper (I can't trace it, but have the cutting): '*Children to Bless You* at The Duke of York's is full of good parts. One of the best is that played by Joan White. Joan is clever and ambitious and has had much experience for a girl in her early twenties. Joan loves producing and wants to run her own theatre."**
>
> **She knew what she wanted even back then in 1936.**

Filming had begun earlier that year at Elstree Studios. You would think that, as a rural play, *As You Like It* would be filmed in the glorious English countryside and woodlands. But no! It was winter. So, they built the 'Forest of Arden' inside a studio with a corrugated iron roof, amplifying the sound of rain. The crew constructed hillocks, a lake with ducks in it, and mighty trees and shrubs, all of which had to be fireproofed.

Finally, for realism, they introduced a herd of cows and a flock of sheep.

During Joan's scenes with Silvius, played by Richard Ainley (Sir Henry's legitimate son), he would go running through the trees calling to his shepherdess, "*Phoebe! Phoebe!*" The crew spent hours completing the sound track. Every time, they were interrupted by strange groans, burps and worse. At last, the cause was discovered. The sheep had been eating the fireproofed leaves with disastrous effects on their digestions. But the lucky shepherd and shepherdess made a lot of money on overtime… thanks to those silly sheep!

The film critic for *The Times* noted,

"Mr. Richard Ainley and Miss Joan White were extremely engaging and the whole cast was to be commended for a serious and often sensitive treatment of the poetry."

As You Like It was the first British talking picture of a Shakespeare play and also Laurence Olivier's first attempt at the Bard on film. The cast was made up of seasoned actors from the London theatre: Henry Ainley, Leon Quartermaine, Felix Aylmer and Peter Bull to mention just a few. At this time, Olivier was also appearing in *Romeo and Juliet* at The New Theatre, playing Mercutio to John Gielgud's Romeo. When he was offered the role of Orlando, even though he had told film producer, Walter Wanger, that he disapproved of Shakespeare on the screen, he succumbed to what Ralph Richardson called *"the artistic satisfaction of six hundred pounds a week."*

But Olivier was never very happy making the film. He doesn't mention it at all in his autobiography *The Confessions of an Actor*. He felt that the Bard was taken out of his element and that his Orlando would not stand up to the test of realism demanded by film. He thought the stage convention, which allows Orlando to mistake Rosalind for a boy, would be preposterous in front of the camera. He went so far as to make his Orlando a little mad in the hope that it would lend credibility to the role. He also hated the lack of continuity between scenes that filming imposed. And the film wasn't helped by Miss Bergner's strong Austrian accent.

Olivier also discovered that filming by day and acting a large role at night was very taxing. Sometimes he would arrive at the theatre, to play Mercutio, so late that he kept on the same make-up, the same boots and the same padding for his calves that he had worn for Orlando. (Yes, that's right. Laurence Olivier padded his calves for many years when he had to wear tights. Those great looking legs were an illusion, like much of acting.)

Olivier went on to prove himself wrong about Shakespeare on film with his later roles. The Bard translates very well to the screen.

As You Like It was a turning point in Joan's life. For the next ten years she knew, mostly, what she would be doing next. The only trouble was being typecast: the bane of all actors. She played a variety of characters, but not one of them was over the age of sixteen. Her most successful part at that time was as twelve-year-old Button Farringdon in *Housemaster*. (Joan was twenty-seven and had already been married and divorced).

Ian Hay's comedy *Housemaster* opened at The Apollo on November thirteenth 1936. It was a huge hit. The reviews were excellent and the play was on for much longer than the usual London run.

During the abdication of Edward VIII, the King and Mrs. Simpson were on everyone's minds: so much so that one night, Frederick Leister the housemaster, inadvertently, referred to the character Mrs. Carey as Mrs. Simpson. There was a sudden silence, then to Leister's surprise the audience burst out laughing.

As they left the stage he whispered to Joan, "*Why did they laugh?*"

She told him and he looked horrified, "*Oh my God! Buckingham Palace will be after me in the morning.*" But, of course, they weren't.

After a few months, the play went on tour to Scotland, and returned to London, this time to The Aldwych Theatre in the spring of 1937.

The Times critic reviewed it again,

"Housemaster is back in London with a practically unchanged cast and takes the stage at the Aldwych with the assurance of an established success." and continued, "With Miss Hilda Trevelyan as chaperone, Miss Rosalyn Boulter for sweetness, Miss Elizabeth Nolan for effervescence and Miss Joan White for sheer farce, the troupe flickers, shimmers and romps through the play, and there is really not much to do but keep an attentive ear to miss as little as possible of the dialogue in the laughs. It is dialogue frankly of the "hit-or-miss" type; but the hits are numerous, although some of the more polished marksmanship seems to fall among the Misses."

**Many years ago, when I lived in Stockbridge, Massachusetts, Mary Thorne, an elderly English lady I knew, remarked that I looked just like Joan White. I said I was her daughter. "*Oh!*" she said, "*I can*" *still remember as a young girl being taken to the theatre in London and there was this girl about my age in the play who said, 'Do you mean funny peculiar or funny ha ha?' So that girl was your mother. I have never forgotten that."* Many people remember that line to this day.

In 1936, T*he London International Theatre Club* was getting organized and it was there Joan again met our father-to-be, Archibald Patrick Moore.

Under Father's management, The Duke of York's had hosted Marie Rambert's *Ballet Rambert* in 1935 with Frederick Ashton, Ninette de Valois and Antony Tudor in the company. The following year, Alicia Markova and Anton Dolin presented a season of classics. This Duke of York's season helped to popularize ballet in England. The next year, Father was involved in founding *The London International Theatre Club*.

During my many months of research, searching for the truth about my Father, I had been unable to find anything about *The London International Theatre Club*. I had searched the Internet, various theatre encyclopedias and biographies. I had been to the New York Public Library and the Library of the Performing Arts searching their databases and coming up empty. Then I got the address of The Mander & Mitchenson Theatre Collection, one of the largest collections of theatre and performance related materials in the UK. In 2008, I visited England and the collection's former home in Greenwich. (It is now housed at Bristol University.) The director, the late Richard Mangan, found me a complete listing of the productions put on by The London International Theatre Club, the duration of its existence and programs of all the LITC plays. Finding this has given me feelings of pride for the father I never knew. My father was a member of a forward-thinking committee that introduced innovative plays to London audiences. It was the New Theatre Workshop or The Donmar Warehouse of the day.

'Bravo, Father. Thank you. You were a man after my own heart — I am proud to be your daughter. I may not have known you, but I seem to have inherited much from you: my long career in arts administration and public relations, and my interest in introducing new works to the local audiences here in New York State. I wish we could have talked about it all.'

The plays The International Theatre Club presented gave only three performances, held on consecutive Sundays, at The Duke of York's for the first year and at The Globe Theatre until April 1939. After all, they had to present their bread-and-butter bookings during the week.

The first production, was "*Susannah and the Elders*" by James Bridie with Father's new bride, Joan White, in the leading role. "*Susannah and the Elders,*" adapted from the Apocrypha, about predatory elders who hide to watch the beautiful young Susannah in her bath, and seek to shame her into sleeping with them. It was a taboo subject back then — dirty old men corrupting innocence and trying to use the law to have their way!

The Times of London made note of this new venture on October 21, 1937:

> "The London International Theatre Club, which has been formed to encourage young playwrights, actors and designers, hopes to keep The Duke of York's Theatre open every Sunday night during the winter."

The Stage wrote, "I certainly hope it (Susannah) will be put on for an ordinary West End run."

Joan was still appearing in *Housemaster* for eight performances a week. She had suggested to her new husband that *Susannah and the Elders* be the first play produced by the LITC. Having appeared in several plays by him, James Bridie was anxious for her to play Susannah.

Bridie wrote to her:

> *"My dear Joan, I have an oath in Heaven that I will not write a play with any particular actor or actress in mind and I think it is one of those oaths worth keeping. BUT I have done a really brilliant Susannah and the Elders (Bowdlerized but Beautiful.) Susannah is all that you describe… If you have decided to stop being a hoyden, I don't think you could do better and I don't think I could either. Love OH*

Following the third performance at the Duke of York's, James Bridie wrote to A.P.

> *November 2nd, 1937.* Re: Susannah and the Elders
> *To Pat,* (variously called A.P., Pat or Paddy)
>   *Thank you for a really first class 'putting on' of "Susannah." I*

do hope it will make a fortune for all of us. I told Joan that she gave a superb performance and I meant it. If there is transfer, she must play the part. Ever yours, OH

The three performances were so successful that producer Bronson Albery wanted to transfer the whole production to the New Theatre. But as Joan was still in Ian Hay's popular comedy, and James Bridie was insisting that only she play Susannah, everything was put on the back burner. Alas, the play was never seen again in the West End,

In December, LITC produced Jean Anouilh's first English foray into London with *"Le Voyager sans Bagage."* The British considered Anouilh controversial. January 1938 brought even more controversy to The Duke of York's stage. This was *"Gentleman's Agreement,"* an English adaptation of Hungarian playwright Eugen Heltai's play *"Jo Uzlet."*

It was about anti-Semitism and given what was happening in Germany, it was timely. There were two more plays that season before productions moved to The Globe for the next year. The LITC, sadly, ceased to exist after just the two seasons, because the War came. It was a noble venture.

Between 1936 and 1939, in addition to *As You Like It,* Joan had supporting roles in many films among them *You're The Doctor* (again with Googie Withers*)* and *A Girl Must Live* (with Margaret Lockwood*)*.

In her monologue, *Alive to Tell the Tale,* Joan writes,

"I met A.P. Moore at a meeting of the London International Theatre Club"

and later *"Meanwhile, A.P. Moore and I decided to get married and we held our reception on the stage of The Duke of York's Theatre on January 27, 1937."*

In 1986, Sue and I went with our mother to The Duke of York's to see Richard Harris's play *Stepping Out.* We sat in the stalls. During the first act, she began to sniffle; soon her sniffles turned to sobs and we had to hush her.

At intermission, Sue said, *"What is the matter?"*

"Oh, dear," sniffle, *"I was remembering that this is where it all began — up there on that stage. Dear Paddy and I had our reception and then you two were born."*

It was the only time that she ever showed us that side of herself.

It is clear that Joan was ambitious, and she was also very attractive. A.P. was ambitious and attractive too, **and** he was the manager of a West End Theatre. He was just what the doctor ordered. Or was he?

> **I often look at the photo of my parents on their wedding day. I see these two shining, beautiful, ostensibly happy people, and the promise of it all. It makes me very sad to think of all that my sister and I were to lose.**

After their wedding and the subsequent production of *Susannah and the Elders*, Joan was still playing twelve-year old Button Farringdon in *Housemaster*, which had by this time transferred from Shaftsbury Avenue to The Strand. Finally, in the summer of 1938, she decided to leave the play. Holidaying in Somerset that autumn, she learned she was pregnant and she was overjoyed. (*In her monologue,* Alive to Tell the Tale, *she does not say, or even hint at, how our father felt, but I assume he was pleased.*)

A few weeks later, on September 30, 1938, Prime Minister Neville Chamberlain announced the advent of "Peace in our Time."

In December, Stephen Mitchell announced (less dramatically) an after-Christmas production of a new play, *Little Ladyship*, with Lilli Palmer and Cecil Parker, both well-known and established British film stars. He wanted Joan for the role of Judy Bingley.

She read the play and realized it was '*socks and gym tunics*' all over again.

> "*A young woman played by Lilli Palmer, recently married to a rich barrister, is bored and is persuaded by her cousin (Judy Bingley) to go back to school. She does and pandemonium ensues.*"

She went to see him immediately and told him of her pregnancy, expecting him to be a little put out. Instead, he rose from behind his desk and gave her an enormous hug. They agreed that she should play the part, until her condition was noticeable. Thanks to costume designer, Molly McArthur, as Joan's girth increased so did her padding. Casting three equally chubby girls to sit near her in the on-stage classroom helped disguise her growing size.

Once again Joan got good notices for her 'socks and gym tunics' role:

The West London Observer "Joan White as Lilli Palmer's cousin is always up to mischief and how well she performs her part."

The Stage "an amusing and completely effective impersonation of a precocious schoolgirl comes from Joan White."

The Birmingham Daily "Joan White contrives to give us a delightful study of a schoolgirl."

The Scunthorpe Herald, "Joan White is charmingly mischievous as the 'holy terror' schoolgirl."

The play was well received and ran for several months until Joan could no longer play a schoolgirl effectively due to her pregnancy.

Joan and A.P. had asked playwrights Ian Hay and James Bridie, costume designer Molly McArthur and actress Roma June, to be godparents.

Roma June, for several years each Christmas, took Susannah and me to C & A's, (fondly known as Coats and 'Ats), and bought us smart Sunday coats with little velvet collars. I hadn't thought of her in sixty years.

A short walk from their Knightsbridge home was the famous old music hall, the Chelsea Palace, on the corner of Sidney Street and the Kings Road. The music hall is gone now, replaced by smart shops. It was very popular in its day and boasted top-line stars; names such as Wee Georgie Wood, Vesta Tilley, and George Robey (in his nurse's uniform telling risqué jokes).

Joan wrote, *"The Palace was especially dear to me, for it was here in the hot summer of 1939 on a certain memorable evening when I was 'large with child' that my husband (insisting that I took my mind off the coming event) conducted me to the Chelsea Palace, where I laughed so much at the comedy trio Seaman, Forsyth and Farrell that our child arrived that very night.*

Some years later, when Miss Farrell and I were playing in different theatres in Manchester, I thanked her personally for causing our child to come into the world. It was her turn to laugh and she positively roared, "Honey, Ah've been accused of doing some funny things in my life but this is a first." Eleanor Farrell was a huge American comedienne with a glorious sense of humor and a rich infectious laugh. Looking back, I think her good nature must have infected my fun-loving daughter."

On July 12 1939 their daughter was born and named Susannah after Bridie's play. When Sue was less than two months old, War was declared, and Ian Hay (Beith was his birth name), by then Director of Public Relations at the War Office, advised Joan and the baby to stay out of London. A.P. resigned his job at the Duke of York's and enlisted in the army.

Life as they knew it was about to change.

Chapter Four

THE WAR YEARS AND "JUNIOR MISS"
1939 – 1946

(Author's note: Now she has become our mother,
from here on "Joan" will be referred to as "Mother.")

When Germany invaded Poland on September 1, 1939, Mother and Father were living at 5 Raphael Street in Knightsbridge with their infant daughter, Susannah. Mother had played Judy Bingley in *"Little Ladyship"* until her pregnancy was no longer possible to disguise.

As soon as war was declared, all able-bodied men rushed to enlist in the services to fight for King and Country. Father, who turned thirty-two that October, signed up and on November 4, 1939, due to poor eyesight and given his managerial background, he was appointed to the War Office as Public Relations Officer for the Western Command. With the war begun in earnest, Mr. and Mrs. Moore gave up their small Raphael Street flat and moved with Susannah to the relative safety of the little village of South Moreton in Berkshire, home of Mother's parents, Henry and Kathleen White.

Father lists his address as *Wheatleys*, South Moreton on Army Form B199A under General List for the War Establishment. He says his parents are British and his religion was Church of England. He lists his status as married, his wife as Joan Moore, their marriage date, and names his daughter Susannah as his only child. He says he is fluent in Spanish with some French and German and that he had spent seven years in South America, as a resident in Chile and Bolivia. He had also travelled extensively in France, Germany and southern Sweden.

He listed his business qualifications as: "Organization of office routine - Welfare - Journalism - Theatre Management - Shorthand - Typing."

In November of 1939, Father was posted to Chester in the North of England.

Mother and Susannah went with him to live in a pretty whitewashed cottage in Hoole, a little village outside the city. In December, *The Chester Chronicle* interviewed Mother.

The headline read   *FILM AND STAGE STAR*
Miss Joan White settles in Chester. Hopes to Entertain the Troops.

> *"We met in The Duke of York's Theatre in London — he owns it you know — when I was playing in Children to Bless You. He would go up to his box, just before my entrance, and sit there looking at me. It was very embarrassing, … we met, and we were married!"* (Whenever she mentions Father, she is very unemotional.) "It is Mrs. A.P. Moore speaking, wife of the Public Relations Officer. Mrs. Moore was Joan White, the well-known actress. A few weeks ago, she and her husband came to Chester; he to take up his new position, and she, for a short time at any rate, to settle down as cook, bottle-washer and 'nanny' to her five-month-old baby, and a most efficient general factotum she appears to be.
>
> "An *Observer* reporter went to see her the other afternoon, and found her surrounded by masses of Christmas parcels and her new baby — a chubby, dimpled morsel of humanity with a charming toothless smile. Eight weeks before this important person was born, Mrs. Moore was playing the part of a fifteen-year-old schoolgirl, in *Little Ladyship* with Lilli Palmer! This of course made them both front page news."

Shortly after Christmas, Mother, Father and others began to put on entertainments to raise money for "*Comforts for the Troops*" and for the local Defense Units. Between January and May of 1940, they presented shows in Chester. The first special event on January 27th was for the Red Cross. Douglas Byng was the headliner. Mother was *Compere* with an assorted cast of performers: Derek Guyler, Richard Bullock and Jimmy Parry, the Españo Trio, the current International Table Tennis Champions and Jack Paterson, a former boxing champion. Assorted indeed!

A local paper said, "*The local committee is very fortunate in having the cooperation of A.P. Moore, Public Relations Officer for the Western Com-*

mand." Five more such events took place between January and May, raising money for "*Comforts for the Troops*" and The Chester Police Ball.

By June of 1940, the Germans were targeting England and on June 8th 1940, Father got an Emergency Commission with Army pay of £600 per annum. He was enrolled as second lieutenant in the Gloucester Regiment and immediately promoted to the rank of Acting Captain. His job was to release information to members of the press: information that had been approved and passed on to him by his commanding officers, who in turn received it from the War Office. For this purpose, he was allowed an "Imprest account" for entertaining the press. For example: 7 shillings and 6 pence per head per meal for the gentlemen of the press. By the number of articles and press releases, the Public Relations Officer for the Western Command was certainly doing his job.

There was much more for him to do, now that the war had begun in earnest.

By late summer 1940, the Blitz had begun and would continue through May 1941.

London and the Home Counties were hit worst by the German bombers. Father's beloved Duke of York's Theatre was damaged by a bomb, as were several other London theatres. Being so close to Liverpool docks, Chester was not the safest place for Mother and Susannah either.

Looking for a place to live, they found an ideal retreat in Snitterfield, a village just north of Stratford-on-Avon in Warwickshire. In July, Mother and Susannah moved there and spent six months in Farmer Cox's stone-built Cotswold farmhouse. The farm had a cow for milk, a heavy hand-pump in the yard for water, wood for the fireplaces and six chickens to augment the one-egg-a-week-per-person decreed by Lord Woolton, *War Minister of Food*. Mother and Susannah occupied the top floor of the house. Mother grew vegetables and became quite self-sufficient, collecting eggs daily from the chickens. Each bird had been given names by Susannah, now a toddler, so of course they couldn't kill them.

Farmer Cox was a genial little man with a great sense of humor. He had been a horse breeder before the war but the Army had requisitioned his horses, and all arable land was now put to use feeding the nation. At the farm, the only loos were six wooden seats with holes, separated by walls and individual doors with a single overall tin roof. Most mornings

Farmer Cox and Mother sat in adjacent stalls exchanging news of the War and latest air raids.

Mother recalled sitting on the porch with Farmer Cox on a moonlit night in November 1940. She wrote, *"To the northeast there was a tremendous fire on the horizon. In spite of the distance, we clearly saw the flames and smoke rising. We learned later that it was the bombing of the city of Coventry. Over 500 German bombers massed for the biggest raid of the war to date — their target, Coventry, a city at the industrial heart of Britain's war production engine."*

Later, Coventry was subjected to two other large air raids in April 1941, when 230 bombers attacked the city, dropping 315 tons of high explosive and 25,000 incendiaries. In all three raids, hundreds of people died and practically the whole city was decimated, including the beautiful old Gothic cathedral.

When the weather turned colder in the North, Mother left the farm where she wrote, *"I had spent some of the happiest days of my life,"* and with Sue moved back to her parents in South Moreton. There, Mother did canteen work, while her parents minded their granddaughter. Mother's war work necessitated learning to ride a bicycle, killing and plucking chickens for the markets and forming a Village Children's Theatre to keep the village children and the evacuees from London occupied on Saturday mornings.

She wrote, *"The local country children were no trouble at all, but lacked talent. The Londoners were like belligerent Cockney sparrows, sharp and talented. But although they were obviously unhappy away from their street corners and fish-and-chips, it was the village policeman's son who bit me. The breaking up of families and forced evacuations was one of the worst things that happened to civilians in World War Two."*

By summer 1941, now the Blitz was over, they were back in London. Father's job with the Western Command kept him on the road, but he was often in London for meetings with the higher-ups. It must have been during 1941 that they found and purchased 36 Paultons Square in the Royal Borough of Kensington and Chelsea.

Paultons Square was, and still is, a lovely square with central, private gardens, off the King's Road in Chelsea, West London. Beautifully maintained and surrounded by handsome Georgian properties, Paultons Square is a favorite place for residents to sit and escape the busy streets of London for a while.

By September of 1941, Mr. and Mrs. A. P. Moore had moved in. It was a lovely Regency row house in the southeast corner of the square. The kitchen and servants' area were down stone stairs behind a wrought iron railing. The kitchen led into the walled back garden, graced by a large laburnum tree and wisteria creepers. On the main floor, entered from the street by three scrubbed steps to a front door with a shiny brass knocker, were the dining room, parlor and sitting rooms. The adult bedrooms were one flight up and on the very top floor were Susannah's nursery and a room for the Nanny.

> *"When they hired Nanny Ball I do not know, it was after I was born; but I am sure that living at such a posh address, a Nanny was a MUST."* Sue wrote to me, *"I think she came to Paultons Square along with the house and the up-style living. I remember Paultons Square and Father coming home in a chauffeur driven car, wearing a Captain's flat peaked cap. I must have been two or three."*

What Sue remembers most about Nanny was that she was very strict. Susannah and I were both rigidly potty-trained. When I came along, as soon as I could sit up, I was made to sit on the potty immediately after breakfast. I was not allowed to get off it until I had *"done something."*

Father did well at his job until spring of 1942, when from his official Army records, the Commander-in-Chief of the Western Command, General Sir Robert Gordon-Finlayson, his superior officer, was promoted and a new Commanding Officer was appointed.

General Sir James Handyside Marshall-Cornwall took over the Western Command in April of 1942.

(Was it required to have a hyphenated surname to be a British General?) It was then Father's troubles began.

I was able to obtain the Court documents through the diligence of my niece Sarah Kennedy in England. When I asked her if she could find these documents pertaining to Archibald Patrick Moore and his court case, she asked me,

"Aunty Judy, who is this Archie chap?"

I replied, *"He's your grandfather."*

"Right," she said, *"I'm on it."* and she was!

In April or May of 1942, Marshall-Cornwall *"reported him (A.P.) as being inefficient and recommending him to be cashiered."* Then, on June 11, 1942, notice was given terminating his services under his contract. Suddenly, court-martial proceedings had commenced before the termination notice was given. Why? They were going to cashier him anyway? If the proceedings hadn't already begun, he would simply have been fired without this major blot on his record. Why all this bother?

The following is a verbatim report in *The Chester Chronicle* June 14, 1942:

FORMER WESTERN COMMAND P.R.O *(public relations officer)* COURT-MARTIALLED ON 29 CHARGES

"I am able to assure you that whatever Captain Moore did with his accounts he did not spare himself when he saw a chance to benefit the troops."

"That tribute to Captain Archibald Patrick Moore, for two and half years Public Relations Officer to Western Command, was paid by General Sir Robert Gordon-Finlayson, former G.O.C-in-C Western Command when Capt. Moore appeared at a

North-West military camp on Thursday on 29 charges relating to misapplication of money. N.B. one charge for each individual receipt turned in as evidence.

Captain Moore was found "Not Guilty" on sixteen charges and the findings of the Court on the other charges are to be announced.

The court-martial was opened on Wednesday, June 10th. Major Manningham Buller was Judge Advocate General. Major Rees was for the prosecution and Captain Pearson defended.

AN ADMISSION

Captain Moore admitted that he adjusted hotel receipts because "I could no longer continue to finance the job out of my own pocket."
He had continued to pay for additional expenses not covered with his Imprest account, until it became a burden. He was frequently

seriously out of pocket. In 1941 he had an additional burden; an A.T.S. publicity officer was attached to his department. She too had to entertain the press. He allotted certain sums to reimburse her for the money she had spent.

He added, "In order to reimburse myself and to recover money spent in obtaining publicity, I began to alter receipts slightly — I see now, quite wrongly."

Asked why he altered the receipts, Captain Moore said, "I wished the Army Paymaster's office to think they were genuine receipts for entertaining. I expected to gain no benefit, only a refund for what I had spent. Obviously, the Paymaster is not aware of the high cost of entertaining."

He said he had some small private means and was not totally dependent on Army pay and allowances. "I have never been dishonest, but here I have been careless."

Second Lieutenant J.E. Powell, giving evidence of Capt. Moore's character, said there were no entries on his conduct sheet and he had not been convicted before. He was 35 and had been in the Army over two years. He held a certificate for good service from the C-in-C of Home Service, and was a Second Lieutenant with the rank of Acting Captain.

Captain Pearson said Captain Moore entered the service of the Army at the outset of the war, having previously been engaged as managing director of a theatre. As a managing director, his co-directors, an accountant and a lawyer — guided him in the financial conduct of the firm. When he entered the Army as a civilian, he was given charge of an Imprest account and had placed upon him responsibility, which according to the findings of the Court, it was clear he was not capable of bearing.

Captain Pearson produced a letter from General Sir Robert Gordon-Finlayson, who said he did not think it proper that as a public man he should be asked to attend a court-martial. However, he was prepared to write a letter.

General Gordon-Finlayson stated, "Captain Moore served under me for two years when I was G.O.C-in-C Western Command, and I saw a great deal of his work in that time, and I would *be grateful if the Court would receive this statement in mitigation of any punishment the accused officer might receive."*

"Captain Moore," he added, *"was the first Public Relations Officer for Western Command,"* and he described how, *"Starting from zero, he worked most energetically. It was surprising how his zeal, energy, and drive overcame various prejudices and misunderstandings about the Army among the local population. In a few months, contacts were established with the Press and local authorities.*

Whatever Captain Moore did with his accounts, he did not spare himself when he saw a chance to benefit the troops."

The General described the various concerts and efforts Captain Moore organized on behalf of Forces charities. He understood that he was to be invalided from the Forces."

A.P. had been arrested in late May, 1942, and had been awaiting trial for twenty days.

The certificate, awarded to him by the Commander-in-Chief Home Forces had stated: *"I am authorized to signify, by the award of this certificate, appreciation of the good service you have rendered. Your devotion to duty shall be made on the record of your service."*

In spite of the above testimonials, for some reason, the trial did proceed and A.P. was cashiered on June 24, 1942. Following the trial, A.P. was sent home to await further instructions. He was ordered to resign his commission.

Because there was a war on, he was sentenced to serve as an orderly in a prisoner of war hospital. Clearly, from time to time he was given compassionate leave to see his family. Both Susannah and Mother's sister Audrey remember him at Paultons Square.

Ironically, his accuser, General Sir James Handyside Marshall-Cornwall was dismissed a couple of months later, in the autumn of 1942, for going outside the proper channels to secure the safety of the Liverpool docks. He spent the rest of the war at a desk job with the Special Operations and MI5 attempting to promote better relations between them. He was retired from the army in 1943.

I have studied the Court documents and the testimonials, especially the one given by his first Commanding Officer Gordon-

Finlayson. I believe the trouble started in early 1942, when the new C.O., Marshall-Cornwall, came in and took against A. P. It was only afterwards, learning what we knew about A.P.'s later life, that we could suppose why the new C.O. didn't like him.

Father's defense to me seems very logical. I can understand that, having had to entertain members of the press corps who, in my career as a publicist, were always up for a free meal and a few drinks. Usually for more than the budget allowed. Nothing changes in that area. I believe him when he says that none of it went to his own personal gain. He had paid for extra charges out of his own pocket for the first year and a half; but he had a wife and child, as well as a house to support, so he adjusted the receipts.

There is so much bureaucracy and Army official jargon in these charges. And why were they spending their time on such a small amount of money (less than £20 over two years). THERE WAS A WAR ON FOR GOD'S SAKE!

Finally, I believe there was a hidden agenda here. This is NOT why he was cashiered. The charges in his court martial were about an insignificant amount, **and** he spent it on entertaining the press corps pertaining to his position as Public Relations Officer. Plus, he was not always able to get proper receipts. It wasn't grand larceny and, according to the testimonials from his superior officers, he had done a good job.

It should be noted that when all this began to happen, I, Joanna Judy, had become more than just a gleam in my Father's eye. Mother was already three months along and I was expected to make my entrance in December 1942.

So back at Paultons Square, 17 July 1942. Mother is four months pregnant with me and Father is out of a job and in disgrace. They own a very smart Regency row house in Chelsea and they have a Nanny to pay and a small daughter to feed. Was Father around then at all? Sue says that he gave her a Teddy bear for her third birthday, July 12, 1942 and she added,

"'Nanny used to put my pet goldfish outside the nursery. She said it used up too much air and wasn't healthy! When my goldfish died,

Father was at home and I remember very clearly how he and I solemnly buried it under the Laburnum tree."

Mother does not mention A.P. at this time in her diaries and notes, not at home in London or anything at all about his trial. He was now working at a hospital in or near London. She probably felt ashamed and angry with him for putting her through this. Did she understand the charges? Did she see the testimonials? Did she attend the trial?

There is no evidence that she did. She didn't stand by her man and she never forgave him. He upset her applecart!

By the autumn of 1942, the London theatres were in full swing, and Mother was very pregnant. It was then that she had a phone call from a leading producer, Firth Shephard, who had bought a New York comedy success and wanted Mother for one of the leading roles. It was a funny, family play called *Junior Miss* and Mother was, once again, to play fourteen years old. She told him about her pregnancy and Shephard said he was prepared to wait.

But from then on, the phone calls were frequent:

"How's that baby coming along?" "

Fine, Firth. Kicking."

"What date is it due?"

"By Christmas."

"Can't you hurry it up?"

But that baby was ten days late.

On January 3rd, 1943, while listening to Susannah's bedtime prayers, Mother's water broke. Audrey, who was staying with the family, had to rush her off to Queen Charlotte's hospital. There she gave birth to a 10 lb. 8 oz. baby girl named Joanna Judy, "Judy" after the role she was to play in *Junior Miss*, Judy Graves.

I have always been grateful that circumstances chose my mother to be playing Judy Graves in *Junior Miss* when I was born. Had she been in *Housemaster,* I might have had to go through life as "Button."

Audrey was in London over Christmas 1942, taking care of the household while awaiting my birth, she told me, years later, that Father did come home to see us. And Sue remembered that she and I spent a lot of time under the heavily blanket-covered kitchen table with our toys when the sirens screamed and the buzz bombs fell in 1944/45.

Mother was usually off at the theatre.

Susannah's birth and the subsequent three years, because of the out-break of war, had allowed Mother to be a mother to Sue in her infancy and as a toddler. Yes, they had a Nanny when they returned to London, but with Sue, she never had to decide whether to act or stay home, be-cause the war was on and few parts were available. Until the offer from Firth Shephard.

However, even with my impending birth, she could still have made a choice, taken a teaching job and been a mother. But, like Maggie Smith and many other actresses before and after her, for Joan White her career always came first. This was to be her pattern throughout her life. I believe she did love her family, in her way, but stepping on "the boards" made her whole.

Six weeks after what must have been a strenuous labor and birth, by February, Mother was in rehearsal for her most taxing role to date. She was on stage almost throughout the play, often seated on the floor, sometimes in yoga positions. Marcel Varnel, the director, would tell her to squat down faster, and she would say,

"I just gave birth to a ten-pound baby, I'm doing what I can."

Junior Miss was a big hit and just what wartime London needed. Mother received accolades in the press:

> *The Times*: Miss Joan White plays the part with an unflagging gusto that cannot be resisted."

> In a full-page spread, *The Sketch* said, *"Junior Miss* at the Sav-ille Theatre is an American comedy based on stories by Sally Benson. It's a gay farcical affair dealing with the sophisticated outlook of Judy Graves, a thirteen-year-old New Yorker and her little friends. Judy's exploits nearly wreck her parent's mar-riage and ruin her father's business prospects, but by a surprise twist her activities turn out to have been all for the best! The child impersonation given by Miss Joan White is outstanding. She provokes storms of hysterical laughter"

> In another full-page spread *The Tatler*, with many photo-graphs, wrote with some relief, "There is no hint, nor talk, of war in *Junior Miss*."

The Scotsman, "Much of the success of the evening is due to the acting of Miss Joan White."

The Liverpool Post wrote "There will be few parents who will not be thoroughly entertained by Joan White, Peggy Simpson and Peggy Cummins. They will be especially charmed by Miss White's swift flight to Stardom."

The Birmingham Post said: "Joan White as l'enfant terrible and Peggy Cummins as her friend have the chief parts and carry them off with spirit."

The Yorkshire Press: "The performances of Joan White, as a child whose over-developed sense of romance nearly ruins the lives of her parents, and Peggy Cummins as her friend are irresistible. Both are only seventeen!" [Well, Peggy was, but Mother was thirty-four.]

The Daily Mirror was not quite so kind to Mother: "The part is cleverly played by Joan White, who always acts like a child even if in appearance she is sometimes a little reminiscent of Auntie carefully made up for the charade."

On opening night, *The Stage* got right to it: "Joan White at thirty-four, gets right into the skin of the alarming but good-hearted and ultimately triumphant Judy Graves."

Junior Miss opened on March 24th 1943 and played at the Saville Theatre for fifteen months. I was to spend several weeks in a basket, under her dressing table, being breast fed until I could be weaned. When the West End run was over, the company went on tour with ENSA playing to the wounded soldiers at Botleys Park Hospital and later to the soldiers and sailors at various bases while they awaited orders to begin the D-Day Invasion — June 6, 1944.

Junior Miss and Mother received new rave reviews from the tour.

"The two friends endeavours are too paralyzing for words." said *The Scots Daily Record* on August 22, 1944.

And from *The Coventry Evening Telegraph*, September 5 1944. "Joan White played the role of Judy with a mixture of innocent air and sophisticated impudence that kept the inconsequential plot moving in a procession of comedy situations and human reactions. She was a Judy with a punch — and an artistic punch at that."

In July, feeling proud of their local "star" *The Chelsea Advertiser* wrote, in part:

"Miss White, (in private life Mrs. A.P. Moore) who has a house in Paultons Square, takes the part of a precocious adolescent so convincingly that it is hard to realize she is the mother of two bonny little daughters. She feels it a wrench to part from them for four months, but she tells me that the spontaneous enthusiasm of servicemen and provincial audiences is a compensation."

Sue remembers Father coming to the house when I was a toddler.

Sue said, *"I remember you sliding down the stairs on your belly and getting Impetigo, a nasty rash, and having your belly painted with battleships in Gentian Violet by Father. I remember Nanny taking us to the Park in that huge Silver Cross pram, with you at one end and me at t'other, and her saying that you had got the Impetigo from gutter-snipes who leaned into the pram to see you. I only got a ride when my little legs were too tired to walk. Nanny also hated it when our cat Tiger sat on your pram."* Sue also remembers Nanny running over her little hand with a hot iron, — to teach her not to touch!

I didn't come along until after Father's troubles and then he only could visit us when he was given leave from the hospital.

The buzz bombs had begun in earnest in 1944 and Mother had sent Nanny, Sue and me to the country to stay with our grandparents. Granny took a strong dislike to Nanny, who then left.

Audrey had returned to North Moreton and was running a small factory, which made *Collier's Universal Hose Clips,* for the war effort in her village and falling in love with the married factory owner, Michael Collier.

In 1945, as the war was winding down, ENSA was no longer entertaining the troops. (*I was told by an elderly cynic that ENSA stood for "Every Night Something Awful"*). *Junior Miss* had closed and Mother was looking for a part to play in which she could break away from being typecast as a teenager — she was, after all, 36 now. She landed the second female lead in *The Cure for Love* with Robert Donat, playing the brazen hussy who had tricked him into an engagement before he went to war. It was the sort of role she had never acted before and she enjoyed playing the "bad" girl; one critic described her as *"deadlier than the Alamein barrage."* The play had a respectable run, opening at the Westminster Theatre in July 1945.

The War in Europe had ended in May 1945. The refugees from the Nazi concentration camps arrived in Britain to be found places to live, and also our soldiers were returning home, some wounded, all weary. Amidst all this, Father simply disappeared.

Mother stayed with *The Cure for Love* into 1946, through the tour. Later, she would decide to get a legal separation from a marriage that was not happy. That is all she would ever say.

> **Where did Father go? Susannah and I didn't know. However, fifty-four years later in 1999, after our mother died, we learned from his remaining sisters-in-law that when Peace was declared, Father took off, going first to Cardiff and from there to points West and parts unknown; Canada and Hong Kong they thought. He probably figured that with all that was going on, no-one was going to be looking for him.**
>
> *"Why did he leave?"* **We asked.**
>
> *"Because my luvvies,"* **Aunt Gina said,** *"Your Dad was gay. And being a gay man in England in those days was a crime punishable by imprisonment."* **And that, I suspect, was the hidden agenda behind the Court Martial: A homophobic Commanding Officer.**

With VE day on May 8, 1945, the war in Europe was over and, while there was much rejoicing, reality had to be faced. Sue and I were returned to Paultons Square, where Mother's school friend from St. Helens, Avril Wood was living in the basement, helping to defray expenses. Tiger, our large tabby cat, had already left for the country, taken by Audrey to become the "factory cat," where he was to live out his life coddled by Mr. Peacey the gardener.

In 1946, the run of *"The Cure for Love"* over, Mother took a role in *G.I. Brides at Seas*, a poorly reviewed play that did not run for long.

She next was cast in the touring company of a light-hearted play of real estate and romance, *This Desirable Residence*. In rehearsals, she left Avril in charge of the house and the children. The tour was to run through the summer and so we were farmed out again; this time to another St. Helen's friend, Violet Slade-Jones, who ran a Holiday Home for children at *Sea Pines*, Milford-on Sea in Hampshire. We stayed there all summer and into the autumn. I think we were happy there. I know I was when I went there for later holidays.

Christopher Fry's *A Phoenix Too Frequent*, a three-character, witty verse play, had had a short run at The Mercury Theatre. The producers decided to give it another run in November 1946, this time at The Arts Theatre with Hermione Hannan and Paul Scofield, he at the beginning of his distinguished career as the handsome soldier guard, Tegeus.

> "Joan White was the absurd and cheerful maid Doto who keeps them company in the tomb." *The Times.*

> *The Stage* waxed eloquent about her performance: "Joan White as the maid who teams up with her mistress because she had no grief of her own worth dying for, has the finest comedy lines of the play and takes full advantage of the slightest inflection. Whether suffering from a hangover or merely regretting having parted with a pair of old shoes, this past mistress in the art of comedy makes us proud of the contemporary theatre, which could surely hold its own with the past as long as Miss White was a member of the 1946 team."

Doto was to remain one of Mother's favorite roles and, through *A Phoenix Too Frequent*, she began a long and enduring friendship with Christopher Fry. She was to present many productions of his plays with her students forty years hence.

Following the too short run of *Phoenix* she was in the film *Youth at the Helm*, always fitting filming in between plays throughout her London years. Now, she probably needed any work she was offered. With Father gone, she was a single parent with two small children. Any income was much needed. And, even though the war was over, rationing was still on and would not end until 1954, when meat and sugar (including confectionaries) were the last to become readily available. Your ration book was as important as your purse.

> **I do remember sweet rationing. Each week we were given a tiny coupon to present to the village shop for a gumball or sherbet straw with our pocket money. If you lost the coupon, no sweeties for you!**

It was while Susannah and I were at *Sea Pines* that Mother heard about The Actors Orphanage, a home *"for children made destitute by the profession."* A 27-room, neo-Georgian mansion called *Silverlands*, it was surrounded by forty-two acres of farmland near Chertsey in Surrey. During the war, the house had been requisitioned as a home for recuperating wounded soldiers, being conveniently close to St. Peter's Hospital. The children, many of whom had been evacuated to the United States, had recently returned. New applicants were being accepted.

For Mother this information was just what she needed. She could sell her house giving herself a financial cushion, and carry on with her career knowing that her children were safe. She applied, learned she was eligible and so, in the very last days of December 1946, Susannah, aged seven and a half, and I, just shy of my fourth birthday, were placed at The Actors Orphanage. I was to remain under their care for twelve and a half years — the remainder of my childhood.

It was good move for her, but was it for us?

Chapter Five

SEASONS OF REPERTORY
1947 – 1950

"What Shall I do with the Children?"

In 1947, after leaving us at *Silverlands*, Mother began to follow her desire to direct as well as act. Again, she made time for filming, one that Sue and I would love to see is her as Madame Lola the tightrope walker in *And Talking of Tightropes*.

In May, under the aegis of The Repertory Players at His Majesty's Theatre, Mother directed and starred in Keith Campbell's *Flat Spin*. It received mixed reviews:

> *The Times* said, "Mr. John Boxer was a delightfully stupid soldier, and Miss Joan White was the most amiable of stupid ladies."

> But *The Stage* wrote, "Any author who has Joan White in his cast should go down on his knees in gratitude." And added "Joan White's direction keeps the fun spinning throughout the evening."

John Boxer was the father of James and Andrew, boys I grew up with at the Actors Orphanage. They arrived a few years after I did and left *Silverlands* before me. *Silverlands* was a stopgap for many respectable working actors: a place to put their children when times were financially hard. Many children were in residence for a year or two, sometimes more. Sue left at age eleven, but I was to be there for twelve and a half years until I was sixteen: more than just a stopgap!

In August, Mother directed a light, funny comedy by Kenneth Horne, later the much-loved radio comedy star of *Around the Horne* and *Beyond Our Ken*. *Fools Rush In* was presented at The Connaught Theatre in Worthing.

As an actress, Mother was anxious to get away from type-casting and light comedy roles, so she went to her old friend Charles Landstone, a respected theatre manager, dramatist, critic and, for a time, General Manager of The Arts Council of Great Britain. He had the solution.

> He said, *"Drop your London salary and get into a good Rep. Go and see Michael Langham, the young director who has just taken over Sir Barry Jackson's Birmingham Repertory Theatre."*

Michael Langham was only twenty-nine when Mother presented herself at his house and told him how much she wanted to tackle roles that were not child parts.

Langham said he knew her work and had loved her since, as a schoolboy, he had seen her play "Button" in *Housemaster*. He hired her to join his company in Birmingham in January of 1948. For six months she played a majestic Duchess of York to Alan Badel's *Richard III;* Ethel Borridge in *The Casilis Engagement;* and, much to her delight, the huge, dirty, drunken and gloriously batty Madame Maniefa in Rodney Ackland's adaptation of Alexander Ostrovsky's *Diary of a Scoundrel,* in which she had to 'burp' on cue. Ackland told her she reminded him of Edith Evans, which pleased her no end. It was for her a wonderful season and a great change of pace.

Susannah and I came, for a brief spring holiday from the Orphanage, to visit her there and saw her in *Richard III*. According to her journal I, aged five at the time, remarked, *"Richard the Third was such a sad man, Mummy."* (Much later I fell in love with Josephine Tey's *The Daughter of Time).* This was to be the first of several visits to see our mother in various roles in various repertory theatres.

Mother returned to London to direct Norman Ginsbury's play *The Happy Man* at the New Theatre. *The Stage* said, "Joan White produced the play in a lively fashion, but it was beyond her power to give it dramatic interest and design." It did however introduce Dora Bryan as a gifted comedic actress.

In September, she starred in Jonathan Field's *The Ten Shilling Doll* at The Torch Theatre. *The Times* said, "Miss Joan White is a gift to the author for the part of his pathetic lunatic who makes dolls and is frightened of the dark." *The Stage* said she was outstanding. She subsequently starred in the television film of the same name. She made two other films that year: *The Weaker Sex* and Richard Brinsley Sheridan's Restoration comedy *The Rivals* in which she played Lucy the conniving maid.

On Tuesday, October 26, 1948 Mother joined fellow RADA graduates in a performance of *The Anatomist* at The Theatre Royal Drury Lane in an All-Star matinee, a benefit for the rebuilding of RADA's Theatre. Her Majesty Queen Elizabeth (later England's Queen Mum) was in the audience.

The War was now over. With the children settled at *Silverlands,* she sold 36 Paultons Square and for a short time, she roomed with her friend Avril on Sidney Street, while she looked for a more affordable home.

In 1949, she signed a contract with the Salisbury Arts Theatre for the season from September 1949 to June 1950. Peter Potter and Denis Carey were producing what came to be known as "the golden age of Salisbury" and Mother signed on for many roles that she had longed to play.

She arrived in Salisbury in August, ready to take on fourteen plays in weekly Rep:

Lady Kitty in Somerset Maugham's *The Circle,* (September 5-9);

Anton Chekov's *The Proposal* and Christopher Fry's *A Phoenix Too Frequent* (repeating her role of Doto (September 26 – October 1);

See How They Run, a popular farce (October 31 – November 5) "Joan White as Penelope Toop exudes good humor and is so delightfully scatterbrained..."

The Rivals (November 7 – 12) "Joan White is an impeccable Mrs. Malaprop never over-emphasizing the misuse of words, but always giving them the right significance."

Under the auspices of the British Arts Council, the Salisbury Arts Theatre sent the actors out to smaller towns to bring "culture to the masses". Immediately following *The Rivals,* they travelled to nearby Chippenham with *A Pair of Spectacles* by Sydney Grundy in which David Carr as Goldfinch was "well-supported by Joan White as his wife." *A Pair of Spectacles* then joined the Repertory schedule in Salisbury (December 12 – 17).

I have inserted the dates of the Salisbury productions to show how hectic the schedule was for actors in those days: rehearse the next show by day, and perform a different show in the evenings and matinees, with one, and only one, day off a week, when they learned their lines.

Mother was next cast as Fairy Rosebud in the Christmas pantomime of *Aladdin*. All 'Rep' company actors appeared in the annual holiday pantomime. Mother wore a tutu and a crown with tinkling bells and, of course, she had a wand.

I got my love of Pantos from those early days when Mother was in Rep. After Mother died and I had remarried, my fond memories of all things Panto returned. Every year, for fifteen years, we produced an original Pantomime for our audiences first at the Spencertown Academy in Columbia County, New York. We formed a company of crazies, the PantoLoons, and while our Pantos kept most of the Pantomime identifiers: *"It's Behind You"*, *"Oh no you won't"*, *"Oh yes I will,"* hissing and booing, cross-dressing and lots of slapstick; they had a decidedly American flavor. Our audiences loved them.

From 2000 until 2014 we presented for three weeks each Thanksgiving these Pantos: *Cinderella - two versions; Snow White and the Seven Frawds; Puss In Boots- two versions; Aladdin and the Wonderful Lamp; Robin Hood - two versions.* We moved to a larger theatre for *The Emperor's New Clothes* (for the 200th birthday of Hans Christian Anderson). Then we began to merge the stories: *HairLoom – Rapunzel and Rumpelstiltskin in DisTress; Lost: the Grimm Years - Little Red Ridinghood with Hansel and Gretel; Menagerie a Trois – The 3 Little Pigs and The 3 Bears; Sleep-Frog (Frog Prince meets Sleeping Beauty);* and finally, *Ali Baba and the Four Tea Thieves (to accommodate our small company).* I played many characters — Friar Tuck, Engelbert Humperdink, Lapsang Suchong, Papa Bear, to name a few; but the Fairy Godmother was my signature role — and I, too, had a wand!

Susannah and I went to spend 'Christmas with Mother' that year. On the train from Chertsey to Salisbury, we bragged to the guard that our Mother was Fairy Rosebud. He was most disappointed that she did not look like Fairy Rosebud or, for that matter, an actress; just a short, rather plump lady in odd clothes. However, Mother gave him free passes to the show. She then took us off to her lodgings in Vivien McCann's lovely Queen Anne house on Crane Street, where she had rented the top floor for the season.

It was a beautiful house, furnished quite unlike any other we had been in before, and certainly the best 'digs' she ever stayed in. There was a lovely garden, which in the spring and summer would be filled with flowers and shrubs. The lawn sloped down to the River Avon. Vivien McCann was a retired professor. He lived with his big old tabby cat called *Da Poosey*. When wishing to make a comment, he would use the cat as his intermediary: "*Da Poosey thinks Miss White should not wear that particular shade of purple!*" or "*Da Poosey thinks Miss White's hat is very unbecoming.*" Sue and I thought this very funny. Mother did not.

While we were in Salisbury that first time, when 1949 turned to 1950, I was not quite seven and Sue was ten and a half. Our Granny's family had come from Salisbury and Mother took us to the Salisbury Museum to see our Great-Grandfather Beach's cutlery on display. We went to the cathedral and listened to the choir sing, as our Great-Grandfather had a hundred years earlier. We went to Stonehenge —which in 1950 was not a big tourist attraction but just a collection of very large stones standing in the middle of a field near the road. I remember lying on the altar stone. When we visited various former family houses Mother said, "*Very changed.*"

But that was all she said. She never told us about her childhood.

Her Salisbury season continued into 1950 with Noël Coward's three one acts, billed as *Tonight at 8:30*. She had roles in all three acts (February 13 -18); then came *The Brontës of Haworth Parsonage* (February 20 – 25), she was Charlotte. In *Caste*, a comedy-drama (April 17 – 22), Newton Blick was her father. They both went immediately into *The Doctor's Joy* (April 24 -29) a British version of Moliere's *Le Malade Imaginaire*. Later in May, the play toured the surrounding communities. John Phillips played the invalid and "was well-backed in the fun-making by Joan White as the maid Toinette.*"

Mother ended this very full season at the Salisbury Playhouse, with Shaw's *You Never Can Tell*. She played Dolly Clandon and they took the play on tour from May 29 to June 3rd, with performances in Basingstoke and Winchester. That was Rep in those days, one week of rehearsal, while performing seven performances of the previous production. Occasionally an actor got a break and wasn't cast in a show.

Stamina! It took stamina!

When her Salisbury season finished in June, Mother returned to London. There, she found and purchased a small house, 16 Linhope Street, not too far from Regents Park and the Baker Street Tube. It was a fairly shabby, narrow, three-story row house and a far cry from the smart Regency house she and Father had owned on Paultons Square in Chelsea.

Downstairs was a hallway with a small living room off to the left. Behind the living room was a small dark kitchen. This backed onto the only bathroom where I remember a sink with rust stains and a deep tub with a Geyser for hot water — it took a good half hour for the water to achieve two inches and then the hot water promptly shut off, so you needed to hop in pretty quick. I always think of Donald Swan trilling "*In the Bath*" when I think back to that tub, with "*the swirl of pipes vibrating*" although there was no "*boiler room below.*" Off the bathroom was the loo; small and chilly, complete with cistern tank and pull chain. It had two doors. One from the bathroom and one from the narrow backyard. If anyone was having a bath, you could access the loo from the yard. On the loo doors, Mother and her various lodgers pinned postcards, most of them of the naughty French and Victorian variety. My small self would sit in there with legs dangling, staring at the pictures and wondering what that man was doing to that lady, or why another lady wore only her corset. Such was my early education in my mother's house.

There were two floors above. On the first was a large room overlooking Linhope Street. This became Mother's bed-sitting room. There was a large bed-cum-sofa behind which she hung an embroidered Jacobean-style wall hanging. On another wall hung an oil painting that Sue told me was by that long-gone, love of her life, Michael Campbell Ross, co-respondent in her first divorce.

When visiting, which was rarely, I slept on the floor of her room or in the bed with her — neither of which was comfortable. I once slept on the extremely uncomfortable Chippendale-style sofa in the downstairs sitting room. Most of her furnishings, throughout her long life, resembled stage props from various productions. Perhaps they were.

I never had my own room in any of my mother's homes.

Behind her room was a small room, which was let to lodgers as soon as she bought the house, and later on in 1954, my sister slept there.

The top floor at 16 Linhope Street had two more bedrooms, one front and one back.

From the moment Mother moved in, according to my sister, every available space was rented to lodgers. Mother's London agent Peter Eade represented Mother, Joan Sims, Kenneth Williams and Ronnie Barker among others. Joan Sims was a lodger, briefly.

While Mother was so often involved elsewhere, she did have us on her mind from time to time. When I was three and a half (before I went to Silverlands), I had blond curls, chubby cheeks and a rather ginny voice. Mother, whose mind was fixed in the world of entertainment, imagined that I could be '*England's answer to Shirley Temple*'; after all I could do a very funny rendition of

O Me Taters and Me 'Ot Fried Fish. / You can eat 'em any way you wish/
You can eat 'em on a plate or a dish, / Or on a little bit of paper!

Using her contacts, she called an agent who represented talented children and persuaded her to meet us. There, I would convince her just how cunning, cute and clever I was. The lady suggested Tea at the Savoy. There, Mother, in her fox fur stole and smart hat, and I, in my green smocked Liberty dress, white socks and patent leather shoes, met the nice lady and we sat down to a splendid tea with little cakes and strawberries with whipped cream. Such delights were most uncommon to a small child with the country on rationing!

Mother tried to talk me into saying something, anything, but to no avail. I just sat there and stuffed my little face with all the goodies set before me. I uttered not one word. I don't think she ever forgave me!

She had better luck with Susannah some years later in 1950. Sue at ten was very pretty, with curly hair and long legs. Above everything else she loved, and was very good at, dancing. We had dance classes at Silverlands in the big assembly room once a week and Sue was the star.

With the support of Noel Coward, Mother arranged for Sue to audition for a place at The Royal Ballet School at White Lodge, Richmond Park. Sue danced and did exercises at the barre in front of Dame Ninette de Valois and Arnold Haskell. They said she had a weak left ankle and would never make a ballerina, which must have been devastating for Sue. But they added she had talent and suggested she audition for the Cone Ripman School (now The Arts Educational School). She did and won a scholarship. This paid for all her lessons except her uniform. She remembers being taken to D.H. Evans and being fitted for a uniform and for ballet and tap shoes.

Mother, at that time, had been signed for yet another Rep season, this time at the Bristol Old Vic. For my sister, Linhope Street was out of the question. Mother couldn't possibly have Sue at home, while she was away. The Actor's Orphanage committee made arrangements for Sue to live at their London hostel. So, at age eleven in 1951, Sue moved to London from Silverlands and for four years lived at 27 Rutland Gate under the kindly eye of Mrs. Rider, and the rather randy eye of Mr. Rider. Duncan and Yvonne Rider ran the rather elegant house, funded by The Actors Orphanage, for those children who, having finished school at Silverlands, were not quite ready for the outside world. Sue was much the youngest. At eight, I remained at Silverlands and missed my big sister.

I stayed once at Rutland Gate when, at ten, I went to Great Ormond Street Hospital to have my incipient wisdom teeth removed, — *"so my lower jaw could go back, and I would look less like an angry bulldog"*—Mother's words not mine. That was not a happy memory.

Rutland Gate closed in 1954 owing to lack of funds. Sue went to Linhope Street and slept in the small room next to Mother for her last year at Cone Ripman. She left school at sixteen. In early1956, Mother left England for Canada and, within a year, Sue went too.

While she was a student at Cone Ripman, Sue was earning money. She and other students were "Ovaltineys" for radio commercials. In December 1953, she was in the first-ever live BBC-TV production of *Toad of Toad Hall*. In 1954 she went on tour with Margaret Lockwood and Felix Aylmer in Agatha Christie's *The Spider's Web*. In January 1955, for two weeks, she was in Ivor Novello's *King's Rhapsody* as Princess Kirsten at the Salisbury Arts Theatre. She told me that she was given pocket money, but she never saw her salary. She has no idea where the money went!

Mother continued working in repertory theatres. This time to the highly respected Bristol Old Vic Company for the 1950-51 season. She was cast in leading character roles.

When actors were hired for any length of time by a theatre, they generally stayed in 'digs.' Some were very pleasant indeed, like Vivian McCann's home in Salisbury, where she had the whole top floor. Others were not so nice, and some were downright insalubrious. You got what you paid for; what your standing at the local theatre was; and the quality of that theatre.

Years later, Mother wrote this about her Bristol landlady, Mrs. Fry, who kept a rooming house for itinerant actors.

> I was on my way to Bristol, a 'good theatre town', and it was to the Theatre Royal that I was bound; a theatre where such theatre royalty as the Terrys, the Seymour Hickses, Edmund Kean and Mrs. Siddons had played.
>
> I took a taxi up to 85 St. Michael's Hill, an address then well known to leading members of the profession. I rang the bell and waited. After a few minutes there was a shuffling noise of someone in bedroom slippers and the door slowly opened. She was tall, bespectacled and suspicious. She peered around it.
>
> "Ye-es?"
>
> "I've come here to stay…weren't you expecting me?" "Who are you?" she muttered.
>
> "I'm the new character actress at the Bristol Old Vic. I'm here for the Season." "I never take anyone but the leading lady."
>
> The door began to shut. Desperately I shouted, "You were recommended by Catherine Lacey." Her attitude changed completely,
>
> "Come in!" she said re-opening the door, "Any friend of Miss Lacey's…"
>
> From then on, I was housed for the season, well-fed, petted and entertained. That evening, after an extensive high tea, she told me her story with all the drama and timing of a professional raconteur.
>
> At the age of twelve she had worked in a butcher's shop, washing dishes for two-and-sixpence an hour. Four years later she became a nurse in a local hospital, subsequently marrying a man she knew could support her and who, in fact, owned this very same house at the top of St. Michael's Hill. They then decided to improve their finances by letting rooms to 'respectable persons'; and, out for a walk one

Sunday, she met two charming, handsome young men who inquired if she knew of any lodgings. Manna from Heaven! She thought.

But it was Sunday. She could not take them directly to her house (the neighbours might gossip); instead, she directed them to the back door, and then showed them her 'desirable well-furnished rooms', they approved and paid a deposit. Soon they returned with their luggage and settled in.

They were not only handsome, they appeared to be well-off; and, when they enquired the way to the Botanical Gardens, her curiosity was whetted and she asked them what line of work they were in. To her horror she discovered they were…Actors! What could she tell her very religious husband? Actors! Residing in his house…! She could not 'show them the door'. They had already paid a substantial advance and were happily settled in. So, they stayed — and proved such reliable tenants that they won over Mr. Fry. Her husband was now dead, but from that day on Mrs. Fry only rented rooms to the acting profession.

As the years went by Mrs. Fry became a theatrical legend; and after her husband's death, she was left 'in the money'. This enabled her to go on cruises (which she loved) when the season was slack.

The next morning, after a good breakfast, I was shown the photos of some previous lodgers. The Great Houdini had made his famous jump (blindfolded) from the Clifton Bridge while living at Mrs. Fry's."

After these theatre tales, Mother, too, was invited to sign the impressive Visitors Book, and went on her way to the venerable theatre where once the great 18th century actress, Sarah Siddons had acted.

The opening production was to be Christopher Fry's play *The Lady's Not For Burning* in which she was cast as Margaret Devize, a small but telling role in which one critic said, "She handled the spring morning music of Fry's verse beautifully."

Next, she gave a brilliant farce performance in Pinero's *The Magistrate* as Agatha Posket, married to that pillar of respectability, the Magistrate of the title. Donald Sinden matched her in comedic invention as the adult stepson, pretending he was only fourteen.

She played her first Mrs. Candour there in *The School for Scandal*. One critic said "...she could make her voice curdle from assumed concern to acidulated malice within a sentence."

Later that season: "Memorably, she was a finely etched Julia Shuttlewaite in T.S. Eliot's The Cocktail Party with Donald Pleasance as the Unidentified Guest, in Denis Carey's compelling production in a setting disturbingly provocative of a birdcage." She was Mistress Quickly opposite Newton Blick's Falstaff in *The Merry Wives of Windsor*. She had acted with Newton Blick in Salisbury and was delighted to play opposite him in Bristol.

One newspaper said, "Newton Blick's Falstaff bounces cheerfully into traps he would have seen a mile off in his wittier, happier historic days." and "Joan White revels in the quicksilver duplicities of Mistress Quickly."

My happiest memory of my mother's repertory days was at the Bristol Old Vic, the Christmas holiday I turned seven. The pantomime that year was *Puss In Boots*. Regular company members, as always, were 'as cast' in the annual Panto. Mother was to play the Empress and 'Uncle Newtie' Blick, the Emperor; both nice cameo roles. Pamela Allen, as Principal Boy, played the Miller's youngest son. Donald Sinden and Donald Pleasence were her nasty brothers — this was quite some time before the West End, Broadway and Hollywood discovered them. During the Panto, the Donalds had to run through the audience with fully loaded water pistols and spray children, who responded with squeals of delight.

One Friday, Mother was queuing up to get her paycheck. Sue and I stood with her plotting to buy water pistols, so we could spray the Donalds. We didn't know Donald Sinden was in the queue. He heard us. That night, Sue and I were seated on the aisle in the stalls. The Donalds came tearing off the stage and, before we could aim our water pistols, they were upon us and let us have it with both barrels. We were sitting ducks. We stood up to return their fire, but their aim was better. Sue and I were drenched and the audience loved it. We would watch *Puss In Boots* every night; pistols loaded.

At the end of every Panto the tradition is to have the actors sing a popular song of the day; one that didn't require too much vocal training. After one particular performance, Sue and I went backstage rather downcast.

"What is the matter?" Mother asked, *"Is anything wrong? Didn't you enjoy it?"*

I looked to Sue, who said, *"Yes Mummy, we always enjoy it, but please do you <u>have</u> to sing when everyone else does?"*

"Well, I do have to. Why do you ask?"

"You see, Mummy," said Sue, *"We heard the lady sitting next to us say 'The Empress is very pretty but she can't sing. It'd be better if she didn't.' So please, Mummy, don't sing."*

It wasn't the only time she was asked not to sing.

After her three Rep seasons: Birmingham, Salisbury and Bristol, all of which she had thoroughly enjoyed, albeit at Repertory wages, she needed a more substantial income.

Chapter Six

THE WEST END, REP AGAIN AND RADA
1951 – 1956

Back in London in April, Ellen Pollock called and offered her the leading role in a new farce, *Storks Don't Talk*, which she was directing. Mother would play opposite Mischa Auer star of over fifty Hollywood films and a dozen Broadway plays. Some of his most notable films were *My Man Godfrey* (for which he won an Oscar), *You Can't Take It With You* and *Destry Rides Again*. He was beloved by moviegoers as 'the Mad Russian' stereotype. Mother was honored to play opposite him.

They were to tour the summer resorts and open in London in the autumn. Those audiences loved the play and Mischa Auer and Mother got great notices. In the Eastbourne papers: *"(Auer)'s performance is a superb example of a comedy played by an expert, with timing, gesture and inflection all polished till they glitter."* Of Mother that critic wrote, *"Joan White invests a delightful vague 'scattiness' into the part of Gloria Cavendish."*

But when they got to the Comedy Theatre in London, Mother had misgivings, West End first-night audiences were more choosey. She was proved right. The audience just sat there, resplendent in their dinner jackets and jewels, and dared the actors to make them laugh. Worse was the reaction from those seated in the normally friendly 'Gods,' (the cheap seats). They booed and hissed and shouted all manner of unseemly epithets. Mischa Auer was distraught. After a lifetime in Hollywood films, he was unused to dealing with audiences that, although 'live', appeared to be dead or obstreperous.

"What shall I do, darling? They do not laugh."

Mother replied, *"They don't think it is funny, Mischa. Let's pick up our cues as quickly as we can and just keep on to the end!"*

Another gentleman friend was Richard Jackson, owner of both the Manor House in our grandparents' village of South Moreton and an elegant flat near Marble Arch. I had my first taste of champagne there, served with a silver swizzle stick by a maid in uniform. It was all very elegant and I remember feeling very out of place in my second-hand clothes.

Until I was about ten, I adored my Mother from afar. To me, she was the very epitome of glamour. She always wore expensive clothes and smelled wonderful. My feelings began to change when one winter Sue and I stayed at the Linhope Street house after Christmas for a few days. Mother had been invited to a cocktail party. Sue and I went along. Sue willingly. I unwillingly. Sue was very sure of herself in adult company. I was not. I was a chubby pre-teen with lank brown hair and National Health spectacles. At the party, I stood near a large plant and tried to look inconspicuous. Sue socialized. Mother was chatting with a lady near my plant and I overheard the lady say,

'*What a lovely child, your Susannah is, Joan dear. So poised and so pretty.*'
'*Yes, isn't she.*' Mother said, '*She's a handful, but she'll grow out of that.*'
'*And how about little Judy?*' asked the friend, '*How will she turn out?*'
'*Oh,*' said Mother blithely, '*Judy will be good looking when she's forty.*'

Forty! I thought I would die right there. When you are ten, at forty, people have one foot in the grave, don't they? My adoration began to wane that evening.

It was sometime in the early 1950s that our Mother, having several years before divorced our father on grounds of him being long gone, decided to go to Court and have our surnames changed, legally by deed poll, from Moore to White. Overnight, I was no longer Judy Moore, my father's daughter; I was Judith White, and somebody I didn't know. My name was changed to "Judith" at the recommendation of my godmother, Judith Guthrie, who thought it would be more fitting, as I grew older. Hah! I had just passed the Eleven Plus exam. I would now have to go to Sir William Perkins Grammar School in Chertsey, all by myself, with a new name. It was all very confusing for an eleven-year-old.

Sue said, "*Mother, don't you see? It makes us sound like bastards.*"
Mother replied, "*I don't care. I don't want you having his name.*"
We didn't know why...then. And even then, what was the big deal!

In 1949, Mother had been invited to teach at RADA. She found that she enjoyed teaching very much and, from then on, it became a major part of her life. She found that the more active she was as an actress and director, the fresher and more up-to-date she was for the students. Her first production there included Ronald Fraser, Ronald Allen and David Baron (better known later as Harold Pinter). Later, she added the London Central School of Speech and Drama to her teaching roster.

In London, Mother continued teaching at both the Central and RADA when her acting and directing contracts allowed. At RADA in 1954, she was directing a first-year class in scenes from Dodie Smith's play *Touch Wood* when one of the young actors caught her attention.

> She wrote, "*I had a feeling in the pit of my stomach that one gets seeing an amazing view or hearing a glorious piece of music. After the class, I went to Sir Kenneth Barnes's office and said, 'I have a 'star' in my first-year class, Sir Kenneth.'*"
> "*Oh, have you,*" he muttered, "*What's his name?*"
> "*Finney,*" she said, "*Albert Finney.*"
> "*Well,*" said Sir Kenneth, "*We'd better keep an eye on him.*"
> And they did.

Mother said she had only recognized "star quality" very few times in thirty years of teaching.

After the debacle of *Storks Don't Talk,* her acting lay dormant for a while, but she was never idle, busy teaching, and getting settled in her new house.

In April 1952, in Jan Fabricus' *Night of Masquerade,* she was to play opposite her old friend Robert Eddison. Directed by Wendy Toye, the play received mixed reviews and ran for a brief time at the "Q" Theatre. Wendy Toye, an actress and dancer and all-round theatre personality, had been in *The Golden Toy* with Mother in 1933. Wendy wrote to Susannah when Mother died,

> "*She was such a brilliant actress, teacher and advisor and so courageous. She helped so many young people. She will be remembered with great love and gratitude by so many people. I'm just one of them.*"

Wendy Toye died in February, 2010 aged 92.

Later that summer, Alan Judd was taking over the reins at the Dundee Repertory Theatre. He invited Mother to join Gerald Cross, as assistant director and actress, and as she wanted to get more experience directing, she gladly said 'yes.' On August 25th they opened with *The Hollow Crown*. Mother played the Infanta of Navarre and assisted in the direction. It received excellent reviews. She directed *The Queen's Husband* by Robert E. Sherwood and played Frau Wolff, leader of a gang of thieves in *The Beaver Coat* by Gerhardt Hauptmann.

In Dundee, she opened a few garden parties and fetes: invitations that West End actors were often asked to fulfill. A visiting theatre personality, in this case Mother, was invited to attend and was introduced by the Mayor or other dignitary. Upon being presented with a bouquet of flowers by an 'adorable child,' Mother would say a few words declaring the event open. Then she would walk around admiring the various stalls, sampling home-made cakes, and generally being charming. I think she rather enjoyed this and, it was good publicity for the theatre.

Back in London at the end of 1952, she resumed her teaching duties at RADA and the Central School. Teaching and directing would become the main forces in her future, although a good role was always a temptation. Towards the end of 1953, temptation came several times. In the autumn, the Manchester Playhouse engaged her to play *"that faded, but irrepressibly gallant Lady Kitty"* in Somerset Maugham's comedy of manners, *The Circle*.

No sooner was she back in London that November, when another acting call came. Again, she was cast opposite Robert Eddison in *The Sun and I* at The Theatre Royal Windsor, this time with better reviews.

Windsor was very near Chertsey and we children from the Actors Orphanage went regularly to the Windsor Panto every year – courtesy of the management. Yet while she was in Windsor, so nearby, Mother did not come to Silverlands.

I spent my tenth birthday at my Grandparents home in Berkshire. But I was inured to it all by now.

During 1953, the year of the coronation of Queen Elizabeth II. Tyrone Guthrie was directing Shakespeare's *Henry VIII* with an all-star cast to open first at Stratford on Avon, before a ceremonial first night at The Old Vic in London in honor of her Majesty.

Mother remembered: *Lally Bowers and I were invited to Stratford to watch the dress rehearsal. Supporting the all-star cast was a
company of Warwickshire yeomen, who made a marvelous chorus,
they being used to follow orders promptly. They had great fun
working with Tony, who called them "Boys Dear".*

*Tony and Judy were living in an outsized punt, being ad-
dicted to the vagrant life be it on land or water. The punt was
packed with bedding, clothing (including First Night formals), oil
stove, kettle and groceries not forgetting the essential whiskey. We
were regaled with a glorious account of how Tony, dressed for a
formal, grant-getting, publicity dinner, returned to the punt only
to step smartly into what he thought was the punt and found himself floundering about in the Avon, white tie and all, and having
to be rescued by his rather hysterical wife.*

Mother stayed in touch with Tony and Judy Guthrie all their lives.

I, as a somewhat awkward godchild, visited them several times in
Lincolns Inn. Climbing the stairs to their rather haphazard flat for a
lunch of hard-boiled eggs and apples. I dreaded their Loo, colder than a
refrigerator and most forbidding. But I fondly remember their cat Myrtle,
who used to get out through the fire escape window and often came
home pregnant. She would give birth to the kittens in the bottom drawer
of the Guthries' bedroom dresser, amongst their underwear. They were
a wonderfully eccentric couple – true Bohemians. Even though he was
much in demand all over the world as a theatre director, he and Aunty
Judy lived most frugally. Much of his income went to the upkeep of his
ancestral Irish home *Annagmakerrig*, a large rambling house in County
Monaghan. (I visited with my artist daughter Abby in 2013.) When he
died in 1971, Uncle Tony left the house to the Irish State as a retreat for
artists and writers.

It was in the summer of 1953, that I was taken to see Robert Eddison
play Oberon in *A Midsummer Night's Dream* in The Open Air Theatre in
Regents Park. Robert Eddison was a wonderful actor. He was tall, very
distinguished and had a deep baritone voice, most effective when he gave
poetry readings. He was also a very kind man. I came to know him better
in Manhattan in the late 1960s, when my daughters were small. In my

mind's eye, I can still see his Oberon, painted green and sitting in a tree in Regents Park, in *A Midsummer Night's Dream* when I was ten. I fell in love with Shakespeare, then.

> **Twenty three years later, I was to take my own children to see that same play performed by Shakespeare & Company on the grounds of Edith Wharton's house, The Mount, in Lenox, Massachusetts. That evening changed my life, and my career direction. I became the Company's Public Relations Director for seven years and from then on, for thirty more years, worked in Arts Management in the States.**

In December 1953, Mother appeared in a melodrama at the Arts Theatre Club called *A London Actress.*

> *The Sketch* said "Joan White, resplendently aproned, and Edward Byrne, very Irish, shoulder the maidservant-manservant light relief that is always the heaviest matter in these old plays. The author has called it a "grand melo-drama" and so indeed it is."

> *The Stage* wrote, "it may not be a good play, but it is a most enjoyable bad one."

Anyway, it saw Mother through the New Year and into 1954.

Director Murray Macdonald offered her the role of Miss Marcy, the kindly schoolteacher, who tries to sort out the Mortmain family's finances, in Dodie Smith's *I Capture the Castle.* The cast included Virginia McKenna, Bill Travers, Richard Greene, George Relph, and Roger Moore.

> Mother wrote, *"Despite a pre-London tour with packed houses wherever we went, the play remained like a well-made car still not firing on all cylinders. Our poor director was fighting boils under his armpits and was certainly not in any state for a West End premiere. On arrival in Southsea, for our final try-out week prior to opening at the Aldwych, he called us all together and said he knew of only one man who could pull the show together at short notice — his old friend, Tyrone Guthrie. He felt sure that we would all work furiously together under his direction, and not*

question any instructions. Guthrie would see the play that evening, call us together in the morning and, throughout the day, introduce his various improvements. Please would we be very patient and co-operative!

Those of us who had worked with Guthrie, foresaw a highly entertaining day as well as some shrewd amendments. We were not disappointed. He opened the rehearsal.

'If anyone has something to say, say it afterwards! Time is short, and we must press on regardless. All right Dodie?'

Dodie Smith, a little woman in a huge black mink coat, had opened her mouth to speak but clamped it obediently shut. Meanwhile, Georgina Cookson had decided to make her mark with this new director by wearing extremely tight leopard-skin trousers — which Guthrie failed to notice. And when it came to her scene with George Relph, Guthrie made her emerge triumphant from the off-stage fight with a broken chamber pot, which she had supposedly cracked over his head.

Dodie expressed horror.

Guthrie was always a little too vulgar for Dodie. When Virginia McKenna was requested to pour 'heel taps' of sherry back into the decanter, there was almost a riot in the stalls, Dodie hissing dramatically,

'Disgusting, Tony, disgusting! My public will never stand for that.'

To which Guthrie, drawing himself up to his full six feet six inches, responded, 'Nonsense Dodie! Judy and I save the sherry like that in our house.' Roars of joyous laughter from the cast.

Georgina never gave up trying to make Guthrie notice her by changing her outfits regularly, to no avail. However, he did suggest that since her eyes were so small, she might embellish them with make-up. She ceased her machinations then. Wicked Guthrie! But what a genius of a director! By nightfall, no one dared hold up rehearsals or complain. The following week, March 4, 1954, we opened at the Aldwych to mixed reviews and ran for several months. Happily, Murray recovered from his boils.

After *I Capture the Castle* closed, Mother was invited to return to Salisbury, to act and direct! First *Dial M For Murder*, Frederick Knott's thriller, to open August 2nd and later, *For Better, For Worse* by Arthur Watkyn, a charmingly funny, domestic comedy, in September. Both would feature Gerald Flood, a Salisbury Playhouse regular who, with his family, became a good friend to Mother and Sue. Between directing these two plays, she was in Paul Jones' *Birthday Honours* (August 9 – 14), followed only two weeks later as the addicted mother, Yvonne, in Cocteau's *Intimate Relations*, (an English translation of *Les Parents Terrible*).

> *The Stage* headed its review thus: JOAN WHITE IMPRESS-ES and followed with "The Salisbury Playhouse Company registered an acting triumph with Cocteau's difficult play, *Intimate Relations*. Joan White, who played the exacting role of Yvonne, the neurotic, diabetic, and ultra-possessive Mother, drolled about in housecoat and slippers, with unkempt hair falling about her shoulders. She was a person of many moods, and by impressive *acting she created a creature to be pitied and loathed at the same time.*"

Richard Scott directed the production, which ran for its scheduled week, August 23 – 28. It was the summer holidays. Susannah and I were in Salisbury for a short visit with Mother, before returning to our respective schools. We sat in the manager's box one night and watched the play. I doubt if I understood much at eleven, but at the end of the play when Yvonne dies on stage, the tears were streaming down my face. We rushed backstage and, apparently, I attacked the stage manager and cried,

"What have you done to my mother?"

Mother was very flattered.

In September, she was teaching at RADA and the Central School, and rehearsing for two BBC-TVs films: *The Last of the De Mullins*, with Wendy Hiller and Michael Evans. Three weeks later, she reprised her role of Janey Jenkins in the BBC-TV production of *The Cure for Love* with Charles Victor.

When 1955 arrived. Mother was teaching at RADA, directing in Salisbury and Cardiff, and still finding time to act in more TV-films. It was to be her last year in Britain for a while.

In February, she played Thirza Tapper in *The Farmer's Wife*. In April, she was Mrs. Snapgood in *Noah Gives Thanks* with her old friend from Salisbury Rep, John Phillips. It was during this 1955 summer session at RADA that she first met and taught Drew Eliot, a young American actor. He became her good friend and worked with her in several plays in America. Drew reminisced with me about the summer of 1955 at RADA.

> *"Albert Finney (had all the girls), Peter O'Toole (even then a frequent tipsy), Alan Bates (a handsome, quiet, conservative chap), Glenda Jackson (a strong woman — a loud and dynamic presence), Richard Briers (quite a clown, always fun), Susannah York (blonde and gorgeously sexy). She had an affair with my flat mate, Michael Wells and later they married. Michael York (no relation to Susannah), was tall, handsome and quietly elegant. There were many more who eventually had very good luck, but the ones I have mentioned here, became stars.*
>
> *"As for the teachers...there were a few who became legends through their results with students. But Joan White was my favorite.*
>
> *"It was about 1955-56 when I first encountered this ebullient dynamo. It was a class with only about a dozen or so students. We were assigned scenes from plays, which we eventually memorized and performed. I loved the role I was given. It was a serious young man who had been a Nazi, and secretly still believed in the Bund. Oh My God! Sounds like today!*
>
> *The best thing about Joan White was that one felt a definite inspiration from the sense that, she was working WITH you — not AT you."*

Drew later acted with Mother in both New York City and Stockbridge, Massachusetts. He died in 2020.

That summer, Mother accepted directing roles at both the Salisbury Arts Theatre and the Prince of Wales Theatre in Cardiff where she was to direct *Quality Street*, *Ten Little Indians* and *Angels in Love*. These plays were staggered throughout the summer and autumn, enabling my ever-intrepid mother to also direct seven plays at the Salisbury Arts Theatre.

She must have spent hours riding British Rail between Salisbury and Cardiff! I can picture her, her valise stuffed with a few necessary clothes and the well-thumbed scripts she would need for the upcoming rehearsals, sitting in one of those long-gone, comfortable railway carriages. Her spectacles would be on the end of her nose, pencil in hand, lost in the action of the upcoming production.

After *Quality Street*, the first production in Cardiff in July, she went to Salisbury to direct two plays over two weeks. *The First Year* by Frank Craven with a very young Ronald Harwood. (Ronald Harwood achieved fame as the playwright and screenwriter for both *The Dresser, The Pianist* and *Quartet*.)

Back to Cardiff for the next production, *Angels in Love* in late August, and then back again to Salisbury to direct Noel Coward's *Present Laughter*, opening in September for one week. The play starred Gerald Flood in his farewell performance. The management of the Playhouse had offered Gerry Flood a choice of roles for his last performance and he chose Garry Essendine. He proved himself up to the role and "kept the audience rocking with laughter as the play unfolded."

Mother then directed Ivor Novello's lighthearted comedy *Fresh Fields*, which opened in October, followed one week later with Moliere's *The Miser*. She garnered wonderful reviews. One short week after *The Miser*, she directed *Saloon Bar* by Frank Harvey with a large cast of Salisbury regulars.

Back to Cardiff, one more time, to direct Agatha Christie's *Ten Little Indians* in early November, and back to Salisbury again, to direct two of her favorite one-acts, The *Bespoke Overcoat* by Wolf Mankowitz and Jean-Paul Sartre's *The Respectful Prostitute*. They opened November 21st and she said goodbye to Salisbury and returned to London.

Somehow, amidst all this directing and travelling, she had managed to appear in two more BBC-TV films. *Yellow Sands* and her last film was in October as Mrs. Fishwick in *Truant in Park Lane*.

Mother had contemplated a change of scene for some time, and a few words with Michael Langham changed the direction of her life. He advised her to pull up her roots and move to Canada. She had heard a lot about Canada and knew that her friends Tony and Judy Guthrie were over there.

In Dundee, she had met the Canadian actor, Donald Davis, who was running the Crest Theatre in Toronto. He had told her about the vitality of the modern Canadian Theatre. So, in the autumn of 1955, she tele-graphed Tony Guthrie, who was in Canada getting the Stratford Theatre Festival organized.

He sent her a cable, "*Come on Mother Courage, I'll guarantee you*".

She said it was the nicest telegram she ever received.

She began putting her affairs in order: selling the Linhope Street house and making plans for a guardian for Susannah. Rutland Gate had closed in 1954, and Sue had lived at Linhope Street while finishing her education. Sue had been working consistently as a dancer/actress and was hired as a Tiller Girl to be in Emile Littler's pantomime of "Aladdin" that Christmas. After that was over, still only sixteen, she would need a firm hand if she was to stay in London. Mother arranged for her to board with Ken and Verity Hudson, theatre friends. Mother's cousin John Coast was appointed Sue's guardian.

During World War Two, John Coast had been captured by the Japa-nese and wrote about his experiences on the infamous *Railroad of Death* in Burma (David Lean's *The Bridge on the River Kwai*). After his release, he returned to London and worked for Columbia Records, managing many stars. Sue remembered him being terribly thin. What she felt about him as a guardian, she never said.

By December 1955, I was almost thirteen and *Silverlands* had a new forward-thinking headmaster, David Slater. Mother assumed I was con-tent to stay put and visit Granny and Granddad in the holidays.

So, in January 1956, she packed her bags and sailed away to New York.

She did call me at Silverlands to say "goodbye." But it was a brief phone call and I'm sure she wasn't aware of the lump in my throat and more feelings of abandonment. Canada was half a world away. Would I ever see her again?

Chapter Seven

O CANADA!
1956 – 1958

Mother never forgot that January day in 1956 when the old Queen Elizabeth Cunard liner berthed on the lower West Side of Manhattan. The sky was cloudless, the air dry and crisp and the city was covered in clean white snow. There was obviously no shortage of electricity, as there had been in London. New York looked like a fairyland at night with all the skyscraper windows lit up.

In the restaurants, the waiters brought plates laden with food, which after twelve years of rationing were too much for Mother's shrunken stomach.

The Guthries were in town. Mother had a message to go to the Van Rensselaer Hotel in Brooklyn, where Judy awaited her. Tony had left for final rehearsals of *Tamburlaine* soon to open on Broadway. She stayed with them for a couple of days, until their Bohemian ways got to be too much, even for her. Another old school friend from her St Helen's days, Denise Farquharson Bryan, invited her to stay in a calmer environment at her East Side apartment in Manhattan. Denise had married Frederick Van Pelt Bryan, who as Federal Judge had ruled *Lady Chatterley's Lover* was not obscene and therefore it could be sent through the post in America.

> **I remember Freddy Bryan. I had "met" him once before, during the latter part of the War, when I was no more than two or three and he was in the American army. He had met and married Denise during the War and they had invited Mother to a smart party. Unable to get a sitter to stay with Sue and me, she had brought us along. After staring at many knees and eating too many little "nibbles," I needed to go to the Loo. Sue was told to take me. There,**

she removed most of my clothes. I was a substantial toddler and Sue couldn't hoist me onto the seat. I'm told that I toddled back to the party, stark naked, and said to the host, *"Please may I have a potty, because I can't reach the seat."* Freddie told me, many years later, he had never forgotten my small self.

Mother went to see Guthrie's production of *Tamburlaine,* at the Winter Garden Theater, featuring a very Canadian cast: Anthony Quayle, Colleen Dewhurst, a young William Shatner, Donald Davis, and her old friend, Coral Browne. Margaret Braidwood was playing Coral's maid Ebea.

Seven years later in 1962, she was Miss Skilling the drunken spinster, and I was Ida the maid in *See How They Run* at the Berkshire Playhouse in Stockbridge, Massachusetts. We shared a dressing room. From Maggie, I learned many useful comedic acting tips, as well as some rather risqué information about the opposite sex.

Mother was lucky to catch *Tamburlaine* as it had a very brief, two-week run. Coral took her to lunch at Downey's. She fell in love with New York and wanted to stay. Freddie Bryan told her it was quite simple, she just needed to go to the Immigration Office in New York and get a visa for the USA.

This she did. Here, in her words, is what happened:

"I am an Egyptian. American immigration has told me so.

I have crossed the Atlantic Ocean and the Bay of Biscay vertically and horizontally at least a dozen times, and been welcomed everywhere, only to be told, quite late in life, by those handsome, humorless American boys in the New York Department of Immigration,

'You're an Egyptian. Sure, you're an Egyptian. Says here country of origin, Egypt.'' He tossed my passport back at me. "If you want to stay here, lady, come in on the Egyptian quota."

He added, "There's a long waiting list for Egyptians. Maybe you've got some special qualities, like translating that could be useful to the U.S. Government?'

But I hadn't. The only Arabic words I knew were 'Impshi!' (Get Out!) and "Tali henna!' (Come Here!) 'Useful in any country,' I added lamely.

'Not here, lady. Sorry!'
They appeared not to want me. Then they softened slightly, and
the interview continued,
'What was your father doing in Egypt?'
"Well, apart from begetting me, he was laying deep sea cables."
They remained unsmiling,
'Did he own his house or rent it?'
I said I was too young to know at the time.
I did not get my visa."

And so, she set off for Canada on the Lackawanna Railway to Toronto. All went well until the train reached the Canadian border where the Canadian Immigration officials came onto the train. Mother produced her ticket and passport. They didn't mind her being an Egyptian, what they were concerned with was her marital status and wanted to see her divorce papers. These were locked up in her trunk in the guard's van.

Suddenly, at the end of the carriage, Donald Davis, recently of the *Tamburlaine* cast, appeared. He explained to the officials,

"Miss Joan White is on her way to Toronto to direct a play at my theatre, the Crest." All was well. She entered Canada and was busy for the next few years.

The always generous, but careful, Guthries had booked her into the YWCA until she could find a flat of her own. She did, almost at once, with a lady named Shirlee Faessler who was distantly related to Mavor Moore, the nephew of James Bridie, in whose plays Mother had often acted. (Theatre is so often about connections.) She settled in comfortably, and found work immediately. She directed *Present Laughter* at The Crest for Donald Davis in March and, in May, made her Canadian acting debut as Miss Marple in Agatha Christie's *Murder at the Vicarage*. She was well received by the Toronto Press.

The Old Vic Company from London came to town and invited her to their opening night party. Returning home at 2 a.m., she had a message from her new Canadian agent.

"You are wanted on the set of The Last of the Mohicans at 8 a.m..... they're shooting the film in Orangeville...the bus leaves at six. Don't worry about costumes; they have it all there. By the way, you'll be riding sidesaddle."

She had auditioned for the part, never thinking she would get it. When asked if she could ride, she remembered her Portugal days on the mules and blithely said "*Yes.*"

With little sleep and ever intrepid, she made it to the bus and arrived on a bright crispy morning in Orangeville, a town northwest of Toronto. The sun was shining and the maple trees were glorious in early reds and oranges. The location swarmed with extras, technicians and horses. There were trailers for the stars: Lon Chaney, Jr., and John Hart, and for the wardrobe department who dressed her in pioneer clothing and a mobcap.

Under the watchful eye of a groom, she was instructed in the painful art of riding sidesaddle on a fractious horse. Somehow, she stayed on and survived the day. For the rest of the week, she could not sit down. The filming was for a television series for Canadian Broadcasting Company, full title *Hawkeye and the Last of the Mohicans,* and her character, Laura Dodson, was in a segment called *Washington Story,* to air in 1957.

Rather sore, she took the bus back to Toronto.

Soon after she was invited to direct a ten-week Summer Theatre Season at The Grand Theatre in London, Ontario.

An official report in *The London Free Press,* June 16, 1956 stated:

> "LLT embarks on a new venture this summer as it presents the newly formed Trans-Canada Theatre Company in a group of ten plays. The guiding hand throughout the season will be that of director Joan White. A veteran of both acting and directing, Miss White played with the Bristol Old Vic and in London's West End, before turning to directing in London and in Wales. Since coming to Canada this spring, she has appeared at The Crest Theatre in Toronto. Miss White and Mr. Ken Baskette interviewed nearly 180 actors and actresses before 19 players were chosen to shape the Company theatregoers will see in London this summer. Hope runs high that this will mark just the beginning of an annual appearance of Canadian companies in summer stock here.
>
> *'We feel that this new venture can be very exciting in the field of modern theatre, just as Stratford has proven exciting in the realm of Shakespearean theatre.'* Mr. Baskette said. *'The accent*

will be on lighthearted fare. The first production "Dear Charles" is
a saucy comedy." Tickets were $1 each.

Following *Dear Charles,* Mother and Ken Baskette presented: *The Seven Year Itch, Anniversary Waltz, When We Are Married, Sabrina Fair, Lucky Strike, White Sheep of the Family, The Tender Trap, I found April, The Happiest Days of Your Life* and *Ten Little Indians.* In future ventures, Mother was to draw on many of these plays. Many of the Canadian actors had been to RADA and the Central School of Speech and Drama in England. She found herself very much at home.

Her new partner and General Manager, H. K. Baskette, was a very original person.

A trained accountant and devoted theatre professional, he had worked at the Grand Theatre for many years. Mother described him,

"In appearance he was not unlike a Buddha, large and rather yellow-skinned with triangular eyebrows, full lips, a bald head and bejeweled fingers. He loved the British and Bourbon, a bottle of which stood in an ice bucket near his desk. The walls of his office were covered with photos of the British stars who had played at The Grand when touring coast-to-coast in everything from Shakespeare to Charley's Aunt. *It was always a comfort to see John Gielgud and Margaret Rawlings smiling at one. Ken Baskette became a valued mentor and a good friend."*

They had chosen a good young Canadian cast headed by Vernon Chapman. All they lacked was a Scenic Designer. Ken Baskette said he knew of a young American who was very clever and who knew this Theatre. Would Mother take him sight unseen? On Baskette's recommendation, she said she would. Letters, scripts and an offer went winging off to Robert Paine Grose at his home in Maine. He turned out to be a brilliant young designer, particularly successful in training young technicians in back-stage crafts and he could create wonderful sets with very little money.

It was to be a happy decision for Mother, for Bob Grose would become her third, and longest lasting, husband, from whom she learned a great deal.

That summer of 1956 proved successful for Mother and Ken Bas-kette, but on the opening night of the sixth production, *Lucky Strike,* calamity struck the company.

> "First-nighters at the Grand Theatre witnessed a rare example of the old stage tradition 'the show must go on', when the leading lady in the comedy Lucky Strike was stricken mute with laryngitis two hours before curtain time and the direc-tor went on in her place. Up to 6:30 p.m. it appeared that Cosette Lee might be able to carry on. But a final check by her physician, showed that it would have been impossible for Miss Lee to carry the heavy role. Director Joan White said she would take the role rather than see the first-night audience disappointed. Miss White carried the script throughout the play and earned, and won, an ovation after the final curtain."
> *London Free Press,* July 29, 1956.

Mother endeared herself to London audiences that summer.

Back in Toronto, between teaching speech and drama, she appeared in two of the Folio TV series. Folio was an ambitious five-year series, in which they offered seventy different programs. Mother was cast as Madame LaFleche in *The Empty Frame* (1957), and Madame Maniefa in *Diary of a Scoundrel* (1958) a role she had loved at Birmingham Rep nine years before.

Meanwhile back in England, Susannah, having finished her formal education at the Arts Educational School, was earning some money through various engagements, and proving a handful for her guardian, John Coast. She was, after all, a teenager, filled with a teenager's zest for life and young men. He wired Mother and said, "*I can no longer handle Susannah and I am putting her on the plane to Toronto.*" She arrived in the spring of 1957 and, for a while, lived rather tempestuously with our mother in Toronto.

The following season 1957, the Trans Canada Theatre Company had been renamed The Maple Leaf Theatre.

> As reported by Herbert Whittaker in *The Toronto Globe & Mail: May 16, 1957.* "A nation-wide theatre project will get

rolling this summer, when Joan White, Vernon Chapman and Robert Grose move into their second year of their summer theatre operation at The Grand, in London (Ont). Miss White and Mr. Chapman will alternate direction of the plays, with Mr. Grose in charge of design."

The plays that summer were *Tea and Sympathy*, *The Reluctant Debutante*, *The Solid Gold Cadillac*, *Light Up the Sky*, *The Spider's Web*, *Picnic*, *Bus Stop*, *The Seven-Year Itch* and *The Browning Version*. Susannah, newly arrived from England with British acting credits to her name, joined the Company and played many roles, large and small.

> **Later in 1960, Sue was to learn from our father, A.P. Moore, (when she and he had reunited in England), that travelling through Canada in July 1957, he had bought a ticket to see his exwife and his daughter playing Sheila Broadbent and her daughter, Jane in *The Reluctant Debutante*. Sue was devastated that he hadn't come backstage, but Father explained that Mother had taken a restraining order against him shortly after the war ended and it forbade him to see us or have any contact with us until we were twenty-one. We have always wondered why?**

In the autumn of 1957, Susannah joined the Canadian Players for their third season. They had two companies with touring productions. One company offering Shakespeare's *Hamlet* and Ibsen's *Peer Gynt*. Sue joined the other company to play Bianca in *Othello* and the maid in Shaw's *Man and Superman* (with Douglas Campbell). The tour took her all over the United States and Canada.

In The Canadian Actors Equity Newsletter in 1999, a memorial to Mother's Canadian days was written by her partner of the summer of 1957, Vernon Chapman. In her long theatre biography, he included a paragraph about that summer:

> *"A lady of boundless energy, tremendous enthusiasm and love of the theatre, she won many friends in the Toronto theatre scene. In 1956, she was hired to direct a summer season at the Grand Theatre. The following summer Joan and I went into partnership with the designer Robert Grose to produce at the Grand what turned out*

to be a disastrous season financially. One of Joan's qualities I most admired was her determination." He continued with more biographical notes and ends with: *...I hope it has revealed enough to inform those who did not know her, and remind Canadian friends, that for a far too brief few years, there came among us a lady of great good humor, guts, drive, determination and with a deep devotion to the art of the theatre. With Joan there was never a dull moment and I am sure she is stirring things up in the Actors' Valhalla."* Vernon Chapman, Toronto.

The season over, Mother was staying with friends in London, Ontario when Bob Grose telephoned her from Florida, where he was teaching at Rollins College. He asked her to marry him. As was her wont when discussing her 'love life', she wrote,

"I could see nothing against it, except he was a little younger than myself. (about 18 years) *We had worked well together for the past two summer seasons, were deeply fond of each other and were both dedicated to our work in the theatre."*

She said *'Yes.'* Not very romantic, but that's the way she was.

Sue says she was furious with Mother for agreeing to marry Bob, who she thought was unsuitable in many ways.

Bob was under contract to Rollins College and could not get up to Canada, so once again she had to apply for a visa to enter the U.S.A. Once again, she was told that she was an Egyptian. Frustrated again, she was at a smart cocktail party in Toronto and she met a charming man who told her how to deal with this 'nonsense.' He told her to get a letter from her father in England. Was he still alive?

"Yes," she said, *"but retired."*

"Get him to send you a birth certificate and a statement from his former employers. What was he doing in Egypt?"

"Laying deep sea cables."

"Good Heavens! Was your father 'Pinky' White?"

(Grandfather's reputation was worldwide and long lasting).

She did exactly as he said. The magic worked. She got her visa and flew to Florida to be married on May 23, 1958 in Winter Garden, a suburb of

Orlando, then a quiet, comfortable town by a lake. Bob and she agreed, it would be a fine location for a theatre in the winter months. Walt Disney had bigger ideas.

Bob's year at Rollins College was over. Mother and he drove up from Florida through the east coast of America to Bob's home in Maine. They made a brief stop in New York City where Hartney Arthur, her first American agent, told her,

"If you should not remain as happy as you look, the role of Agnes Gooch in the London production of Auntie Mame *is yours, if you phone me..."*

It was temptation indeed, but as a happy bride, she firmly refused and they drove on through Connecticut, Massachusetts and New Hampshire to the lovely state of Maine where, in the little town of Dixfield, Bob's sister Susan was about to be married. Mother was immediately immersed in meeting all her new relatives.

Her new mother-in-law, Leona Grose, was a lady full of fun and not at all upset that she and Bob had married quietly without any of the fuss and confusion that was currently ensuing. Where was Bob's father, the missing Mr. Grose? Leona had married and divorced him three times and said that he had carelessly drowned ice fishing before she could marry him the fourth time. She was a character!

Mother found herself organizing Leona's new outfit and taking care of the grumpy old grandmother, who was not happy that her beloved granddaughter was marrying a Catholic! Then she was put in charge of the "drinks" table, which was a relatively easy task until a large-bosomed visitor managed to knock many of the shining wine glasses onto the floor. Mother swept them up.

The ceremony proceeded without further incident, until Leona came home from the church to find a note that some elderly aunt had passed away. Not only had the lady passed on, but she had been completely forgotten in the wedding kerfuffle, and was apparently in the local funeral parlor. The family must go! Oh dear! They hadn't sent any flowers. It being Sunday, no florists were open. Mother and Bob, used to improvisation, gathered flowers from various bunches on display for the wedding in the church and Bob fashioned them into a funeral bouquet, much to the old grandmother's displeasure.

Later, Mother joined the family as they progressed past the open coffin. It made Mother slightly faint to look at the old lady lying there in a fancy nightgown, a bible clutched in her be-ringed hands, her face heavily made up and her hair beautifully dressed for the occasion.

All of this unaccustomed domesticity was too much for Mother. She quietly phoned Hartney Arthur to see if the Agnes Gooch role was still available. He told her it was cast, and she should be happy. So, she tried.

They went from Dixfield to the Chase Barn Theater in Whitefield, New Hampshire, where Bob had been hired as designer for the Summer Stock season. There she met the company, including the stage manager, Charlie Davisson, an old friend of Bob's. They spent a mostly quiet and happy summer in Whitefield.

Returning from the Canadian Players tour, Susannah had done summer stock in Vineland, Ontario in *The Pajama Game* and *The Boyfriend*. For some reason, she was unable to complete the season in Vineland. Lacking any income, she joined Mother at The Chase Barn Theatre in New Hampshire. Sue, at nineteen, was at this point unsure of her future. Eventually, she returned to Toronto, to stay with friends. It was there, that winter, that she met and soon married James Walker, a Scot from Aberdeen, twelve years her senior, working in Canada as surveyor.

Charlie Davisson would become my mentor and father-figure in my early New York years. He trained me to be a good stage manager, took me with him, in 1961, to be his assistant in Charlotte, North Carolina for a season of musical Stock, and dried my tears when I was overcome with lonesomeness. We stayed in touch through all the years. He met my children when they were small, and my grandchildren when they came along, too. He knew my first husband, the actor Colgate Salsbury and also John Staber, my second husband, whom he liked very much. John and I visited him, several times, in his little house near Whitefield, where he lived out his years with his cat Albert and with all his souvenirs from past touring companies, New York productions and yard sales…he was an inveterate yard sale goer. He gave me an elegant, fluted teapot, but I coveted the colorful cushion that said, "Fuck the Golden Years" in exquisite silk cross-stitch embroidery.

They continued as quickly as they could to the end and took one embarrassed curtain call. The Stage ended its review on July 19, 1951, *"However, the play is dead and we can only hope to be spared anything so deplorably dreary in future."*

Storks Don't Talk closed after three performances. Even now, it is still considered one of the all-time West End flops.

> My sister Susannah, then just twelve years old, remembers, *"I was taken to the first night of* Storks Don't Talk *by one of Mother's gentleman friends, I think it was Llewellyn Rees. It was at the Comedy Theatre, (which is now the Harold Pinter). I can remember that night leaving the theatre with Mother through the stage door and her fans all waiting, and one saying in a very Cockney voice 'Oh Miss Whoite! Why did you 'ave to come back to us in such a load of tripe?'*
>
> *I was acutely embarrassed."*

Even though Sue was now in London, from time to time she came down to Chertsey with some of the others from Rutland Gate for a weekend in the country! Mother had a series of gentleman friends during this time in her life. Sue and I remember how, when Mother was not away acting, one by one, they would escort her in a smart car, usually the sporty kind, to Silverlands on a Visiting Sunday (always the third Sunday of the month) and take us out to tea at the Chertsey Bridge Hotel. Mother would arrive *after* we'd been to Church and had lunch. Then Sue and I, sometimes just I, would be waiting in our best dresses, freshly ironed by Matron. Hands and faces were washed and we were admonished to be on our best behavior. After introductions, we would climb in the back — if it was a sports-car we sat in the rumble seat — and be driven to Chertsey, inhaling petrol fumes, Mother's *Je Reviens* perfume and the gentleman's strong, expensive aftershave. By the time we got to the hotel, we were often nauseous. We'd have tea with cakes and sometimes ice cream, and make polite conversation, which Sue was good at. I probably grunted. I remember Llewellyn Rees because he took us punting on the River Thames as an extra treat. My friend, and fellow 'orphan,' Liz remembers coming with me when Mother's date was Herbert Lom (of *The Pink Panther* movies*).*

After a fun and restful season at The Chase Barn Theatre, the summer was over and Bob had to return to Rollins College in Florida to teach the autumn term. Mother headed south with him and they stopped off at Robin Craven's for a party in New York City. (Craven had been in the cast of *Housemaster).* While there, she learned that Herman Levin's casting director was looking for a Mrs. Higgins to join the National Touring Company of *My Fair Lady.* Cathleen Nesbitt was leaving the Broadway production and Margery Maude, currently playing the role on tour, was to replace her. Mother went to Hartney Arthur's office in New York and said,

"Hartney, I want you to put me up for Mrs. Higgins in the National Company of My Fair Lady*!"*

He replied, *"Don't be silly, darling! You're no Cathleen Nesbitt. Besides, I can't do that for several reasons. One, I am representing Margaret Bannerman for the role. Two, you are too short, and three, you are too earthy to play Mrs. Higgins."*

Mother was so angry that she slammed down the phone and called another agent she knew, Sara Enright.

"What a good idea," said that lady, *"I'll arrange for an interview tomorrow."*

She did. The management would see her at the Mark Hellinger Theatre at 11 a.m.

Now she panicked. Her clothes were packed for Florida. Her hair was red and pulled into a pony tail, and she was wearing a summer frock. She was as unlike Mrs. Higgins as could be. But she was an actress. She quickly made a hair appointment, and unpacked suitable clothing.

Armed with her resume and photos from her Bristol Old Vic days, she arrived at the Mark Hellinger on time. As she strode across the huge stage, a cluster of men rose and cried,

"Wait a minute! You are far too young! And too short!"

Mother decided to brazen it out.

"Gentlemen, I am a producer and director myself and I would not waste your time or mine auditioning for a part I was not right for."

"How old are you?"

"That's my business," she sweetly replied. *"I can play between fifty and a hundred."*

"Read." They said, so she did.

A tall man came up onto the stage and said he liked her reading, but he had to leave. It was Moss Hart. His colleagues from the stalls followed him onto the stage. They asked her if she could 'open' in the role next Monday in Chicago. She said she'd have to consult her husband. She did and it was agreed, he would go on to Florida without her.

Two days later, Hartney's secretary came into his office and said,

"*Mr. Arthur, Miss Joan White is here. She will not leave until you have seen her.*"

Hartney said, "*Show her in.*"

Whereupon Mother swept into the office waving a piece of paper and said, "*I just wanted to show you the contract that I got and Margaret Bannerman didn't.*"

Chapter Eight

MY FAIR LADY USA
1958 – 1959

Moss Hart had directed the Broadway production of *Junior Miss* in 1941. Firth Shepard bought the London rights in 1943 and Mother played the lead role of Judy Graves for more than two years to press and audience acclaim. I suspect that Moss Hart knew this, either from Mother's resume, which would have been submitted to the casting people, or perhaps because he had seen her sixteen years ago in London. I think he wanted her because she had the 'chops' to play the role the way that was needed.

Costume fittings, wigs, the fabulous Ascot hat with grey ostrich feathers, not to mention her salary, were all taken care of in twenty-four hours. She travelled to Chicago to rehearse with the stage manager that same Thursday and would meet the cast at a special dress rehearsal on Saturday morning. She went on, in fear and trembling, the following Monday, less than one week from agent Sara Enright's phone call. It was September 1958.

My Fair Lady was beautiful to look at and well-acted; the company was well disciplined and well managed. Business in Chicago was first-rate. In the cast were some of her English actor friends: Charles Victor playing Doolittle, Hugh Dempster as Colonel Pickering, and Michael Evans as Higgins, a dead ringer for Rex Harrison. Ann Rogers was a lovely Eliza.

The Company was a large one, but everyone was on friendly terms and had great fun. Self-discipline was paramount backstage. No actress must ever let her dress trail on the floor, and the chorus boys had to remember to throw their white gloves in the basket when they walked off stage after the Ascot scene or the Grand Ballroom scene.

Of course, on stage, behavior was strict too, even when tempted into giggles, as on a memorable night during the Ascot Gavotte. Cecil Beaton's immaculate, black and white chorus was suspended in a breathless pause, watching the Derby, when a chorus boy, nearest to where Mother was in the wings waiting to go on, muttered *sotto voce*, *"Bob Held farted… and not even on the beat!"* Those on stage nearest to Mother must have heard but not a muscle moved, not an eyelid blinked. Mother gave into silent giggles, then straightened up, took a deep breath and made her dignified entrance.

The score by Frederick Loewe was, and is, magical, and Mother always managed to join in with the cast in the Ascot Finale to Act One. One day, at a brush up rehearsal, the Music Director Anton Coppola had some trouble with the ensemble during that number. The sound was not quite right. Suddenly he stopped the orchestra and asked,

"Joan dear, are you singing?"

"Yes, Anton," replied Mother happily.

"This time, darling, just mouth the words, will you?"

Mother was crestfallen, but she complied.

"That's it!" Anton triumphantly announced. *"Just mouth it, dear."*

Mother then remembered the conversation with Sue and me in Bristol many years before.

Later during the tour, an elderly member of the orchestra, against Equity rules, made a recording of her lines as a gift for her parents in England. She sent it off.

I was often there when such gifts arrived at Christmas time. Mother invariably sent only gifts pertaining to her career. I don't think she ever thought of giving anything else. Granny always received Mother's 8 x 10 glossy photos, press reviews or recordings with a *"Humph. Joan showing off again."* But when my grandparents died, Mother found a folder containing all her reviews, articles and photos. They had saved them all. In their way, they were very proud of her.

The Company was in Chicago for at least three months. They were wined and dined by the Wrigleys of the chewing gum fortune, and many others. Mother found plenty of time to visit all the museums and go to the shops with Katherine Hynes (Mrs. Pierce) with whom she shared a dressing room.

Come Christmas, Ann Rogers left and Diane Todd was brought in to replace her.

Diane had a lovely singing voice and gave a delightfully fresh reading of the role. Rehearsals were called.

Moss Hart arrived to coach Diane into the role of Eliza the way he had directed it.

Mother wrote in an article for *The RADA Magazine*:

> *"It was fascinating to watch Moss Hart at work. In the kindest, most subtle way, he transformed Diane into an exact copy of Ann Rogers. Every step, every pause, every inflection had to be exactly as Ann had done it. I had been rehearsed by Eddie Preston, our stage manager, and had had an equally exacting time: line readings, exact beats and bits of business had been my lot and, as I had so few rehearsals, I did as I was told without arguments about 'motivation, inner dialogue' and the general discussion of which American actors are so fond.*
>
> *Eventually, the character became part of me, and worked well.*
>
> *Now I enquired why this rigorous copying of the original principal was necessary.*
>
> *"The formula works" was the reply — and they were right. Moss Hart knew exactly where every laugh or mood should come and how to achieve it without showing the audience the technique.*
>
> *We all know that perfect timing is essential for good comedy playing. Unless you are born with this gift in your make-up as Rex Harrison, Athene Seyler and Noel Coward undoubtedly were, the way to achieve it is for an actor to follow Moss Hart's infallible and precise direction. Then it works. Laughs are money in the box office; they put 'bums on seats.' No wonder fortunes were, are and will be made for years to come from My Fair Lady."*

After all those exacting rehearsals, they were given a company party in Chicago. No one had ever said a word to her about her Mrs. Higgins. So, emboldened by a couple of drinks Mother approached Fritz Loewe, the composer, and asked him why no one had said anything to her.

He turned to her in surprise. *"My dear, we don't have anything to say to you. You are excellent — the best after Cathleen Nesbitt."*

"*Sucks to Hartney Arthur,*" she thought. But that conversation with Mr. Loewe helped. All actors need to hear compliments about their work; it's like a pat to a dog.

The tour was to span the USA and Canada. The Company always travelled on Sundays by train. After Chicago, the National Company continued on its way across the USA and Canada. First stop was Detroit, a large industrial city and center of the automobile world. The only theatre there that could house the Company was a large cinema on the outskirts of town. Next, they played a week in Rochester, New York, home of Eastman-Kodak, and on to Cleveland, Ohio for two weeks.

They played only the major cities and travelled by train, with sleeping compartments for the long hauls. They had reserved carriages, and she and Katherine Hines (Mrs. Higgins and Mrs. Pierce) always shared a roomette. They journeyed on to Cincinnati where several years later she would return to play Mrs. Tarleton in Bernard Shaw's *Misalliance* and Lady Bracknell in *The Importance of Being Ernest* at the Cincinnati Playhouse in the Park. Onward to St. Louis, Missouri, where they crossed the great Mississippi River and visited a Show Boat still presenting old time melodramas.

From Kansas City, their last stop before the West Coast, to San Diego was a two-day journey across the Southern Plains. For that, they had a whole train to themselves: The *My Fair Lady* special.

A few years later, I too toured the United States, with *A Man For All Seasons*. But ours was a Bus and Truck tour. No special trains and fancy hotels for us!

Several times during the tour, the management tried to get Mother to commit to staying on another year. She didn't want to sign on any earlier than Equity said she had to, two months prior to the end of her contract. The management wanted her to commit because they would like her to hold understudy rehearsals in addition to her role. She was cagey because I, her younger daughter, was finishing school in England and was coming for a holiday before returning to England. Also, her new husband, Bob Grose, was leaving his college position and wanting to start a new life with her in New York.

San Diego was a wonderful town to visit and she loved the town and especially the Zoo. Bob joined her there and they rented a car and drove to the next stop, Los Angeles. *My Fair Lady* was to play in a huge auditorium in Pershing Square for three weeks. On Sundays, the *My Fair Lady* Company's day off, this theatre became a temple where people were baptized in large tanks on the stage. Saturday nights the set had to be struck and all costumes and props carefully stored away from any dampness. She was not impressed with Los Angeles, but for the next four weeks they were booked into the Opera House in San Francisco, which she loved.

I arrived in town shortly after the Company, at the end of July, landing at San Francisco International Airport. This, my very first flight in a plane, was from Heathrow to San Francisco over the polar route on TWA! Once I got through customs and the embarrassment of my cheap, blue cardboard suitcase with my teddy bear packed on top. I went out into the arrivals building looking for Mother. I hadn't seen her for nearly five years. Then she had been taller than me. Two rather short ladies wearing tracksuits approached me. One asked,

"Are you Judy?"

"Yes." I said *"Are you my mother?"*

She was and introduced me to Velma Royton, who was playing Mrs. Hopkins. (I was to play that role in 1964). We took a taxi to the apartment she was sharing with Velma and Katharine Hines on Sutter Street. I would be sleeping on the sofa.

I saw *My Fair Lady* every night; made friends with the Company and helped the costume department with wig dressing backstage, loving every minute of it all.

> Mother wrote, *"If I had been thirty years younger, I could have lived the rest of my life in San Francisco. Alas, the show pressed on to Portland, Oregon and Seattle, Washington. After a wonderful fishing trip with members of the Company on the Puget Sound, it was time for Judy to leave."*

I told Mother, I wanted to stay in America and make my own way, maybe even in the theatre. After all it was in my blood and, by now, I was stage struck with *My Fair Lady*. Mother's words, and they were not something I will ever forget, were:

"Whatever am I to do with you?"

I said, *"Don't worry about me. I can get a job anywhere. I can cash in my return ticket and I have my Post Office Savings Book."*

I was rather starry-eyed, free at last, not very realistic but, very determined. My mother was only partly mollified. But Bob, my new stepfather said,

"Let her do it, Joan. She's had enough of that Orphanage."

I often wondered what he, and her other friends, thought of her lack of parenting.

I sat for the College Boards in Seattle, but college for me was not really on offer, as I found out later.

So, it was arranged that I would fly to New England and stay with some friends of Mother's until the tour ended. Meanwhile, Bob would go to New York City to find a suitable apartment for the three of us.

Mother gave her notice and, after weeks in Vancouver, Calgary and Edmonton, she left the tour in October 1959 and came to New York to, if one interview is correct, "be a homemaker." But that had never been in the cards.

Irony of ironies, Hartney Arthur's client from the year before, Margaret Bannerman, replaced her as Mrs. Higgins!

Back in Toronto, Susannah had married Jim Walker. Soon, she was pregnant.

Their son, Jamie, was born on August 13th 1960. I went to Toronto that autumn to be his godmother. Turning twenty-one that year on July 12th, Sue could now, legally, see her father again. He had kept in touch with news of his daughters all along through his brother, our Uncle Arthur. He called Sue in Canada and paid for her, Jim and baby Jamie to return to England, which they did shortly after the Jamie's Christening.

Meanwhile, there was I in the States, ostensibly for just a summer holiday. I was meant to return to the care of the Actor's Orphanage and train for a suitable job for a young woman: — a nurse or a teacher or a librarian. Uncharacteristically, I had spoken up and said I wanted to stay in America.

Poor Mother! Newly married and having had some success in North America, she was suddenly upset by both long-neglected daughters. Mother was not pleased with either of us, but what could she do? It was out of her hands.

Mr. and Mrs. H.W.G. White

Henry and Kathleen White,
Amelia Sabina Beach with Joan aged 2

Awaiting the cable tankers at Carcavelos

Joan White 7 ½ years
Audrey White 4 ½ years

Joan in 1933 photo ©Houston Rogers
courtesy Victoria and Albert Museum, London

As Euodias in James Bridie's
Jonah and the Whale *1932*

Robert Eddison in The Anatomist, *1932*

*Sir Tyrone Guthrie, who gave Joan her
start at The Cambridge Festival Players*

As Bella Hadley in The Barretts of Wimpole Street *1935* photo: Morter

Googie Withers and Joan White in You're The Doctor *1937* British Independent Films

Now thou art mine.

As Phoebe in the Paul Czinner film As You Like It *with Richard Ainley as Silvius*

Joan in 1938
photographer: John Vickers

Housemaster *by Ian Hay, which ran from 1936 through 1938. Joan as Button Farringdon is seated second from the right.* Photograph from her scrapbook

Little Ladyship *1939 Joan and Lilli Palmer*
photographer© J.W. Debenham
courtesy Victoria and Albert Museum, London

Joan as Judy and Peggy Cummins as Fifi in Junior Miss *1943-5*
Photographer: John Vickers

[LEFT] *The Duke of York's Theatre St. Martin's Lane, London*
Managed by A.P.Moore 1932-39

[RIGHT] *Father and Mother on their wedding day January 21, 1937* photo by H. Allen/Getty images

Father with Judy and Sue 1943

Susannah 6 and Joanna Judy 3

Silverlands – the front entrance.

Arts Theatre, 1946 with Paul Scofield in
A Phoenix Too Frequent
Photographer: John Vickers

Birmingham Repertory Theatre, 1948
Madame Maniefa in Diary of a
Scoundrel Photographer unknown

Bristol Old Vic 1951 The
Cocktail Party
as Julia with Peter Cook
Photographer: Desmond Tripp

Annual Pantomime Puss in
Boots, *Bristol Old Vic 1950*
Joan as Empress with Newton
Blick as Emperor
Photographer: Desmond Tripp

The Circle. *1949 Joan as Lady Kitty with David Carr and Robert Cartland*
Photo: Salisbury Playhouse

Aladdin Panto *1949 as Fairy Rosebud*
Photo: Salisbury Playhouse

[ABOVE] Caste *1950 David Dodimead, Joan and Robert Cartland.*
Photo: Salisbury Playhouse

[LEFT] *Noel Coward's* Tonight at 8:30 *as Myrtle Bagot*
Photo: Salisbury Playhouse

*The Grand Theatre in London, Ontario where
Joan and Bob produced 1956-58*

photo courtesy of the Grand Theatre

*Susannah at 16, before
Joan left for Canada 1955*

As Mrs. Higgins in the National Company of
My Fair Lady *1958-9 and later
at The Berkshire Playhouse in 1964*

Stockbridge photo by Louis Hansen

*Robert Paine Grose, 1961
her third husband*

Chapter Nine

NEW YORK CITY AND
STOCKBRIDGE MASSACHUSETTS
1959 – 1960

I was a green girl of 16 years and 9 months when I first moved to New York City in October 1959. Having left England and the Orphanage in late July, to visit the mother I hardly knew, new doors were opened for me. For five weeks, I tagged along as she toured with the National Company of *My Fair Lady* as Mrs. Higgins up the West Coast of America. After five weeks of exposure to that wonderful musical, of course I fell in love with the theatre.

When I announced that I did not want to return to England but wanted to stay in America, she was shocked and, I think, unsettled by the prospect of having to deal with me, at last. However, Bob, my newly acquired stepfather, took my side and when Mother's tour was over, we all moved to Manhattan, where Bob had found a decent apartment in the theatre district.

463 West 49th Street was a second-floor railroad apartment. The area was then called Hell's Kitchen now, gentrified, it is known as Clinton. The apartment was between 9th and 10th avenues and the crosstown bus stopped outside. Quite nice as apartments went, but small for three people. The front door opened into the large front living room furnished with the uncomfortable antiques that my collector stepfather assured me were "*the real thing, Honey.*" It was a square room with a fireplace that hadn't worked in years, two tall windows fronting the street and an alcove, really a pass-through to their bedroom. Beyond was a good-sized kitchen with a window looking over a sad back yard with one Godot-like, forlorn tree, a fence, another equally sorry yard and the rear of the building on west 50th street. The bathroom was off the kitchen.

Where was I to sleep? In the alcove, on a narrow, lumpy, but very decorative couch. My blue cardboard suitcase, shoved underneath, was where I kept my meager belongings. At night, unused to the street noises and frequent sirens of the great city, I kept my pillow tightly over my head. Since my bed was part of the living room, when company came over, and that was more often than not, I couldn't sleep until the guests were gone. It was an awkward and unwelcoming set-up, even for me, who had been used to thin mattresses and iron bedsteads in rooms shared with four, sometimes six, other girls. I was not made much of as the long-lost daughter newly come home!

But I was not to be there for long.

While Mother's tour was ending, I had been shipped east to stay with the Farquharsons, old school "chums of Mum's", at their weekend house in Mill River, in the southern Berkshire Hills of Western Massachusetts. They were very kind. They introduced me to American ways and also to *Flanders and Swan*, for which I have been forever grateful. David Farquharson also introduced me to a friend, his name long forgotten, who promised he'd give me a job at Macy's in New York. I was only sixteen.

When Mother and I arrived in New York City that October, I *was* given that Macy's job. It was in the currency office of Macy's, Herald Square. There I translated the invoices that came in; from pounds, shillings and pence, or francs, or marks, or lira, into American dollars. Then I entered them into the comptometer, an awkward type of adding machine that I managed to master.

You might wonder how I landed such a job — I, who had perennially flunked mathematics. During my interview, it came out that I was able to translate other currencies into pounds sterling; it was a short step from that to dollars. I credit this minor talent to years of stamp collecting. (I was that kind of girl.) However, soon the American bureaucratic machine found me and decreed I must go to school, one day a week, until I was seventeen, unless I could prove I had graduated properly from High School or the English equivalent.

I wrote to Miss Margaret Sames, MA Oxon, my former headmistress at Sir William Perkins School for Girls in Chertsey. In my school days, I had spent many an anxious hour standing outside her office for some misdemeanor or other. However, she wrote me a kind letter saying I had been a good student and had earned several O-level passes.

Her letter arrived, but not before I spent several Tuesdays at a "High School for Dropouts" on the lower east side. It was torture. I was assigned to classes for "English as a Second Language" (huh?) and "American History." I kept my head down, as I had learned to at the Orphanage, and finally when Miss Sames' letter arrived from England, I took it up to the teacher, hoping she would just let me go. But oh no! She had to wave it in the air and tell the other students that I had seven years of French, four of Latin, and had four O levels in History, English Literature, English Grammar and French. I felt my face turning red. I took the letter and ran from that classroom to the uptown bus, changing to the crosstown bus at 34th Street for Macy's.

It was early December now and getting on for Christmas. Carols were in the air everywhere. Macy's was a Wonderland. I spent my lunch breaks gazing at the decorated, animated store windows and looking longingly at all the laughing people. In brightly colored hats, scarves and coats, carrying boxes and shopping bags, they hurried past the "false Santas" furiously ringing bells for the Salvation Army. It was indeed "*beginning to look a lot like Christmas.*"

The situation at the apartment was uncomfortable. I needed my own place. Paying rent to my mother and her new, much younger, husband, for the privilege of sleeping on their faux Empire sofa in their West 49th Street railroad flat, was not conducive to happiness.

It was the very beginning of the Sixties, January 1960, and I was turning seventeen; four months new to New York City.

Santa came in the guise of Don Brassington. Don had been in the *My Fair Lady* Company and now, back in New York, was giving singing lessons. I had sung in the Lyne Church choir in England and, having made up my mind that I was going to be in the theatre, I took him up on his offer to teach me. He charged me a pittance. He was a dear soul and a good listener. He 'got' my situation and just after Christmas, he told me there was an affordable studio apartment in his building, just two blocks away on West 51st Street.

He said, "*You need your own place, kiddo? An apartment in this building is empty. Do you want to take a look?*"

It was perfect. One room with a galley kitchen plus a small loo and shower.

Seventy dollars a month. I took it. Now I *had* to get a better job right away.

With my British Post Office savings account from England and my cashed-in return ticket for down payment, as well as my current salary as surety, it was mine. The large square room, about 20 by 20 feet, had no furnishings except, to my delight — an upright piano. This was painted bright blue and was only a little out of tune. The former tenant had left it behind. Too difficult to move. I bought a bed at the Salvation Army and, with my employee discount, some sheets and towels from Macy's. Little by little, I began to assemble my household.

Until I married, I never had much in the way of possessions. Somehow that was okay because everything that I gleaned, no matter how small, was a gift. I was free! Free to explore New York, free to find new friends and to get on with my new life.

When I arrived in America and had refused to return to England, I told Mother I wanted to be an actress and to work in the theatre. This may have seemed strange after spending twelve and a half years at the *Actors* Orphanage all because she, Mother, was determined to continue her career as an actress and work in the theatre! As ironic as this may seem, that's what I wanted now!

Mother, who has been dead for some time but still roams around in my head, used to resort to metaphors when giving advice. She, who had never done anything else in her life but work in the theatre fully supported, by either her father or her husbands, when work was scarce, said,

"You must have another string to your bow. You'll need to keep the wolf from the door."

She even offered to pay for me to take an evening secretarial course to afford string and avoid wolves. I learned to touch-type and to write *"Dear Sir: Thank you for your letter"* in Gregg shorthand.

As I lugged my blue cardboard suitcase out of her door, Mother remarked,

"Well, I hope you haven't bitten off more than you can chew."

Ever ready with the idioms.

After a few weeks in my new home, I left the job at Macy's and got 'temp' jobs at *Time Magazine* and Dictaphone, probably thanks to my clipped British accent. But I was always looking for more interesting ways to pay the rent. Free from the Orphanage, I roamed New York City full of wonder and awe.

In the evenings, I worked with new friends Peg Shirley and Margie Bolton as a substitute usher on Broadway. For the next three years, we saw almost every production — flops and hits — for free. My only expense was a black sweater and skirt from Lerner Shops – our white collars were provided.

Mother and Bob had let me go without a murmur or a question. I'd love to have gone to college, but that was not on offer — ever. I was an alien; scholarships and other financial awards were not available to aliens in those days; my studies for life came straight from the School of Hard Knocks, and for theatre from Herbert Berghof, who took me on as a scholarship student at the HB Studio on Bank Street and taught me so much. I was eager, tidy and with my English accent I had no problem getting part-time jobs.

That was about me and I should stop digressing and return to my mother, Joan White, for she is primarily what this book is about. But I wanted to say how it was.

Well, I moved out and Mother got used to New York City and all it had to offer an actress of her experience. Her agent Sara Enright, who had sent her up for *My Fair Lady*, began to submit her for roles and almost immediately she was cast as Mrs. Page in David Susskind's television production of *The Citadel*. Based on the novel by A.J. Cronin, it was directed by Paul Bogart and starred Ann Blyth, James Donald and Carol O'Connor; great company for her New York City debut. The production aired on February 19th 1960 and she earned a favorable mention in *The New York Times*, …"and Joan White as an unprincipled shrew." Her next few months were spent auditioning and becoming known to casting directors.

During the early 1960 winter months The Berkshire Playhouse in Stockbridge, Massachusetts advertised for an Artistic Director and an Administrator. Mother and Bob applied and, on a freezing winter's day in an unheated car (Bob's Florida car, a yellow Cadillac named Urina), they drove for three hours, through trees weighed down by wet snow, to meet the Board of Directors of the Three Arts Society.

Designed by the talented, and somewhat notorious architect Stanford White, The Berkshire Playhouse was originally The Stockbridge Casino. The building had been moved to its current location at the east end of Main street where, in 1928, it became a reputable summer stock theatre, one of the oldest in the States. Every summer for many years, in the charming New England town of Stockbridge, (made famous by Norman Rockwell) the Playhouse offered the local people and their summer visitors ten plays in ten weeks; a daunting schedule for actors and designers alike. Many famous actors, and those who would become famous, trod the boards in Stockbridge. Eva LeGallienne had opened the very first season with *The Cradle Song*. During the 1930s James Cagney, Katharine Hepburn, Ina Claire and Ethel Barrymore appeared at the Playhouse, and later Tallulah Bankhead, Ruth Gordon and Shirley Booth came to star with their names writ large above the play titles. Summer in Stockbridge, in a long-coveted role, was a happy engagement for many Broadway actors and even movie stars. An added attraction was staying at the Red Lion Inn, although when the Playhouse first opened, it had been difficult to find housing for "actors."

It was a charming little theatre with a large barn on the property for the scene shop and rehearsal studio. Early on, the barn even housed students and apprentices in the former cow stalls. Eventually the townsfolk came around to renting rooms.

Billy (William) Miles had successfully operated the Playhouse from 1935 until 1957, with time out for World War Two, but now he was ready to hand it over to younger people. He had hired many well-known actors, as well as building a company of 'local stars.' He had even enticed Eva LeGallienne to return to the Playhouse in 1949 to play the lead in *The Corn Is Green*.

Billy wanted to end his tenure by co-producing the 1957 season with a popular playhouse actress, Eleanor (Siddy) Wilson, who he hoped would succeed him. But Siddy decided, after one exhausting ten-week season, that she preferred to be "on the other side of the footlights." For the 1958 season the producers were two inexperienced men. They ended up deeply "in the red" and were not asked back. Then came Nikos Psacharopolus, an exuberant Greek director. He was running the nearby Williamstown theatre and thought he could easily run the two theatres simultaneously.

It didn't work. Nikos returned to Williamstown to run his theatre there successfully for twenty-seven more seasons until his death in 1989.

In 1980, when I was marketing and public relations director at Tina Packer's newly-formed Shakespeare & Company at The Mount in Lenox, Massachusetts, my friend and colleague was Ellen Lampert, who held the same job at the Williamstown Theater Festival. We sometimes met for lunch and made plans to lure the New York and Boston critics for a "two summer theatre" experience. Picnicking on the Williams College lawns, we would amuse ourselves, and passersby, with imitations of our bosses. Ellen had perfected Nikos' Greek-American vernacular and I could do a pretty passible Tina Packer-British (RADA with just a touch of Nottingham). Ellen now lives on St. Barthelmy in the Caribbean and writes about her beloved island home.

Early in 1960, Billy Miles had been introduced to Mother and Bob in New York City and was impressed enough to recommend them to the Board of the Three Arts Society; hence that wintry drive.

Mother remembered "*a tall lady with incisive diction and a searching eye. As Treasurer, Bertha Skeffington was all-important in the hierarchy. I was terrified of her until a mutual friend told me Mrs. Skeffington had remarked, 'I'd be rather be with her than against her...' Me? But she proved a loyal friend and supporter – and also introduced me to Jack Daniels!*"

Other board members included Robert Wheeler (then owner of The Red Lion Inn), Pete Miller (publisher of *The Berkshire Eagle*), Mrs. Laurie Deeley, Frederick Lord, Brier Stoller and Rosamund Sherwood, sister of the late playwright, Robert E. Sherwood.

Eighteen years later, as a *Berkshire Courier* reporter, I interviewed Billy Miles and remember him fondly. He talked about running a Summer Stock theatre in those early days; of the importance of choosing a season with the local residents in mind and of finding lodgings for the actors nearby.

He told me, "We had a very good stock company who came back year after year. Some of these actors were so well liked that if we

couldn't get a star, we would feature one of them and no one knew the difference. Some of our regular actors were: Gaye Jordan, William Swan, William Roerick, Mary Wickes, John Straub and Tom Coley. We had a lot of very famous names too: Ethel Barrymore three times; Jane Cowl five times, Thornton Wilder twice, Edward Everett Horton three times (and only one of those was *Springtime for Henry*). We had Anna Russell as a legitimate actress — well as an actress, I'm not sure how legitimate, but she was very funny."

We talked about other company members: sets, costumes and props. "We had an electrician, not a lighting designer, just a good electrician. We tried to accommodate people too. One set designer said 'I'll do the season but my wife is expecting a baby and I must have time off when the baby's due. So, I said, 'No problem we'll do *Our Town* that week.' No sets needed you see."

Billy Miles ran The Berkshire Playhouse for twenty-two years. Mother and Bob inherited much of his good sense in how to manage this particular theatre. Unfortunately, over the years, things had become more and more expensive.

Mother and Bob were hired and they returned to New York to select plays and personnel for the 1960 summer season. They invited me to join their staff.

That first summer, I sublet my new apartment to a dancer and off I went to Stockbridge to apprentice at The Berkshire Playhouse. In order to earn a little money to pay for my lodgings, I agreed to work in the box office, instead of back stage where I would have had a better chance for a small part on stage. The box office proved to be an invaluable experience, organized and run by Bert Gruver. Bert wrote *The Stage Manager's Handbook*, which I read while waiting for the phone to ring. I learned the need for planning ahead and how to be polite to anyone, no matter how rude.

The characters I met then have remained indelibly fixed in my mind: Gertrude Robinson-Smith, a short, square, doyen of Stockbridge society, who purchased season tickets for four, but always came alone with her chauffeur, insisting vociferously, when picking up her fourth-row center tickets, "*I will not be seated next to tourists with hairy legs in those ugly short trousers.*"; Bertha Skevington, a terrifying giantess in a toque hat, reminded me of my old history teacher. She demanded prompt and courteous service of us all and, because she was on the Board of the Playhouse, we jumped; and there was deaf Mr. Simpkins, who would yell "louder" at the poor actors when he forgot his hearing aid.

Bert Gruver was a wonderful and patient teacher who taught me much about dealing with people and front-of-house etiquette. Mother and Bob wanted Bert back for the second season in 1961, but he was contracted to tour with William Gibson's *The Miracle Worker* and sadly, he died during that tour.

Later on, in 1963, when I was hired as assistant stage manager and understudy for the Bus and Truck tour of *A Man For All Seasons*, the production stage manager was Frank Hamilton, from whom I learned even more about Stage Management. Frank had written the 1972, revised edition of Bert Gruver's book. I own a copy of it and consider myself lucky to have been influenced by both these giants of hands-on theatrical stage management.

Having set a high value at the top, Mother and Bob added backstage and publicity staff and set about selecting their first season.

Mother wrote in her journal about that first season:

"I was determined to have a good sound company, with no insistence on 'star' names. Bob and I agreed to build up from a small cast, adding actors (each week) as more roles were added. The cast could not get much smaller than our opening production, William Gibson's comedy, Two For The Seesaw with Gaye Jordan and Kendall Clark, local favorites from past seasons. Bill Gibson, who had a home in Stockbridge, said he liked our production better than the Broadway one, which was encumbered with unnecessary revolving stages. My husband was a genius at designing simple, effective and economical stage sets."

Mother and Bob's philosophy was that each season should have something to please every taste. For their second play they chose Alan Melville's comedy *Dear Charles*, with Mother, Kendall Clark, John Malcolm, and Drew Eliot (her former student at RADA). The plot: a woman who had three illegitimate children by three internationally known fathers. Walter Howard, writing in *The Berkshire Eagle*, said,

> "It isn't easy to crack jokes about bastardy for three acts, but Miss White can do it. In a magnificent drawing room set designed by Robert Paine Grose, she moves about with ease and grace, savoring every little comment she has to make about the wild oats of her past."

Pauline Flanagan took the lead in Agatha Christie's *Witness For the Prosecution* with Kier Dullea, who, in Stanley Kubrick's *2001, A Space Odyssey* as astronaut David Bowman, had the much-quoted line "*Open the pod bay doors HAL!*"

The fourth play was Shaw's *Misalliance*. Shaw had subtitled his play *A Debate in One Sitting*, and insisted on this program note: "*The debate takes place at the house of John Tarleton of Hindhead, Surrey, on 31 May 1909. As the debate is a long one, the curtain will be lowered twice. The audience is requested to excuse these interruptions, which are made solely for its convenience.*"

I own Mother's copy of the play, complete with her directorial notes and rather extensive cuts. It's a very long play, especially for summer audiences.

Misalliance was presented the week of July 18th with Playhouse 'stars' from Billy Miles's days, Eleanor (Siddy)Wilson and John Malcolm as the Tarletons. During the run of the play was a moment which introduced me to the venerable art of ad-libbing. John Malcolm was on stage with two young actors. Siddy was due to make her entrance on cue. Well, she didn't appear and didn't appear. They couldn't just glide over her entrance; what followed was key to the plot. So, John Malcolm ad-libbed for what seemed an age about how his mother made orange marmalade — getting many laughs! Suddenly, a toilet flushed somewhere offstage and, shortly after, a rather flustered Siddy Wilson appeared in the doorway and said, "*Now, what are you going on about, dear.*" And the scene continued with the audience none the wiser.

The Member of the Wedding, featured Patricia Fay as Frankie and an eight-year-old boy as her cousin, John Henry. When not needed in rehearsal, he could be found selling lemonade at 2 cents a cup to passersby, outside the Playhouse. His name was Richard Thomas. A dozen years later he became known worldwide as John Boy in the television series *The Waltons*. Mother noted, "*He was a good actor and a small person of great charm.*"

After the genteel American south, next in the line-up was Jean Anouilh's bitter French farce *Waltz of the Toreadors:* a savage lampoon of a man of honor, filled with Anouilh's humorous relish of grotesque animosities, which gave Mother a chance to show off her versatility opposite Paul Ballantyne.

Following their philosophy of "something for everyone," they brought Margaret Hamilton back to Stockbridge. She had played there before, in a number of productions, and she would return again under Mother's aegis. In *The Happiest Days of Your Life*, Maggie was the headmistress of a girls' school about to merge with a boys' school. I got to act that summer in *Happiest Days*. Having never seen *The Wizard of Oz*, Margaret Hamilton didn't scare me, in fact I loved her. We all did.

Happiest Days was my stage debut, I played Barbara Calhoun, a cheeky Scottish schoolgirl. Upon meeting a trio of schoolmasters, I lifted up my skirt and, in my best Scottish brogue, said, "*And we're girrrls, see.*" It got a laugh every night! That's when I was sure an actor's life was for me.

I made a lifelong friend in this play. David Vaughan, another Brit, came as an actor in 1960, stayed for two more Stockbridge seasons before moving on to his true calling: Dance. He became Merce Cunningham's archivist. David and I exchanged Christmas cards for fifty-six years until he passed away in 2017.

Margaret Hamilton stayed on for a cameo role in *Angel Street*, and returned in 1962 to play the title role in *Miss Lucy*. Maggie Hamilton was a kind woman. While she was known all over the world as the Wicked Witch of the West in *The Wizard of Oz*, she never behaved like a star. She was the consummate professional, learning her lines, taking direction and quick to befriend the younger actors, indeed all young people.

There is a lovely story about a young son of friends who, when Maggie was visiting, climbed up on the couch where she was sitting and stared at her for some time. Finally, he spoke, "*I've seen the George Washington Bridge, Niagara Falls and a fire eater, and now I've seen you.*" She was enchanted.

After *Angel Street,* came *The Gazebo,* a comedy murder mystery with Pauline Flanagan and William Swann as a blackmailed couple and Drew Eliot as their comic contractor. For the final production they produced a musical. Musicals were Bob Grose's forte. He was an excellent director and he designed gorgeous Victorian-style sets for *Dear Miss Phoebe,* a musical version of J.M. Barrie's *Quality Street.*

The Board invited Mother and Bob to return for the 1961 season with the *proviso* that they not do so many English plays. They were also asked to keep to a tighter budget. In those days there were no government grants, no Ford Foundations and very few wealthy patrons to fall back on. Summer theatre depended on a good box office.

Mother and Bob followed Billy Miles' example and cast a solid repertory company: William Swan, Gaye Jordan, Eleanor Wilson and Mac Morgan; and some who became repeat performers each season such as Drew Eliot, David Vaughan, Pauline Flanagan and Kendall Clark. To bring in the audiences, they also contracted with film and stage stars of the day, luring them with rooms at The Red Lion Inn and other amenities. As well as Margaret Hamilton, there was Gloria Swanson, Sylvia Sidney, Anna Russell, Geoffrey Lynn, Joan Copeland and Gloria Grahame. Many of them, like Maggie, returned for more than one summer season.

That first summer in 1960, Stockbridge was nothing like the tourist mecca it is today. It was just a sleepy New England town. I had a tiny room on Elm Street. We apprentices went to nearby Lee to eat because Rossi's restaurant offered "*all you can eat for $1.99*". The telephone system was very simple: most phone numbers were simply "Stockbridge," followed by three numbers. I was trying to call Bob Grose one day, when the telephone lady cut in and said,

"*He's not home dear, I just saw him cross the street and go into the Red Lion.*" Norman Rockwell lived on Main Street, Tanglewood was still an easily affordable summer music festival and parking was no problem. That was Stockbridge in 1960.

It was my first summer and I learned a lot about putting on the productions.

There were guest directors, but mostly Mother directed and sometimes acted, with Bob designing the sets and directing the musicals. That summer, they also started a Summer Theatre School which was well respected and continued throughout their tenure for next five years.

My first theatre job in New York after Stockbridge was with a dreadful revue called *Darwin's Theories*. A fast flop, it ran for two performances in an Off-Broadway theatre above Vic Tanny's Gym. Bob, my stepfather, designed the sets and I came on board as assistant stage manager to Charlie Davisson, and as dresser to future luminaries Alan Alda and James Coco. Howard Taubman, critic of the *New York Times* wrote:

> "The line of dialogue to heed was 'I don't know about you, but
> I'm going home.'"

This show is not on my resume!

David Harper had been the technical director that Stockbridge summer, and it was through him I went to volunteer at Equity Library Theatre, the Union showcase for actors, now sadly no more. I ran props for *Merry Wives of Windsor* and Dina Harris designed the costumes. She has been my close friend ever since. Soon to be dear friends, Edward Payson Call directed and Ron Bruncati was stage manager. Jordan Charney, as Fenton the young lover, asked Dina if he could put socks in his codpiece. She said "*Sure, why not*".

He was the *only* cast member to get an agent. His was clearly an enhanced talent!

I liked ELT and I guess they liked me because I was offered the job of production manager for the Children's Theatre in the late autumn. We toured the five boroughs that winter with two plays: *Nicolo and Nicolette* and *The Stone Tower*. In the spring of 1961, we gave free performances at the Wollman Skating Rink in Central Park — after it thawed!

The following year, Equity Library Theatre for Children moved to Joseph Papp's new outdoor theatre, the Delacorte. I remember, with nostalgia, sleeping on the stage under the stars with the rest of the crew after we had finished putting up the set. Ah, those long-gone days of innocence; you couldn't do that now.

Chapter Ten

LIFE UPON (AND OFF) THE WICKED STAGE
1961 – 1963

In January 1961, with my newly acquired box office skills, I was hired as the assistant box office manager at One Sheridan Square. This supplemented my always meager earnings. One Sheridan was at the confluence of Seventh Avenue, West 4th Street, Waverly Place and Christopher Street in the heart of the West Village where so much was happening. The play was Michael Shurtleff's, *Call Me By My Rightful Name* (with Robert Duvall in his first major role). Each night, when the performance was over, the theatre space became a nightclub. Because of this designation, everyone had to have a cabaret license in order to work there. My license had a clause that said that I would not be considered naked as long as I had my shoes on. I kept them on at all times!

I shared box office hours with a blond, buff guy with the improbable name of Bobb January. Three b's in his Bob! I worked mostly evenings – right there in the hub of it all. In the 1960s, Kelsey Marechal was proprietor of One Sheridan Square. Down the street was The Limelight Café. It was immensely popular. I saw *Peter, Paul and Mary* there. *The Clancy Brothers & Tommy Makem* made it their headquarters. It was a center for joyous gatherings, informal concerts by patrons, and sitting all night over one beer without being ejected or carded.

Folk singers no one had yet heard of were popping up all over the Village. Bob Dylan was just a kid with a guitar at the Café Wha. At that time, there was a local ordinance against folk music in Washington Square Park. The police would arrest anyone who so much as plucked at the strings of their instrument.

On many a night Kelsey would ask, *"How much money in the till, Jude?"*

And I'd say something like, *"A hundred and thirty-two dollars and fifty cents."*

And he'd say, *"Better give me a hundred. I've got to bail the boys out so they can do the show."*

My theatrical education was many faceted.

Meanwhile, my indefatigable Mother had returned to New York, to work as an actress and dialect coach, and to prepare for the next Stockbridge season. She wrote:

> *"For the next four years, Ken Baskette was now our business manager. He remained a real 'theatre person' through and through, an excellent showman and a strict disciplinarian. He held a nail inspection every night before the public was admitted, and no apprentices were allowed to go 'downtown' collecting theatre props, unless they were cleanly and decently dressed. Charlie Davisson, who joined us as stage manager towards the end of the second season, was equally strict backstage. He and Bob trained excellent technicians, and the Barn scene shop was always tidy and on time with beautiful sets. It was Ken who advised us to engage an occasional 'star' to help boost publicity. When Gloria Swanson thanked us for a week spent in 'the best-run Summer Theatre I have ever visited', we were justifiably proud. Gloria Swanson was theatrical royalty. Her week's contract ran into several pages, and even stipulated Poland Water, organic food and a private Loo. Her progress from New York to Stockbridge was announced by her secretary on the 'phone from each New England town she passed through, and she arrived in her Rolls Royce on a hot July day in 1961 in a full-length mink fur coat. She was definitely a* Star. *She was also hard-working and self-disciplined; a wonderful example to our young company in rehearsals and on stage in* Between Seasons.
>
> *"As was Sylvia Sidney, when she came to star in* The Pleasure of His Company *in 1962 and returned for Sidney Howard's* The Silver Cord *in 1964. Another star, Gloria Grahame failed to appear on the first night of* The Marriage-Go-Round. *She eventually turned up at 11 p.m. having gone to Sturbridge, Massachusetts by mistake. Ken Baskette had to return thousands of dollars to the disappointed audiences."*

(In defense of Miss Grahame, that was a common mistake to make – Sturbridge and Stockbridge were both much visited Massachusetts towns during the summer tourist season, — and besides, surely the fault was by Miss Grahame's driver, not hers. I am sure she was frantic. No cell phones in those days! Anyway, the lady was invited to return to Stockbridge later that season as Susannah in James Bridie's play *Susannah and the Elders,* the role Mother had originated in London in 1938).

Mother continued:

> *"We had a more than usually wild time with Anna Russell, who broke her arm (not her leg!) on the first night of* Breath of Spring. *She had caught her toe in the jaw of a tiger skin hearth rug. She played the rest of the week in a cast. We finished our second season with a joyous production of* South Pacific, *with all our apprentices and theatre school students on stage."*

My work with the Equity Library Theatre for Children that spring had led Lyle Dye, ELT's managing director, to offer me the job as his secretary (general dogs-body) for the grand sum of $100 a week to start in the autumn of 1961. I think it was my English accent that sold him, but whatever it was, I was on my way. This would cover my rent and other expenses.

But first, I was off to The Ovens Auditorium in Charlotte, North Carolina to learn the ins and outs of stage management under the benevolent eye of Charlie Davisson, who was to become my mentor, father figure and dearest friend. It was a summer of stars, musical theatre and eighteen-hour days. We did a different show every week with a resident company of singers, dancers and featured actors. The big-name stars, Elaine Stritch, Hugh O'Brian, Alan Case, Darren McGavin and others, would check in two days before their shows opened. My job, aside from the prompt desk stage right and "walking" the stars' blocking during rehearsals, was to run lines with these headliners and give them their moves when they arrived.

Elaine Stritch, before each performance of *Plain and Fancy,* would place a tall glass of clear liquid on my prompt desk, saying with a wink *"Watch my water, honey."* She would take a swig from it before going on stage, where she wowed the audience every time. Elaine was a joy to work with in spite of, or maybe because of, being fueled with vodka.

Hugh O'Brian on the other hand was quite the most boring Destry in *Destry Rides Again*. He could have used a shot of vodka to jolly up his performance. Sweet Darren McGavin simply could not comprehend the South's dry laws. As I ran lines with him, for *The King and I*, in the diner next door to the theatre, from time to time he would mutter "*No wonder they lost the war.*" Then he would flavor his coffee from his silver hip flask commemorating his *Riverboat* TV series.

That summer, we had a director and a choreographer for each show. Our director was Adrian Hall, later, distinguished artistic director of Trinity Square Theatre in Rhode Island and the Alley Theatre in Houston, Texas, but this was early days for him in 1961.

Adrian hated doing the musicals – his forte was drama – so whenever the chorus dancers and singers were to come on, he would walk out and leave it to the choreographer. Adrian was temperamental, to say the least. During rehearsals for *Where's Charley*, an actor went up on his lines. I, as prompter, usually gave them a moment to see if they remembered. This time, Adrian yelled,

"*Where is that f***king little English girl?*"

I stepped smartly around the proscenium from stage right and said sweetly,

"*The f***king little English girl is right here!*" The company applauded.

North Carolina in 1961 was segregated and I was a British naïf from New York City. Having been coldly reprimanded by the box office manager for making friends and chatting with the African-American groundskeeper in front of the theatre, I took against the South. But, my happiest memory of Charlotte that summer was ice-skating. Next door to the theatre was the Charlotte Coliseum with an ice hockey rink. The janitor would leave a small work light on for us and, after the show, many of the company would go over and skate, making our own music. I learned to ice skate in Charlotte, taught by some of the nimblest show gypsies. It was glorious fun, skating and stumbling around that huge rink in the semi-dark, singing the songs from the show we had just done.

Charlie and I did six musicals and one play, *Mr. Roberts*, before we left Charlotte in somewhat of a huff. Charlie had had a serious disagreement with producer Ben Kapen over the way the shows were run, and he finally quit – which meant me too, as I was part of the package.

Mother and Bob were having difficulty with their stage manager and Charlie was just what the doctor ordered. He signed on and was the Berkshire Playhouse's stage manager for the next two years.

Returning to New York, I decided that I must get contact lenses if myopic me was ever to become an actress. I went to Pearl Vision on Sixth Avenue and was fitted with hard little lenses. I could see! And without the thick glasses I had worn since I was five! I went to work at ELT for a couple of years and learned a lot, even though for the first few months I frequently had tears streaming down my face as I broke in my new "eyes."

ELT's office was in the old Actors' Equity building on 47th Street in the heart of the theatre district. In the geriatric elevator, I often stood thigh to thigh with the likes of Jerry Orbach and Gwen Verdon. ELT's showcase theatre was up on 103rd Street and Riverside Drive at The Master Institute. I typed up the programs for all the plays and cranked them out on the ancient Mimeo machine. I answered the phone, ran errands and was the first line of defense for my boss, Lyle Dye, should an irate actor or director demand to see him because *they* hadn't been chosen to direct or act in a play. I would say in my crisp English accent,

"I'm terribly sorry, sir, but Mr. Dye is out of the office just now."

Whether he was or was not.

Early on in my association with ELT, I was sitting eating my lunch when a disheveled man came in wearing a long, rather dirty raincoat and a worn fedora with the brim pulled down.

"Uh Oh" I thought to myself. *"Here's trouble."*

He asked to speak to Lyle and said he was an old friend. His name was Lore Noto. I phoned through to Lyle who came right out and embraced this man. Impeccable, rather fussy Lyle embraced him! They went into his office. A little while later they came out and Lyle introduced the five staff members present to Mr. Noto, who told us he was producing an Off-Broadway show, an exciting new musical with a small cast and wonderful songs. We could all be in on the ground floor if we bought a share — only $100 each. Larry Metzler and I declined being the lowest paid. Joy and Packy McGinnis bought one share and so did Dave Harper. Lyle bought two. Larry and I considered sharing a share, but it sounded too complicated and anyway the show could be a flop and our money would be gone. The musical was *The Fantasticks* and to his dying day in 2019, Lyle got a monthly royalty check.

Ah well, as they say, "*That's Show business!*"

Their second season in Stockbridge over, Mother went straight from Stockbridge to Boston to play Julia in *The Cocktail Party* at The Charles Playhouse. Kevin Kelly, critic for *The Boston Globe*, wrote "*The production is an interesting failure…but the performances are excellent. Joan White is perfect as an interfering busybody who is also intended, I think, as a handmaiden of the Lord.*"

Nicholas Kepros, who'd been at Stockbridge in 1961, wrote to me when Mother died in 1999:

> "*Dear Judy,*
>
> *I was sorry to hear of your mum's passing, but it made me think of all the wonderful things about her, and how she had always encouraged and cheered me with her joy and lively spirit.*
>
> *I remember we were once at the Charles in Boston, in different plays, but living at Mrs O'Keefe's, in that incredible house full of English antiques. Joan invited me, and Brendan Burke, upstairs to dinner in her room, where there was an upright piano. Brendan played and he and Joan sang a lot of old Coward songs — "I'll See You Again," "I'll Follow My Secret Heart," "Mad Dogs and Englishmen," and I suddenly felt I was in theatrical digs in Bournemouth or somewhere — completely transported! What fun we had.*
>
> *We had met when she hired me, practically sight unseen, for four plays at Stockbridge in 1961, a tough but rewarding experience, and she was supportive throughout. Her enthusiasm for the theatre, and for people, never faltered through the years. I hadn't seen her for many years (since she returned to the UK, in fact) but I will miss her nevertheless. She was a great and unusual woman, Judy.*"

Well Nick, she was certainly an unusual mother!

After the Charles Playhouse, Mother returned to New York. She auditioned for and got the role of Mrs. Telfer in the Equity Library Theatre production of Pinero's *Trelawney of the 'Wells.'* I was already working for ELT by then as Lyle Dye's secretary, but rarely had contact with her. I suppose I must have seen *Trelawney*, I don't recall, but it was to be the following production, *The Story of Mary Surratt* that opened new doors for me.

Mother takes up her story here,

"Bob had gone off to design sets in Wisconsin and I was booked to play Mrs. Turton in Donald MacWhinnie's production of "A Passage to India" starring Gladys Cooper and Eric Portman. We rehearsed all through Christmas in a large ballroom above a Jewish restaurant on Second Avenue. My husband in the play was to be my old friend from London and Housemaster, Robin Craven.

As we neared production, a host of ladies 'in hats' and busy-looking gentlemen appeared. They sat in groups, noting every nuance of the rehearsal; and afterwards they conferred in tight-knit bunches.

'Who on earth are those people?' I asked Eric Portman.

'My dear, they are the backers. They want to see what they have bought.' "I was amazed. So was Gladys. But apparently it was the normal practice.

We suffered the same scrutiny at our final rehearsal at The Billy Rose Theater. Then we were off to Boston for our only date prior to opening on Broadway.

"Boston critics were not kind to us, accusing the producers of caricaturing the British Raj, hardly a fair criticism since the Raj was a pretty good caricature of itself. However, the Theatre Guild did not wish to offend the British, and the women especially were modified in both costume and manner.

"Socially, Boston was fun. The British Consul and his fun-loving wife gave a lovely party for us, the Old Vic Company (who were in town) and the Irma La Douce Company. The highlight for me was at 3 a.m., with Gladys Cooper accompanied by Denis Quilley singing "Two Little Girls in Blue."

Returning to New York, we opened on January 31ˢᵗ at The Ambassador Theatre and, with a favorable review in The New York Times, *enjoyed what could be called a 'success d'estime'. We ran for about three months, closing on May 5ᵗʰ 1962. By then I was preparing for our third Summer Theatre season in Stockbridge. This entailed endless long-distance calls to Bob in Wisconsin and the Three Arts Society Board in Stockbridge. We ended up with a good selection of plays, including* A Streetcar Named Desire *with Ray Reinhardt and Marcie Hubert,* Life With Father *with local Berkshire stars Mac Morgan and Eleanor Wilson and a twenties Cole Porter musical* You'll Never Know, *in which I was to sing!*

"Being the producers of a popular summer theatre was not simply directing, acting and managing the theatre; a certain amount of hobnobbing with other artistic venues in the area was part of the job, and expected by The Three Arts Society. Often Bob and I attended other performing arts organizations benefits and hosted them in return. We visited nearby Jacob's Pillow Dance Festival run by Ted Shawn and Ruth St. Denis; the Boston Symphony Orchestra's Summer home at Tanglewood; Hancock Shaker Village and, of course, Nikos Psacharopoulos' Williamstown Summer Theatre.

"In New York, Bob and I had moved uptown to the Dorilton at 171 West 71ˢᵗ Street earlier that year. It was a beautiful, high-ceilinged Victorian palace of a building, and we had a large spacious apartment, much more conducive to entertaining prospective talent and friends like Gladys Cooper and Eric Portman.

"At the end of that third Stockbridge season, Bob and I took a sea trip to England where Bob met my parents for the first time. While we were in London, we ran into Anna Russell who told us she wanted a change from her one-woman shows. She was keen to act with a company again and suggested rejoining us in Stockbridge the following year. Knowing her ebullient personality, I thought that a melodrama might provide the best transition, and we agreed then and there to work together on the book of Lady Audley's Secret *and to transform it into a musical, Anna providing the music and lyrics in her own inimitable style."*

Meanwhile, I spent my days in the office at ELT and many evening hours up at the theatre on Riverside Drive watching rehearsals and performances, subbing for the box office manager, and absorbing it all. I made a new friend in Julie Sommars, who had a role in *The Story of Mary Surratt.* She asked me to be her room-mate so, after a happy, but lonesome, time on my own in Hell's Kitchen, I moved into her basement apartment on 75ᵗʰ street near Central Park West: one huge space with a bathroom. We bought screens for privacy and learned to cook bizarre and cheap meals. It was Julie who introduced me to the HB Studio and Herbert Berghof.

Julie said, *"If you really want to be an actress, you need to take some classes, Jude. Come with me to the Studio and sign up."*

Well, I didn't have much money; pretty much what I earned went to just living: food, rent, second hand clothes and bus fare, but I went.

Herbert Berghof himself interviewed me. He and his wife Uta Hagen had founded the studio on Bank Street and it had a terrific reputation. Still does. I think Herbert liked me, and he invited me to stay and watch a class that evening. After that class, which was like no class I had ever taken, I desperately wanted to be part of it all. Herbert asked me if I could afford the tuition and I mumbled *"not really,"* embarrassed by my penury.

"Vell darlink," (he was very mittel-European), *"vould you like to be my key student. You vould just get my classroom set up and you can come to any other class you vant, on scholarship. I think you have promise."*

Would I? I almost kissed him. I had to be at the Studio four evenings a week, which was do-able with my ELT schedule. Later, also for my tuition, I stage-managed some of the Studio's productions. We did one of Robert Frost's one act plays, *A Masque of Reason*: Earl Hyman played God, Bill Hickey was Satan and Ion Berger and Lily Lodge were Job and his wife. Those classes were Nirvana. I learned so much, and not just technique but, well everything. I got to audit other classes, whenever I had time. Uta's classes were amazing. She could teach you how to walk across an old linoleum floor as if you were on a thick pile rug. Bill Hickey's classes taught me a lot about technique, and Charles Nelson Reilly gave me the wherewithal to do comedy. He told me,

"You're a natural born comedienne, kid. Go for the schtick and leave the drama for others."

But I showed my dramatic side later, with my first Equity role.

Often after class, a few of us would go back to Herbert's house on Washington Square. In his basement, we sat at his feet, drank hot cocoa and listened to his stories about German theatre, before the war and the Nazis came. He had us spellbound with stories about Max Reinhardt, Bertolt Brecht, Lotte Lenya and Marlene Dietrich.

As well as preparing scenes for class, during this heady time, I acted in a few showcase productions Off-Off-Off Broadway. In the spring of 1962, I auditioned for a season of summer stock at the Red Barn Theatre in Northport, Long Island and was cast as Jo, the ugly duckling, who-gets-pregnant, heroine, in *A Taste of Honey*. Nancy Andrews played my mother. I had become used to hearing an audience laugh, but in my big final scene, I learned what it was like to make people cry. It felt weirdly powerful. I went on to play Molly, and understudy Polly Peacham, in *Threepenny Opera* with Felicia Sanders, Mitch Jason, Gene Rupert and Nancy again.

Mother and Bob had meanwhile been having a very successful season – which probably accounted for neither coming to see me in my first big Equity role. They had decided to add an eleventh play, a farce, to end their season. My summer contract fulfilled, they invited me to play Ida the maid in *See How They Run*. After the drama of *A Taste of Honey* and the melodramatic *Threepenny Opera*, it was wonderful to let my hair down and have a rip-roaring time.

> The press called it "a really funny farce" and "wild and rambunctious."

> *The Berkshire Eagle* said, "The cast is wonderful and to single out anyone would be unfair."

> *The Springfield News* raved about us all and said of me, "Judy White in the role of a cockney maid took out every bit of stereotype and brought to it a sublimely ridiculous air."

I returned to New York on a high note. My roommate Julie was leaving, for what was to be a very busy future in Hollywood, so we had to give up our basement flat. For a couple of weeks, I bounced around sleeping on friends' couches, until Charlie heard about an apartment for $45 a month on East 28th Street – across the street from him and around the corner from Bellevue Hospital – sirens day and night, but hey, it was New York. 342 East 28th Street between 1st and 2nd Avenues was in a row of brownstones complete with stoop and iron railing. (The whole block has long since been razed.)

My new home was a fifth-floor walk-up with three rooms. The entrance went right into the kitchen-cum-bathroom with a tiny loo – so tiny you couldn't shut the door when sitting down. A claw-foot tub was beneath a large enamel counter-top next to a very deep sink, into which hot water rarely ran. The living room was big enough for my bookshelves (planks on bricks – I hauled those bricks, a few at a time, up five flights), an armchair and a small, black and white television that sat on an old chest, which held blankets and clothes.

My bedroom window looked south and had a fire escape. From the fire escape was a washing line, which was connected to the building across the alley. I shared this, quite literal, line of communication with an actor named Jerry. We rigged up a bag in which we shipped each other LPs, scripts, onions, cheap wine and other sundries. I don't know what happened to Jerry. I only knew him across the clothesline.

It was from the fire escape that robbers came one night when I was out working. They took the TV and flipped open every book, looking for the money that I never had. I did have a police lock on my front door and besides they would never have got past Tom on the stoop. We didn't have a doorman, but we had Tom, our resident wino. Tom knew us all by name and any stranger who tried to enter, was questioned by him. In the winter, he slept in the front hall. For almost two years I was happy there, enjoying the aromatic cooking of my Chinese, Japanese, Jewish and Italian neighbors as I climbed the stairs after long days and nights of two, sometimes three jobs in a day.

The best thing about this apartment was that my beloved Charlie Davisson and his roommate Glen lived across the street and they were always ready to feed me.

Having earned my Equity card in *A Taste of Honey*, life became a crazed cycle of acting jobs in short run shows, auditions, classes and little supplementary jobs: bussing tables at *Marie's Crises*, a funky restaurant in the Village; and selling honeymoons at *Honeymoon Holidays*.

This last job came about after my Long Island summer. Robert Dean Hooks had played the sailor to my Jo, and we had both gone into *Threepenny Opera*. Other members of that cast — Herb Edelman, Henry Howard and Simm Landres, along with friends Harvey Jason, Morna Murphy and Don Buchwald, had gone to Brooklyn College with Jordan Wolfe.

Jordan ran a travel agency with a sideline in honeymoons. "Honeymoon Holidays." Several evenings a week, a few of us, depending on our acting work, would gather at his office and sit at the phones with a list of names and a script. We worked on commission and sold honeymoons in the Poconos to putative brides. I did quite well, probably because my British accent lent an air of something to the Poconos. A sample script went something like this:

"Good evening. I understand you are getting married soon. May I offer you, my congratulations?" Pause *"Would you and your future husband be interested in a romantic honeymoon in the Pocono Mountains. Our intimate inn rooms feature heart-shaped bath-tubs, champagne, roses and red satin sheets."* Etcetera, etcetera.

And of course, like all telemarketers, we were calling at dinnertime! Sometimes one of us would get the first sentence out and there would be a muffled sob on the end of the line followed by *"He's left me for someone else."* After a few hours of this, we would go to Rattner's for Huckleberry Blintzes and Seltzer or Matzo ball Soup. I learned never to ask for a glass of milk — but a glass of tea was fine. Morna and I were the only *shiksas* and Bobby was the only *schvarze*, the others were all Jewish and they taught me to say Chanukah and Chutzpah and Chuckleberry with that glottal *Ch.*

That winter I auditioned for an ELT production of *The Magistrate*, a rollicking comedy by Arthur Wing Pinero, to open in March 1963. Tom Gruenewald was the director.

> Leighton Kerner in *Show Business* said, "ELT, if it wants to and it can get the money, can move this production of Pinero's farce 'The Magistrate' into an Off-Broadway Theatre and have a hit on its hands."

> And Tom Hammond in *West Side News* wrote, "'The Magistrate' is truly funny and stylish. In short it is a ball." About me he said, *"Judy White, as Popham, is delightfully whacky."* This showcase did its job.

Three of us went on to appear in *The Saving Grace*. Connie Booth as Beattie went on to fame and fortune as John Cleese's wife, writing partner and Polly in *Fawlty Towers*. She was so much fun to act with. Leon Benedict, who played the Magistrate, was to work with me later that year. Tom Gruenewald got a directing job at The Berkshire Playhouse that summer.

Mother came to see this production in her capacity as a producer. It was the only show that I appeared in that she came to, unless of course, I was acting at the Playhouse. I can hear her saying now,

"But Darling, I would have come, but you know how busy I always am!"
But in all fairness, I rarely saw her act in New York.

I, along with Patricia Falkenhain and Arne Weiner, went almost immediately into rehearsals for *The Saving Grace*. Directed by Richard Altman and starring John Cullum, we opened at the Writers' Stage Theatre on East 4th Street on April 18th after three weeks of rehearsal and a couple of previews.

All the New York critics came and the reviews went from lukewarm to terrible.

Edwin Harvey Blum had written, what he intended to be a farce, about the British horsey set and fox-hunting. It ended up being a polemic about everything he could think of and filled with dreadful British caricatures. In seventeen publications, the critics were kind, or they faintly damned, or outright damned, or excoriated.

> *The Daily News* said "I had not encountered a play that was all bad — until last night."

It improved from there. I came off favorably in quite a few and got a glowing review from Edith Oliver in *The New Yorker* – the best review I ever received.

> "The find of the company is a young English actress named Judy White, who plays the marriageable daughter. One can almost feel her damp palms as she writhes or prattles or sulks or achingly tries to be a credit to her mother. Her "Ay don't remember, Mummy," as she gasps like a fish with shyness, is very funny, and her love scene ("Ay feel so frightfully common") with the marriageable son is the high spot of the show."
> *The New Yorker* no less!!

Mother did not see *The Saving Grace*. Perhaps she was in England dealing with her parents. Perhaps she was plotting the coming 1963 season or writing the script for *Lady Audley's Secret*. Whatever she was doing, she missed the show, but she certainly knew about it as I have a letter from

Edward Greer, a well-known director and a leading member of the Actors Studio. He wrote a short note to Mother (which she sent me):

Dear Joan   What a surprise to find one Judy White tread the boards downtown last week in The Saving Grace. Even if you'd want to you couldn't deny her – so like you in face and form. And <u>such</u> a delightful performance!

I never write a fan letter, but I know you'll be proud to have this enthusiastic reaction from me, as well as the usual friends in the audience, to her fine work. Aren't you lucky? Greetings ever, Edward Greer.

I received other kind letters too: (from Norman Roland, screenwriter and actor)

Dear Judy: Just a note of heartiest congratulations for your excellent work which I thoroughly enjoyed last night. Your Penelope was a sheer joy! Yours sincerely,   Norman Roland

And a letter from Patrick Waddington, former headmaster of Silverlands, who had returned to acting and was currently in the States in rehearsal for a revival of *The King and I*. He had stayed in touch with me and was my supportive non-parent at this time.

I want to congratulate you on your excellent performance in The Saving Grace. You were, Praise God, not a caricature and you alone among the grotesque figures made it possible for me to believe in you. Affectionately, Patrick.

The Saving Grace lasted a couple of weeks.

Chapter Eleven

ON THE ROAD AGAIN
1963 – 1964

The Merry Month of May in 1963 came. Once again, as an actress I was out of work but I filled my time doing box office stints, handling props for the Jewish Educational Theatre for Children, working at HB Studio under Herbert's beneficent eye, and auditioning around town. I did go up to Stockbridge for a week that summer on the two-coach train

Late in 1962, Mother and Bob had returned by ocean liner from England, where Bob had picked up a few choice antiques. They began planning the 1963 Stockbridge season with a date for Anna Russell to return with the premiere of *Lady Audley's Secret*. The coming summer would have seven productions rather than ten, three of them musicals, to run for two weeks each. Bob had to return to a commitment in Milwaukee, and Mother began working, long distance, with the redoubtable Anna Russell. Christmas came and went. In the New Year, Mother was Mrs. Gladstone in Hallmark Hall of Fame's *The Invincible Mr. Disraeli*. Starring Trevor Howard and Greer Garson, the production went on to win two Prime Time Emmy awards, airing in April 1963.

Shortly afterwards, Mother wrote,

> *In early summer I flew back to England, this time to help transfer my elderly parents back to Gibraltar where we had spent so many happy days when my sister Audrey and I were young. So much had changed: the dockyards were no longer full of naval ships, and high-rises now towered on both sides of the Rock. Two good things though: the Barbary Apes were still there and the native Gibraltarians were firmly pro-British.*
>
> *Having settled my parents in a rented house over-looking the Straits, I returned to New York. I knew, eventually, something*

would have to be done about their house in South Moreton and its furnishings.

Back again in Stockbridge, I found the Theatre School and af-filiated Apprentice Group both doing well. We had revived The Berkshire Playhouse Drama School from the days in the 1930s when Katherine Hepburn had been a student there. Under the leadership of Charlotte Fitch, with students from all over the world, about twenty students came for the summer to "find their feet" in the world of theatre. They don't all end up on stage; they might become stage managers, designers and one chap we had, found he loved doing publicity.

Our Summer Theatre season was a strong one with The Grass is Greener *and* A Shot in the Dark, *playing to excellent houses. I was back in time to direct* Lady Audley's Secret *or* Who Pushed George *with Anna Russell in the leading role, ably abetted by Geoffrey Webb as George."*

I sat in on rehearsals for *Lady Audley's Secret,* now in development for the World Premiere in July. It was while I was there, that I remember talking to Anna Russell at a party. She asked me why I was sad. I told her I had just heard that my father had died the previous winter, December 9th, 1962, in London. He was only fifty-five and I was saddened that now I would never know him. Susannah had told me that he died of a myocardial infarction brought on by a severe beating. Sue had been to see him in St Mary's Hospital, Paddington before he died. She said his face and upper body were covered in bruises. The hospital told her that because his death was from heart failure that is what would be on his death certificate. As a gay man he was vulnerable. Anna told me she had met him several times, so I asked her to tell me about him. She was a bit in her cups, but she said to me *sotto voce,* which for Anna was stentorian,

"I did know your father, dear girl. He was a very nice man. I'm sure your Mama hasn't talked to you about him, very down on him she was after the War business, but I can tell you he was very well-spoken, short but good-looking, and very intelligent. Be proud, dear."

Her words have meant a lot to me. Few people have spoken to me about my father. Mother and her side of the family were, at best, negative. *Lady Audley* received wonderful write-ups and reviews in the local press.

The Springfield Union said, "Even with high-caliber competition, it is Anna's show. When she isn't filling the scene with her ridiculous villainy, the songs with her absurd words are in the mouth of the cast." And "Just as her satire is more like burlesque, and her whimsy is more like buffoonery, her audiences' laughter becomes uninhibited guffaws. Which is to say she is more of a clown than a comedienne. Either way, she is a great artist."

Milton Bass in *The Berkshire Eagle* began: "What a joy and delight to report that an impeccable cast is playing a parody of a Victorian melodrama right to the bloody hilt at The Berkshire Playhouse in Stockbridge. Farce is the most dangerous of games, but Joan White and company have brought off "Lady Audley's Secret: Or Who Pushed George" to a deliciously charming turn."

Here are excerpts from an extensive interview with Anna Russell in an earlier edition of *The Berkshire Eagle* by Arthur Myers "Anna Russell looks like a proper English Dowager gone wrong." "The play has 21 songs, all written by Miss Russell. They go by such titles as "Oh Perfidious, False, Deceitful, Perjured Profligate" and "Ah Me, What Terrible Doom."

The show was such a hit that Mother, Anna and Bob began plans to bring it to New York City, and indeed they were invited to bring the production to the New York World's Fair on Long Island in April 1964.

Mother wrote, "*Other ambitious plans for it ensued, but with the tragic assassination of John F. Kennedy in November of 1963, and planning our upcoming season in Stockbridge in 1964, nothing further happened.*"

Following the riotous success of *Lady Audley's Secret*, the Playhouse season continued with *The Cat and the Canary*, a murder mystery; the Broadway musical *The Pajama Game* directed by Bob Grose; *The Corn is Green* by Emlyn Williams — Mother had wanted to play Miss Moffatt for some time, and now she was the right age. They ended the season with the Off Broadway hit *Little Mary Sunshine*.

Attending an Equity Library Theatre production of Pinero's, *The Magistrate* earlier that year, she had been impressed with the work of the director, Thomas Gruenewald.

She hired him to direct *The Corn Is Green* and, liking his work invited him to direct the following 1964 season.

Thanks to *Lady Audley* and the other two musicals, the Playhouse did well that summer. In late October, Mother and Bob returned to England to organize the sale of her parents' South Moreton cottage and its contents. I was not consulted at all about this, even though I had spent my holidays there, and where I had my own room. My treasured books were sent out to a jumble sale. Much of the furniture was sold, although they did save some family paintings, photographs, silver and other odds and ends. The house was put on the market. Some items were sent to Gibraltar, at Audrey's request. Bob and Mother brought some pictures and silverware back to the Dorilton.

Now, everyone is gone and I have inherited some of my family's treasures.

AN INTERLUDE THAT CHANGED MY LIFE.

In September of 1963, I was hired as assistant stage manager and understudy for the Bus and Truck Company of *A Man For All Seasons*. I was both excited and nervous about the adventure ahead, and also in a bit of a muddle career-wise. The contract I signed with the producers, was for six months; to me that meant six whole months employment in a career that was at best ambiguous. It would give me a chance to put some much-needed money in the bank against an uncertain future. BUT and there is always a BUT, doing this tour meant leaving New York City, home of the Big-Time; the opportunity to land a Broadway show and perhaps even become a musical comedy actor?

My dilemma became reality when, early on in rehearsals, my agent sent me to audition for a new musical *High Spirits*, based on Noel Coward's comedy *Blithe Spirit*. Coward himself was to direct it.

I went to the backstage door of the Alvin Theatre, joining the line of other hopeful ingénues and, when my turn came, I nervously walked onto the stage to read with a stage manager. From the dark hole of the auditorium came a voice from my past:

"Judy dear, is that you? Weren't you at Silverlands?"

Amazed he would remember me I said, *"Yes, Mr. Coward."*

Silverlands was the home of the Actors' Orphanage Fund where I had lived for twelve and a half years, most of my childhood, before coming to the States four years ago. Noel Coward, as President of the Fund, had been an intermittent presence in my young life.

I read a scene from the script.

Then I heard The Voice again. *"Do you sing?"*

"Yes, Mr. Coward." I said stammering, *"B-b-but I didn't bring any music, sir."*

"Oh, never mind that, dear," he said, *"Just sing something a capella."*

JUST sing something *a capella*! Knees knocking and heart pounding, I tremulously sang a few bars of *"Maybe it's because I'm a Londoner."*

"Thank you, Judy. So nice to see you again."

That was it. I left the theatre and went back to the dingy rehearsal space on Eighth Avenue convinced that I hadn't done very well at all.

Eva, my agent, called the next day to say I had been offered understudy for Edith the maid. Me! Offered an understudy in a Broadway Show! After rehearsal, I went straight to see Terry Fay, casting director for *A Man for All Seasons*, and explained my dilemma.

"I'm sorry, my dear," she said, *"but I can't let you out of your contract. The only way we can legally let you go is for you to pay us the full amount of your contract."* *"But, Miss Fay,"* I stammered, *"I can't possibly afford that, it would be thousands of dollars. ($185 x 25 weeks or $4,625). Surely, you could find someone else to take my job."*

"My dear girl," she said, *"young actresses who can sing are a dime a dozen in this business, but an understudy who brings stage management skills with her is golden. I am sorry, but you are not easy to replace."*

That was that. I was stuck. Who knows where my career would have gone if things had been different, if I hadn't gone on tour and everything else that followed? But there it was, my fate was sealed and so, to see America I would go.

I went to have dinner with Mother and Bob before leaving town. I told them that I had been offered the understudy in a Broadway show, but the only way I could do it would be to buy my way out of my contract with *A Man For All Seasons*. Bob was very sympathetic. Mother just said,

> *"You are a lucky girl to be able to see America at such a young age. Why, I had to wait until I was almost fifty when I got to play Mrs. Higgins. You'll have other opportunities. Besides Stage Management seems to be your forte and perhaps you should stick to it."*

I thought to myself, *"Thanks for the encouragement, Mother dear! Perhaps you don't think I have much talent as an actress!"*

Anyway, there was no offer of help from her. Could she have loaned me the money? Could she have borrowed it? Still, I sometimes wonder, what if things had been different...

Back at rehearsal, probably because I was the youngest on the stage management crew **and** the only girl, I was initially given the lowliest jobs — going for coffee, running out to the shops for Scotch tape, pencils, push pins, flashlights, chalk, masking tape, as well as hearing the actors' lines, running messages over to the producers' office, taking lunch orders, and on and on.

It wasn't until we got to Rochester, and began rehearsals on the actual set with the actors' in costume, that Frank Hamilton, our Production Stage Manager, having evaluated his three assistants, put me in charge of the Stage Right prompt desk, and there I stayed for the duration of the tour. I became Frank's right hand 'man' and through him I learned more than any college course could ever teach about the art of stage management and organization, and how important that is to the smooth running of any production. It was to serve me well throughout my life.

In Rochester, New York on Tuesday, October 1st 1963, I spent the first of six nights at The Manger Hotel. The hotel's room charge was five dollars a night. My dinner that evening was one dollar and forty-five cents, and breakfast the next morning, just eighty-five cents. I know this because I kept a little black notebook of my daily expenses back then. I kept that notebook because, being a girl of very small funds, I was watching my pennies, hoping to send most of my paycheck to the bank.

Rochester was our final week of rehearsal and there we would open at the Masonic Auditorium on Thursday, October 3rd.

I was twenty years old, in my fourth year of America and a member of Actors' Equity Association — a gen-u-ine theatre professional with a Union card to prove it. For the next six months I was off to see the United States. As a Bus and Truck Company ("truck" because all our scenery and costumes traveled in a large semi) we would play in smaller American cities and towns, such as Schenectady and Tulsa for one-night stands – sometimes two, and rarely for more. Over the next hundred and seventy-three days we would perform at theatres and auditoriums in one hundred and twelve towns and cities, in forty-six states and two Canadian provinces. When the tour was over, we would have traveled thirty-six thousand miles by bus. It would be years before I got on a long-distance bus again.

National Touring companies, like the *My Fair Lady* Company Mother was in for a year playing Mrs. Higgins, traveled by train and plane and played all the major cities, with the cast and crew settling into fine hotels, often for weeks at a time; able to see the sights. Some of our stops were so brief that we only got to see the inside of the hotels (mostly cheap) and the theatres (often ill-equipped), and we ate at nearby restaurants for the quickest of meals. We played one-night, sometimes two-night-stands in bright college auditoriums, colorful former burlesque houses or dingy movie theaters.

Those old burlesque houses reeked of history, with faded posters of Bert Lahr, Jimmy Durante, Sally Rand and others. Dick O'Neill, our Common Man, once found a tatty red G-string and one tasseled pasty in his dressing room. Sometimes, the local stagehands had raunchy stories to tell as, with our crew, they set up each evening's show.

I was Stage Right Prompt Desk. I had had that position before in that one-a-week musical stock in Charlotte, North Carolina. There, my mentor and friend Charlie Davisson had first taught me what a stage manager did. But now, with this big national touring company, my promotion was a very big deal. Frank's position was Stage Left where he cued the light and set changes and ran the show. At Stage Right, I sat in the wings on a high stool at a lectern-type desk with my script in front of me. My script was marked up with all things that happened from Stage Right:

"Warn the Spanish Ambassador's entrance." "Warn candle for Cardinal Wolsey" "Check letter on desk for Common Man," "Clear exit for Cromwell." Etcetera.

And all the while I had to keep my eye on the script in case one of the actors "went up." If they did, and sometimes they did, I would say clearly, never shouting, the line that was needed.

During performances, Stage Right was my job. The other two assistants, Roger and Leon, had their assignments, as well as understudying several roles each, as I did.

Roger's job was to call "half hour," "fifteen minutes," "five" and "places," and during the play be aware of who was **not** waiting in the wings ready to go on stage. In those days, few theatres had backstage loud speakers, and Roger had to be pretty spry on his feet. Often some dressing rooms were three flights up. He had to knock on each door and call the time, ("half hour, Mr. Harris") and try to reach all the dressing rooms within five minutes, all the while trying not to get waylaid by Jeff Morrow, the actor playing Cromwell, who always had some niggling complaint. Roger also had to tell Laurette, the wardrobe mistress about any costume problems and tell Frank if any actor was not feeling well. A tired Roger slept easily on the bus. Leon pretty much stayed near Frank and did whatever was needed. Leon was the same Leon Benedict who had the lead in *The Magistrate* at ELT the year before. The theatre can be a hard and erratic mistress.

But Stage Right during the performances wasn't the only responsibility I had.

With all touring companies, the scenery and lights, props and costumes travel with the crew either in special train compartments or, in our case, in a long trailer truck. On a one-night stand tour, such as ours, it had to get to the next destination to start the Load-In several hours before the actors and stage management team arrived on the bus. Art, a tall, burly, bald-headed man, was our Master Carpenter and drove the trailer truck and, because he drove the truck, he was also a Teamster. Two Union salaries! The rest of our crew were Harry, chief electrician, Al, property master, and Carl, assistant electrician and follow-spot operator. All four were members of the New York chapter of the International Alliance of Theatrical Stage Employees or IATSE. They were great guys who loved the theatre and had been stagehands for years. Some had inherited their job from their fathers and, while they were all dedicated professionals, they were not above patting my bottom.

Artie was the crew chief; getting the truck unloaded and the scenery into position was his priority. They carried 20-foot-high flats and several elaborate cutout pieces that formed different arches, all set on long ramps. Each flat had to be hung from the flies and rigged just right for smooth scene changes. The set had been designed to be versatile so that it could form different configurations to create Wolsey's chambers, a Tudor street scene or Thomas More's home, etc. and finally the scaffold. Along with the flats, there were risers to create levels on the set, also doorways, staircases, and tormentors or "torms" – the black drapes that masked any openings to the wings. Behind the whole set was an enormous white cyclorama or "cyc," which was hung as a backdrop and changed color with the light cues. And there were the set dressings – a wall hanging here, a crucifix there, and moveable Tudor style tables and chairs — which the prop master placed once the set was up.

All this scenery had to be unloaded and set up in a matter of hours, and every theatre had different dimensions. Some stage houses were huge and cavernous; others were shallow with low prosceniums. Even Artie couldn't put this huge set up by himself, although sometimes he very nearly had to. Each theatre we played had local IATSE members, many of whom were simply movie projectionists, however the contract with each theatre said we must hire, *and pay*, five union stagehands – whether we used them or not. Sometimes these men (always men) were useful and sometimes useless.

On a several occasions, the useless ones sat onstage behind the scenery, playing cards, smoking huge, soggy, stinking stogies and scraping their chairs, — all while the play was going on behind them. They only got up off their bovine butts when Artie personally came and told them to "*Stand by for a set change.*" They wouldn't take any direction from Frank ("*You're not in our union, mate!*) And they totally ignored me, even when I implored them, "*I say chaps, please could you be quiet!*" during a particularly dramatic scene. (I was still working off my British-ness, in those days). Fortunately, those incidents were few and far between. But we had to have these men. Union Rules. Besides we were only in each town for a night or two, so why complain? We just put up with them.

Al, as Property Master, had to make sure all props were set out on or near the prop tables, on each side of the stage. Props entering stage left would be placed stage left; the same for stage right. The actors would retrieve their prop, perhaps a candle, before an entrance and leave it on the nearest prop table upon exiting. Personal props, handkerchiefs and chains of office etc., — were checked by Al before each show. If a prop got worn out with too much use, which happened with letters, — and we had many different prop letters — Al would create another one. New candles were used every night, and back-up props were kept in case anything went missing.

I know all about Al's job because in late January when we were heading into Waterloo, Iowa, Al left the tour suddenly complaining of pain. (We learned later that he had a cancerous growth on his prostate). Herb came to Frank, and then they both came to me and asked me to take over Al's job until an IATSE replacement could be found. Herb had checked with our crew, and they all agreed that I was the logical stand-in, knowing the play as well as I did. Herb told me that he had asked the producers and they had, grudgingly, agreed to pay me IATSE minimum wage for the duration. I filled in for two weeks until New York found Al's replacement. The crew made me an honorary member of IATSE. My paycheck was three times my Equity salary!

Then Leon sat at the prompt desk every night, and I ran props until Joe came to replace Al. It was a big responsibility but I guess I handled it okay because I got a letter, in his big round handwriting, from Herb, which I still cherish:

> *Dear Judy,*
>
> *Thank you so much. When we needed you very badly, you came through. But then, of course, you always do and I appreciate very much all you do every day – day after day after day.*
>
> *Herb Cherin*

Herb Cherin was a good man and we were lucky to have him as our Company Manager. I heard some horror stories later about some who were sticklers for procedure and who were all too willing to fine actors for sins of omission or just tardiness. Herb was a generous and kind human being who sadly, a year after the tour's end, drowned while swimming in Florida. I can still picture him: a short man, bright-eyed and dark haired with a little brush mustache. He always wore a navy blazer or windbreaker, an open-necked shirt and chinos. On more formal occasions he sported a spotted bow tie.

Harry and Carl, our electricians, were small, strong, wiry men. They set up the lights and the few sound effects for the show. Now, remember that this tour was back in the dark ages before computerized consoles, remote control phones, hi-tech sound systems etc. Long-gone are those days when one needed muscles to run the lights in a theatre – nowadays the operator sits before a small console in the rear of the auditorium and pushes a button with one finger activating a pre-set of instruments to light up when the stage manager says, into his tiny Bluetooth-like headset, "Cue Fourteen Go."

Back in the nineteen-sixties, stage lights were controlled by a wall of dimmers; ten to fourteen massive levers, usually on-stage right. Each dimmer had to be wired to a configuration of different lights (instruments), so when its lever was pulled down a specific area of the stage would light up — how far the lever was pulled would depend on the brightness of the lights. Those levers were stiff and large, some dating back to the 1930s. To pull two or more at the same time took a great deal of strength and a wide arm span, which is why the way the dimmers were wired was crucial. Once the show was up and running, Harry would be behind me, a half-smoked cigarette tucked behind his ear, moving like a ballet dancer, pulling those dimmers to just the right level when, from the other side of the stage, Frank gave the cue over the walkie-talkie into his headset.

While Art and his pick-up crew were putting the set up; Harry and Carl would unload the instruments from the truck, set them on the apron of the stage and bring in "the pipe." This pipe was forty-foot long and it always traveled with us, for on it were hung the main lighting instruments. It was carefully marked where each Fresnel, Klieg or Leko should be clamped. Once the instruments were attached, the pipe would be hoisted into the air, approximately over the front row of seats. Then, like acrobats, they would climb ladders and, once up on the catwalk, they'd plug the lights into outlets, tape up the excess cable, affix the barn doors, slide in the colored gels, and that done, begin the job of hanging more instruments on side pipes to fill in different areas. Some would be hung behind the proscenium and shine straight down onto the stage, flooding an area where a principal scene might take place. When everything was hung, Harry would go to the dimmer wall, pulling the levers and checking that all was in working order and that the levels could now be set.

(Ever since, whenever I go to the theatre, I count the number of instruments hanging high over the audience).

Meanwhile Carl would go up to the very rear of the theatre's balcony and set up the big follow spot. Often, he could set up in the projection booth, if it was a movie theatre, where he could operate without being seen. From day one, Carl knew his cues: who should be in the spotlight and when. These guys were pros.

Once the set was up and the lights in place, the crew took a short break and waited for Frank. By now, our bus had arrived and we had all checked into our hotel for the night. The actors would rest or have a meal. The stage management crew went straight to the theatre. Frank would assign dressing rooms and then Roger and Leon would help Laurette, the Wardrobe Mistress, unload the costumes and hang them in the dressing rooms. Laurette would set up her ironing board and take care of getting all the "smalls" presentable for the show.

Then Frank and I would "walk lights." In theatre parlance this meant that, with Harry on the dimmers and Carl standing by on the ladders to adjust the focus and Frank in the audience, I would stand wherever actors stood for the different scenes. This would usually take about an hour, sometimes less, and sometimes more if a light didn't work or the focusing was difficult. When the lights were focused, the set looking presentable, the costumes hung in the dressing rooms, props in place and everything shipshape, then and only then could we all go and grab a bite to eat, before coming back to the theatre before the half hour call for curtain time.

Once the play was over, the curtain down and the audience gone home, then the set was struck and loaded, all the props accounted for and stored in the prop chest, the lighting instruments unplugged and carefully stored in the truck, the pipe in its special place. The costumes were hung on the racks, shrouded in sheets, the dressing rooms were checked for any lost items, and all was ready to move on the next day – sometimes fifty miles, sometimes two hundred – to our next one-night stand, where we would do it all over again. Spending two nights or more in one town was a gift to be cherished.

A Man for All Seasons is about Sir Thomas More. He was King Henry VIII's councilor from 1521, and became Lord Chancellor of England in 1529. He resigned in 1532 and was executed in 1535 for not condoning the King's divorce and subsequent marriage to Anne Boleyn. The play deals with More's stand for his conscience. It is a moving and powerful drama and it was a privilege to be a part of it for so long. I believe it kept us sane just to know we would be presenting this moving and literate play to another new audience, after the endless drives across America's hinterland.

The memories of some of the towns we visited are lost in the mists of time, but some still stand out more than fifty years later, many because of production mishaps or, sometimes, when the outside world burst in.

On November 22, we had stopped for lunch at a roadside café in a tiny dot on the map called Medicine Bow, Wyoming. We had played the University of Wyoming in Laramie the night before and our next stop was Casper, some two hundred miles away. Our bus driver Willie had taken the back roads – a more direct route but decidedly slower and bumpier — and Medicine Bow was the only possible place for lunch.

We all piled out of the bus to stretch our legs, have a smoke and peruse the menu pasted in the café window. Not much on offer – grilled cheese, hamburgers or tuna on white. But we were used to such fare by now. Most of our Company squeezed into the tiny café. The man behind the counter and two other customers were transfixed watching a tiny television set hung on the wall. He raised his hand to silence us.

"*What's the matter?*" someone asked.

"*Kennedy's been shot.*"

Without a sound, we turned as one and watched Walter Cronkite as he removed his black-rimmed spectacles, wiped his eyes and said,

"*It has been confirmed that President John F. Kennedy died at 1 p.m. central standard time.*"

There were gasps, someone sobbed. We somberly left the restaurant and got back on the bus. No one said anything. We drove on to the Henning Hotel in Casper and, after checking in, we clustered around the television set in the lobby. (No televisions in the rooms in those days).

We wondered aloud if they would cancel the show. They didn't. The reason was, according to Herb, that this was our only stop in Casper and people had paid to see us. Also, it was well known that Victor Samrock, our producer back in New York, was ever mindful of money and not even a dead president was going to stop the cash flow.

Theatres across America were dark that night, but not Victor Samrock's productions.

As it turned out only eleven people came; I could count the house through a crack in the curtain. We paused for two minutes of silence before the play began. Dick O'Neill said, "*Well, at least we aren't doing Jean Kerr's* Mary Mary.*"*

No. Our play was more fitting, about another Catholic martyr.

We had many adventures on our journey across America. Our acting company was a mixed bunch with some fine actors and some journeymen. There were only five women in this company of twenty-four. Three of the women, Lois Kibbee, Vanya Frank and Amelia Romano, had parts in the play, I understudied Vanya and Amelia and Amelia understudied Lois. Laurette was the wardrobe mistress. I never did figure out when she did the laundry, she barely had time to iron everything. Of the men, four were IATSE crew, three were stage management — Leon and Roger understudied too, the others were actors.

It was an inspiring play and we were seeing America in a way that few people do. Standing in the wings every night, waiting for the curtain to rise, and watching the play unfold through the dust motes dancing in the stage lights, I was never bored. Harry, our master electrician, was often alongside me pulling down the great levers that raised and dimmed the lights. He had as fine a touch as those who operate those small dimmer consoles in to-day's theaters. In some theaters these huge dimmers were located on Stage Left and I would forego Harry's whispered curses — and having my bottom patted. But then I'd get big Artie who raised and lowered the stage curtain or handled the fly ropes that set the flats for scene changes. I loved my job.

The rest of us were members of Actors Equity, except Willie the bus driver and Laurette the wardrobe mistress, and we were paid whatever our agents had negotiated. I got union scale plus a per diem, which was more money than I had ever made in my life! Like I said, I understudied two of the women —Margaret More, Sir Thomas's daughter, and a lower-class woman. I only went on once; which was just as well, I had enough to do. The others on the bus were actors and stage management: some nice and some not so, some talented and some mediocre.

College auditoriums were the cleanest and best equipped and had the most helpful union crews. The University of Indiana at Bloomington, when we played there, was the largest performance space in the country. It boasted two seats more than Radio City Music Hall. And plays were not miked back then; actors were trained to project.

Arriving in Bloomington, as in every other town, we checked into the hotel. The actors went to their rooms and rested. We, on the crew, dropped our bags and went straight to the theater. The stagehands put up the set, hung the lights and set up the props. Leon and Roger checked out and assigned the dressing rooms, and Frank and I inspected the set-ups and set our prompt books at our stations. If we were moving on next day, we'd strike the set right after the show, catch some sleep and get back on the bus early next morning.

We were booked for two nights in Bloomington. We would get to sleep in!

Roger had called the half and there was no sign of Jay, our Cardinal Wolsey. Frank took me aside, "*Check the nearest bars, he's bound to be in one of them.*" It was October 30th, 1963 and we had arrived in Bloomington a few hours earlier. Our booking was the University of Indiana auditorium. We had come directly from the Hotel McCurdy (four dollars and fifty cents a room) in Evansville, after yet another one-night stand at the Victory Theater, an old vaudeville house.

When Frank sent me to search the bars for Jay that night, I had done it before. Jay was an alcoholic, a good actor and a kind man, but with a yen for booze. Because of my age, Frank had tried sending Leon, but Jay was belligerent with him; he would come quietly for me. Usually, I found Jay after he had only one or two drinks, but it had been a short hop from Evansville and that evening he'd had plenty of drinking time. He was in the second bar I entered. I touched him on the shoulder and said, "*Show time, Jay.*" He took my hand and came with me, docile as usual, but this time his speech was slurred and his step uncertain.

At the stage door, Frank and Herb were pacing. They heaved a sigh of relief seeing Jay. Frank led Jay to his dressing room and told Leon to get him into costume. Leon had already dressed to go on in his stead.

I told Herb "*He's drunk. He can't go on.*"

Herb said, "*He has to, kiddo. If he doesn't go on, I'll have to fire him and he's got a wife and six kids.*"

Frank came back looking worried. I pleaded, "*Couldn't you both say he's sick?*"

Herb said, *"No we can't. Rick is the Equity deputy and you know him. He would report us. Jay's best shot is to go on and hope he gets through it."*
Cardinal Wolsey had just one pivotal scene with Thomas More in the first act.

Frank said, *"I'd better warn Bobby."*
Robert Harris was our Thomas More, a lovely English actor and, as we learned that evening, a real trooper.

When Frank returned, he said, *"Bobby's prepared to do the scene as a monologue. He's acted with drunks before."*

He turned to me, *"Go find Roger and Leon and tell them to bring their scripts. I want someone on book in every entrance during that scene."* I turned to go.

"Don't tell anyone else. They'll know soon enough. Oh, and tell Roger to call five before he comes."

Herb said, *"Good. We'd better not go up late. It's a packed house.*
We went up on time.

Dick O'Neill said the Common Man's opening line, *"It is perverse."*
And I thought to myself, *"Damn right it is!"*

The play moved smoothly along, the actors in fine form, not a prompt needed anywhere. A third of the way through Act One, Jay appeared through the gloom of backstage at my station, dressed in his red Cardinal's robes. I signaled Frank. It was few minutes before the scene. He'd been pumped full of black coffee but was still slurring:

"Shudy, lemme kiss the book. I'll know my lines if you shust lemme kiss the book."

I let him kiss my script, handed him his candle and pushed him out on stage as the lights went down for the minor set change.

They got through the scene, with Robert covering Jay's incoherence, and it looked as if everything would be all right. Robert exited. Jay had been directed to frown at Robert's departing back, pick up his candle and exit down stage right. This time he picked up his candle and staggered down to the footlights. My stomach lurched. He stared out into the darkened, two thousand five hundred and two seat houseful and said,

"I'm sho shorry," and exited down left, clutching the stage curtain.

Herb had to fire him and Leon went on for the next two weeks until New York found a replacement to join the Company in Wichita, Kansas.

The replacement for Jay was Jay. New York reported that he was the best man for the part, and that he had promised to behave. Did he? Well, that's another story.

Robert Harris, our Sir Thomas, had an impressive British resume. Dick O'Neill, the Common Man, had been married to my friend Dina, so he and I were already friends. Jeff Morrow, our Thomas Cromwell, was an aging television star; nicknamed "Bill Box" by Dick because Jeff's contract said he should have his name in a box on all publicity materials. This infuriated Dick. Bernie Hyatt, the Spanish Ambassador, became my travelling buddy. There were other actors, but I guess for me the most important was Colgate Salsbury, a tall, good-looking man playing Will Roper, More's son-in-law.

I should mention here that in this company of mostly men, I was the youngest of the women by twenty years. I was also, when I had time to think about it, lonely and needy, but then I had always been needy. It came with my childhood. I stifled it by putting my job first. Anyway, Colgate befriended me and took me to his bed or mine, more than once; and I confess I went willingly. I thought I was careful, but Texas did me in — we were there for almost a month of one-and two-night stands.

After a whole week over Christmas and New Years in glorious New Orleans, we moved on to Houston for four nights. On my twenty-first birthday, January 3, 1964, the British Consulate in Houston threw a jolly fine party for us — no doubt because of the play. Houston was at that time a dry town – no liquor anywhere – so when we arrived at the Consulate, we were each given two drink tickets, my first *legal* drinks…and I drank them, and allowed myself to be led back to the Rice Hotel and put to bed.

A few days later, in Dallas, just seven weeks after JFK's assassination, the air was heavy with unspoken protesting: *"Don't Blame Us"* and *"We didn't Kill him."* Yet, it was in Dallas that we all stood around the hotel lobby TV set and watched the Beatles on Ed Sullivan. Most of us were enchanted, but Rick Branda, our Henry VIII, sneered at them and called them "sissies" because of their mop-top haircuts.

We did have days off, we didn't do the show seven days a week, and it was on our days off that I most remember our camaraderie. In Des Moines, Iowa, a group of us went to dine at a "good" restaurant one evening; low lights, flocked wallpaper and practically everything on the menu "flambé".

In our party were Frank and I, Colgate (called Gate), Dick O'Neill, Lois Kibbee (our Lady Alice) and Robert (Bobby) Harris, our very erudite leading man. At one point, after the flambé flames had died down and we'd all had a few drinks, Dick called Bobby a "*silly old faggot.*" Bobby rose to his full five foot nine and said in his best pear-shaped British,

"*I may be a pervert and I may be a homosexual, but* (he paused) *I am NOT a faggot!*"

Another day off in Fresno, California found us at Ernest and Julio's Gallo wine-tasting tour and bar. The winery hadn't seen tourists for some time, it being winter, and we tasted everything from aperitifs to port. Reeling out of Gallo's, Dick pointed across the street to a large sign "*Christian Brothers Brandy Here!*" We used our better judgment; besides we already had hangovers.

In Enid, Oklahoma, as we were checking into the only hotel large enough to accommodate us, the men were informed, *quietly,* that the ladies of the evening were on the third floor. Lois on hearing that, turned to me with a wink, "*Good, that'll give us a rest.*"

February 1st and 2nd we were to play The Pabst Theatre in Milwaukee and to save a hotel fee, I stayed with my stepfather Bob Grose in his lodgings for those two nights. He was directing at The Swan Theatre and probably spending hours on long distance with Mother in New York planning the upcoming 1964 season. It was okay for me to stay with Bob, for he, like Mother's previous husbands, 'batted for the other team.'

The tour continued with seven more weeks of mostly one-night stands through Michigan, Ohio, a jog up to Ottawa, and then down to New York State and much of New England.

I went back to my 28th street walk-up on March 22. Much richer in money and with so many memories.

By the end of the tour, I had missed my period. The doctor, a nice man, had said I was three months along. (I did the math and thought "Houston.") I had not been nauseous and I hadn't seemed to miss my monthlies — there was always some spotting, so being young and fairly naïve, I thought all was well until I *really* missed one.

Chapter Twelve

MARRIAGE AND STOCKBRIDGE
ONE MORE TIME
1964

I was pregnant and there was only one possible father. I didn't want an illegal abortion. I also didn't want Gate to do something he'd regret.

What to do? I had to tell Gate, but I didn't want him or anyone to marry me unless they really wanted to. I made the mistake of also telling Mother.

I distinctly remember lying supine on my bed on 28th street with Gate and Mother leaning over me as though I was an inanimate object, while they talked about me. Mother saying *"What a silly girl you are and now you must do something about it."* Once again, no real help from Mother here, for no way was I having an abortion!

I announced I wanted to go to Gibraltar and see my Aunt Audrey and my grandparents. This would give Gate and me a chance to think about our options.

I made the arrangements and flew to Gibraltar via London in early May. Audrey met me at the airport and I spent a week with my family. I said nothing about my condition, but Audrey, wise lady that she was, knew me too well. She was kind and said she knew I was a sensible girl and would do what was best. My grandparents, now in their late eighties, were glad to see me. Granny was rather frail and was in bed much of the time. Grandfather, up and about, was suffering from some dementia and as a life-long diabetic was not allowed alcohol. My aunt, in sympathy, put cold tea in a whiskey bottle and he got quite tipsy on that. He was not clear who I was much of the time. But after a few days, he suddenly said,

"Who are you?"

I replied, *"I'm Judy."*

"My Judy? They didn't tell me you were coming."

I was so very glad I had gone to Gibraltar; my grandparents had been my safe haven during my teens. It was to be the last time I would ever see them.

On returning to New York, Gate was at Idlewild (now JFK) to meet the plane. He said to me later he had talked to his parents. He agreed with them that he should marry me for the sake of the baby or he might be full of regrets later. So, we got married quietly and had a good marriage, with some ups and downs, for eighteen years with three children.

June 10th 1964 was a sunny-cloudy day. We made our way downtown to City Hall in lower Manhattan. Gate was wearing his good audition suit; I wore a white sheath dress with a sleeveless lacy black cotton overcoat. My bump didn't show yet, I was only five months along. My long hair was coiled on top of my head. I hoped the hairpins would hold.

On the steps of the huge, ornate building we met up with our witnesses: one best friend each. No parents and no other guests. Dina had fashioned a small bouquet of petunias, snapdragons and coleus from her window box for me. Steve Aaron (Colgate's room-mate from Harvard) had brought two white carnations – one for him and one for my groom. He pinned them on.

We went up the steps, through the center columns, and entered the building through the main doors, following the signs for the wedding chapel. Couples passed us in their Sunday best: laughing, kissing and hooting. In a cavernous room, with rows of wooden folding chairs, were clusters of people. Most of the men were dressed in suits: striped or plaid, wide and narrow-lapelled, shoes spit-shined for this special day. The women were frilled, teased and perfumed, costume jewelry glittered around their necks and on their arms, their dresses were tight, white or colorful, flounced with taffeta and net.

I felt dowdy; nervous.

We signed in at the desk, presenting our marriage license and paying the modest fee. We would be called fourth. We each took a seat. Dina held my hand. Steve fumbled in his pockets. Looking for the ring? Gate stared straight ahead.

Was he as nervous as I was?

Ahead was the door to the chapel. Suddenly it burst open and a couple, followed by a passel of witnesses, spewed forth; she, in frothy white lace, he, flamboyant in a red vest, full-sleeved shirt and tight black pants. They were all falling about with laughter. We four observed them with disdain and, tacitly, we solemnly vowed that *we* would not behave this way. The next couple entered the chapel and later, they too exited amid gales of mirth. And so did the next couple.

It was our turn. We rose and solemnly entered a small room with a stained-glass window – very secular – just flowers and clouds. A man was standing in front of the window, not a real window at all. He was of late middle age, greying and balding, the first assistant to the Assistant Commissioner of the Borough of Manhattan.

"Come in. Come in." He said jovially. *"Bride and Groom stand up front with me. Witnesses take a seat. Do you have the ring?"* He asked Steve.

Steve inched forward and handed Colgate the narrow ring of gold, bought at Tiffany's the day before and sat back down next to Dina, her hanky at the ready.

He began. With words of great solemnity, he questioned our intentions and whether anyone present had any objections. He uttered each sentence as if we were in church, or perhaps at a revival meeting. He intoned each word with the rolling vowels and enthusiasm of an evangelist. I did truly believe he meant to make this rather swift and humble ceremony into something special, even holy, for us.

He succeeded only in making us shake with laughter.

Gate was holding my hand during this and I felt a tremor pass between us.

"Dooo yooo Colgate take this woman, (pause - clear throat) *Joanna Judy, to be your wife?"*

"I do"

Behind us we heard muffled giggles coming from Steve and Dina, of handkerchiefs being stuffed into mouths.

"And dooo yooo Joanna Judy take this man, Colgate, to be your husband?"

By now, we were both shaking with mirth… I was terrified I would snort. I managed a subdued *"I do."*

"By the powers vested in me by the State of New York, I now pronounce you Man and Wife. (He paused again) *You may kiss the bride."*

Gate leaned in. His shoulders were shaking, and he was grinning from ear to ear. So was I.

The deed done, we thanked the gentleman, signed the book and fled the room, laughing quite as hard as those who had gone before us, and receiving stern looks from those now waiting.

Outside, we all fell into a taxi, full of joy and merriment, and went to our reservation at Pete's Tavern on 18th Street near Gramercy Park. There we drank champagne, ate shrimp and steak and chocolate cake, and took the Number 5 bus home to the Upper West Side.

> Dina wrote: *I will never ever forget your wedding ceremony at City Hall. It is just burned into my brain till the end of time. I may have mentioned to you, I heard Mel Brooks describe his wedding to Anne Bancroft in New York City Hall by the clerk, who also thought he was Elmer Gantry, kind of like yours was. But that is the only other time I've heard that story. Steve Aaron and I were laughing so hard we were crying. Perfectly okay for a wedding!* (Brooks and Bancroft were married August 5 1964, so I'm guessing it was probably the same marrying man).

Following our wedding and the move to a new Upper West Side apartment, we went to Hartford to meet my new in-laws, Charles and Edith Colgate Salsbury. Mother and Bob had offered us jobs for 1964 season at the Berkshire Playhouse; Colgate to be the resident leading man and I would be Bob Grose's assistant and also play three character roles later in the season, as I grew great with child.

With Mother and Bob's fifth season to open on June 27th with *Time of the Cuckoo*, rehearsals were to start almost immediately after our wedding. We had found an apartment on the fifth floor of 915 West End Avenue: two bedrooms, living room, large entryway, kitchen and bath. The building was neither modern nor historic, but it was a short walk to Riverside Park and, at 105th and West End, was just two blocks from my old ELT theatre at the Master Institute. We bought some rudimentary furniture, arranged for some bookcases to be installed – we both came to the marriage with too many books – and took the train to Stockbridge to begin the summer season at the Berkshire Playhouse.

In Stockbridge, someone found us an apartment near the Red Lion Inn. We bought an old blue station wagon at the local garage for five hundred dollars — and were lucky enough to sell it for the same at the end of the summer. It was to be Gate's car, I couldn't drive, — yet!

Time of the Cuckoo, a bittersweet romance by Arthur Laurents, starred Eileen Heckart as the lonely American spinster who falls in love with Mitchell Gregg, a charming married Italian. Colgate and Dorothy Tristan were young newly-weds and Mother directed.

The second play of the season was a comedy, this time Neil Simon's *Come Blow Your Horn* with Gertrude Berman, Lou Gilbert and William Swan. Directed by Bob Grose and assisted by myself. Once again, the producers were trying hard to meet the dictums laid down by the Three Arts Society at the end of each season: less British and something for everyone.

It was the next two plays where they ran into difficulty at the box office and in the local press. Sidney Howard's play *The Silver Cord*, was an early excursion into Freudian philosophy: the pathological side of mother-love. It shocked some people and titillated others. Hollywood film star, Sylvia Sidney, was the mother and William Swan and Bill Shepherd were her sons. Sidney Howard was considered a "local playwright," having lived and died in nearby Tyringham. This play did not win over the critics.

> One writer said, "But a shoddy production is a shoddy production and no amount of meddling with a dated play will make it any timelier."

Nor was the next offering, *Journey to Bahia*, any better received. Mother had told the translator, Stanley Richards, they would produce Dias Gomez's play, winner of many awards in his native Brazil. The English production simply did not translate well. Colgate was burdened with the role of Joe, a poor farmer who vows to carry a cross thirty-nine miles to a church, to give thanks for the cure of his mule. But once he gets there, the priests won't let him in.

> Milton Bass in *The Berkshire Eagle* wrote, "a first-rate, deeply felt and closely thought-out performance by Colgate Salsbury. He is the only one who makes any ripples in the limpid pool of symbols, metaphors, similes and bad jokes that make up the dialogue."

He went on to give a thorough review of the production's faults and merits,

> *"It is impossible to assess the performance by Rosita Diaz (as Joe's wife) because of her difficulties with the English language."* Rosita was the imported 'star' for this production.

I remember Gate's frustration with this play, his character and Miss Diaz. Later, we were able to joke about her inability to pronounce the letter "J". Instead of saying *"Yes, Joe."* She would say *"Jess, Yo."* After she returned to Brazil, the password of the season became *"Jess Yo."*

Having received bad reviews from *The Berkshire Eagle* for both productions, Mother and Bob did a *big no-no*. They criticized the critics, which engendered letters to the editor. One such writer wrote,

> *"The Berkshire Playhouse has presented some fine productions in the past. It would be more fitting if the directors called a flop a flop."*

So, onward! The next production was to be the big musical of the season, *My Fair Lady*. Mother wrote in her memories of that summer:

> *"Nemesis was near. We were due to present a full-scale revival of My Fair Lady. But the new president of the Three Arts Society insisted on a 'star' name for Professor Higgins. She knew just the right person: the Hollywood actor Murray Matheson, veteran of a host of Hollywood successes, but in my opinion no 'star draw'. In addition, he was white-haired and we looked like brother and sister, not mother and son."*

Mother was reprising her role as Mrs. Higgins and a young British actress Anne Wakefield came to play Eliza (and several other roles). We became good friends, that summer.

> Mother continued: *"However, the production played to packed houses and, the season having proved so successful, we optimistically prepared to return to Stockbridge in 1965. But Nemesis hovered. Our Hollywood actor's salary plus percentages and royalties proved our downfall; one we had to face and overcome. I was reminded of Tyrone Guthrie's words in any crisis: "Rise Above It!"*
> *So, I did."*

But there is more to the tale of Stockbridge and how their time there ended.

For a Summer Stock production, this *My Fair Lady* was very elegant, with sets designed by Bob Grose, costumes by my old friend Dina Harris augmented by the rental of some of the Broadway original hats and Ascot gowns. The small orchestra was extraordinary under the baton of Robert Blafield. Barton Mumaw, from Jacob's Pillow, choreographed. Colgate got a breather during this show, playing Zoltan Karparthy – the hairy Hungarian. I finally got on stage as Mrs. 'Opkins,

"All she wants is 'er birdcage and her Chinese fan. No clothes."

Bob directed, with me again assisting. While staging the Ascot Gavotte, he called

"Freeze!" Everyone froze and, as I was marking down the positions, Bob turned to me: *"How ever did I manage to freeze this scene with the least interesting couple down front and center?"*

Tom Gruenewald arrived to take over directing the next two plays: Shakespeare's *As You Like It* and Emlyn Williams' *Night Must Fall.* (The Brits again)! This was to be fun for me as Tom had previously directed me in *The Magistrate,* but he was new to Colgate. They got on very well that summer and remained friends for years.

As You Like It was to celebrate the 400th anniversary of Shakespeare's birth.

Colgate was to play Orlando, Angela Wood was Rosalind, with Anne Wakefield as Celia. Ray Reinhart wound up his summer contract by following his bawdy Alfred Doolittle with a melancholy Jacques.

I was cast as Phoebe, the role Mother played almost thirty years earlier in the film. Phoebe's wooer is the shepherd Silvius, played by the actor Bill Shepard. It had become clear to many that he was wooing and being wooed by my stepfather, Bob Grose.

Practically everyone in the resident company and all the apprentices were on stage for this one. Dina Harris dressed us in neo-18th century costumes, me as a rather plump Dresden-style shepherdess to hide my ever-growing bump. Dan Walker arrived to play both Charles the Wrestler and Corin the old shepherd. It was during this summer, he romanced Dina, now divorced from Dick O'Neill. Dina and Dan would be married within the year.

Our final play of this season was *Night Must Fall*, Emlyn Williams' melodrama, more of a 'how-it-was-done' rather than a 'who-done-it.' Gate was the murderer Danny, carrying around a hatbox, purported to contain the head of a former victim. (Much discussion in rehearsals as to how much a human head weighed). Enid Markey, star of stage and screen, the original Jane in the first Tarzan film, played the old lady to be murdered. Anne Wakefield and I played the servants. As Dora the maid, I had the memorable line, "*Aow, come quick! There's a 'and in the rubbish dump.*"

There was one more production to put on for that 1964 season, the musical *Guys and Dolls*. But Gate and I were done and we needed to return to our new apartment in Manhattan. Gate was signed to a supporting role in Jean Kerr's *Poor Richard* on Broadway, with Alan Bates and Gene Hackman. I was to present our son Corin on October 1st at Columbia Presbyterian Hospital and take on my new role as mother.

For me, life changed. I solemnly vowed I would forgo any acting dreams and be the mother that my own mother had never been.

Mother wrote no more about that season. I think she knew that Nemesis had arrived. Even though the critics had, overall, been kind. *The Lakeville (CT) Journal* summed up the season thus:

> "With a merry tune and a gay flip of the heels, the Berkshire Playhouse bids a flirtatious goodbye to a successful season. Robert Paine Grose and Joan White have offered a variety of selections, something for every taste. From the very old to the untried new; musical comedy and dated melodrama; mystery and pure farce. The settings have been fine throughout the season, colorful and imaginative. Costuming too, has been excellent. It is with regret that we see the closing of the Berkshire Playhouse for another year, already we are looking forward to 1965."

The Playhouse would reopen, but without Mother and Bob. Despite their budget over-run, another cloud was hanging over their partnership. The meetings of the Board of the Three Arts Society, throughout their tenure, had centered on money; not quality but money. Mother and Bob had managed to keep their heads above water for four years, but this final year had, in spite of excellent houses for the most part, showed in the red.

Much of *My Fair Lady's* two weeks of packed houses was eaten up by royalties, musicians' fees and the "exorbitant" fee for the leading man, Murray Matheson, ironically insisted on by the President of the Board herself. This could possibly have been overcome had the Board not had a very different reason for their dismissal.

In the minutes of the Board meeting on September 1, 1964, after some financial back and forth, the minutes reflected, and I quote:

> *"Following this discussion, Mr. (Jack) Talbot asked for permission to read a lengthy report he had prepared outlining the strengths and weaknesses of the present management. He concluded with a motion asking for the resignation of the Groses."*

There is no copy in the archives of Mr. Talbot's report. What it said, I don't know, but with hindsight, it was probably damning about Bob's dalliance. The next paragraph of the minutes was blacked out! However, the blacking out was not very successful, and, after all this time, I have deciphered it and got the underlying gist that they were trying to avoid unseemly publicity:

> *"Discussion followed, particularly in regard to whether or not the option clause held with the Groses was enforceable. Suggestion of offering a contract, which was reasonable but not attractive, was proposed. It was decided that this was not a logical solution. Suggestion was then made that overtures to the Groses be made in such a way that they would offer to resign, rather than asking for their resignation.*
>
> *"The question was finally put to a written ballot and the vote was unanimous to ask for the resignation of the present management. It was decided that the Executive Committee would be asked to do this on a date to be determined by them.*
>
> *Respectfully submitted, L. Deeley secretary.*

So that was that. No more Stockbridge seasons. It was a bittersweet ending for them, especially for Mother who was, once again, faced with yet another husband's preferences for men. Stockbridge, being rather Puritan in those days, did not like it.

She "rose above it," and she and Bob returned to New York City and their elegant apartment in the Dorilton. They must have been chastened by their dismissal, after working so hard for five years, and I suspect their marriage was now on rather rocky ground.

Susannah and I always felt that our Mother knew about Bob's preferences, in fact Sue says she is sure Mother knew back in Canada. Their marriage, much like the one to our late father, was a marriage of two theatre people pooling their talents. They worked well together and I know there was fondness between them. I knew, from knowing Bob, that he cared for our mother very deeply. He told me he resented being known as "Joan White's husband." What they did with their sex life was their business and I have no idea about that. So far, their union had made them happy, avoiding any public unpleasantness (until that final Stockbridge Board meeting).

This part of Mother's story has made me remember Christmas, 1987.

I remember that Christmas well. Sue and I were both recently divorced and I was visiting England. It happened to be the first time my sister and I were with our Mother for Christmas since I was three almost four, just before we were placed under the care of the Actors' Orphanage and went to live at Silverlands.

Mother had relocated to England in 1983 and bought a flat in Chelsea on Mallord Street, around the corner from Paultons' Square, where Sue and I had been babies. We had gathered, just the three of us for Christmas, and were talking in her sitting room.

Mother had been to see her accountant, Norman Bishop, the day before. She said, "*You two are single now. You could do worse than marry a man like Norman. Oh, if I were twenty years younger I would to put my shoes under his bed.*"

Sue snorted, "*Mother, Norman is a lovely man, but he is as queer as a three-dollar bill.*"

Mother spluttered, "*How can you say that?*"

Sue, "*You obviously can't tell. You have been married three times to gay men!*"

Mother shouted, "*I have not!*"

Sue said, "*Look, we know that Father was gay and so was Bob Grose. That's definite. And as for your first marriage, with John Vesey Baines looking like he did, well, I wouldn't be surprised about him. Besides, he divorced you, because you were having an affair, within a year after marrying him.*"

Mother was, for once, speechless.

Chapter Thirteen

MOTHERHOOD FOR ME
AND "ON A CLEAR DAY..."
1964 – 1969

On October 1st, after eighteen hours of labor, Corin Salsbury arrived at Columbia Presbyterian Hospital. He was a healthy baby, but I had been given a dirty catheter and got a nasty infection. As a result, I could not see my baby, let alone nurse him, and it was a most unpleasant stay. The overworked nursing staff wouldn't tell me that it was I who was ill and there was nothing wrong with my son. I was glad to go home. Because of the infection, my milk was not nutritious and I had to crash wean my baby to formula. This was very uncomfortable and upsetting.

I don't remember Mother coming to the hospital. I did learn later that she had been busy organizing a Cabaret for the Legal Aid Ball at the Waldorf Astoria around that time. Colgate was dividing his time between the hospital on the Upper West Side and rehearsals for *Poor Richard* at the Helen Hayes Theatre on West 44th street. It was Gate's Broadway debut and he was naturally nervous. The Jean Kerr play was directed by Peter Wood and a potential box office draw. It was a big opportunity for Gate, and for us.

When I came home, in a rather weakened state with our beautiful baby boy, Mother did visit. She also came to our rescue with a practical solution. She found a baby nurse to live in and teach me the rudiments of baby care. (*I know, I know, your mother is supposed to do that, but my mother wasn't ever that kind of mother and, actually, for that I am grateful. Lord knows what she might have taught me!*) The nurse's name was Peggy Hyde and she was an elderly, very English lady who had been a Park Avenue Nanny.

She was very sweet, yet rather over-bearing, and after one month, we were glad to see her leave.

While Colgate was rehearsing, so too was Mother. She was directing *The Brownings – a Foot on the Stair* with Byrne Piven and Nancy Wickwire at the Theatre De Lys to open in November.

Poor Richard opened on December 2 and ran through March 13, 1965. It received mixed reviews. Colgate got a nice mention in <u>The New York Times</u>.

Mother wrote in her journal:

> "*In December, I received a telephone call from my sister Audrey in Gibraltar:*
>
> "*Come at once! Father is dying.*"
>
> *Immediately I flew via Madrid, and for the first time approached that magnificent Rock from the air. Audrey and my older daughter, Susannah, met me. Father had died on December 9th as I flew over that damned Atlantic. We buried my favorite human being in the cemetery, under the shadow of the Rock, little knowing that my Mother would join him there only three months later.*

Audrey told me, years later, that when word got out about Grandfather's death, several men in black coats came to the house and carried his coffin on their shoulders to the cemetery. They were members of the Gibraltar Masonic Temple and knew that Henry White was member of the Order of Free Masons. They came to bury one of their own. Audrey said he hadn't been to a meeting since leaving England, yet they knew he was there. (So *that's* where he went on Tuesday evenings, when I was staying in South Moreton as a girl!)

In March,1965, Mother wrote a rather long letter to Gate's Mother, Edie, whom she had only recently met but would correspond with for the next few years:

> "*Had a wire from my sister saying our mother had died peacefully. I know we all expected it. It was a merciful piece of news really and not a shock but...well...one's very good friend is one's mother. (Huh?) I am not going out there again though, as she did not wish me to do so.*"

Granny had never approved of Mother's way of life and was quite vociferous about it.

Mother continued in the same letter about spending an evening with Corin and me,

> *She (Judy) is deeply devoted to her most important job, Colgate and the baby. She seems to grow more sensible daily, and her philosophy is such that, whatever may befall her in life, I really do think she will be able to cope without the need for fashionable psychiatry (never approved of by my father, and I rather agree) or other outside aids.*

This coming from a woman who did not have a clue about what I felt about anything. She never talked to me about my childhood; about my father; or my years alone in New York.   She never expressed any curiosity about my tour of the States or asked what I wanted from life. And this was early days yet into my marriage. After her mother's death, Mother wrote in her journal about the coming summer with Bob Grose.

> *When I had returned to New York, Bob told me of the availability of a small theatre on Cape Cod. It sounded a possible place for us to continue what we had begun so successfully at Stockbridge. The Yarmouth Playhouse was a white clapboard New England house containing a small auditorium and a proscenium stage.*
>
> *We immediately bought the theatre, and Bob transformed it into a beautiful and practical gem. We collected a good young Company and planned a light program of plays for people on holiday. Anna Russell agreed to open the season with her one-woman show.*
>
> *Publicity went out and V.I.P.s were invited to the Opening from as far afield as Boston and New York. To follow Anna, we were rehearsing the Hart-Kaufman play, George Washington Slept Here. All was going as planned.*
>
> *Then Anna suddenly informed us that she had 'mistaken her dates'. So had her agent, manager and secretary. This, a week before the Opening!*
>
> *Nothing could be done. We had to replace her – but how? Frantically I telephoned Hermione Gingold, who like the splendid trouper she was, merely drawled, "How very naughty of Anna! When do we*

start?" And the crisis was over. But programs and billing had to be changed, and audiences notified. This cost us a fortune. So, when I was suddenly offered the role of Lady Insdale in Alan Jay Lerner's new Broadway musical, On a Clear Day You Can See Forever, I accepted, and left my partners to continue at Yarmouth.

This is the first time that Mother mentions a partner, beside Bob Grose. That partner was William Shepard. Things may have been awkward and she needed an "out" to leave Cape Cod. The offer came at a very fortunate time.

She continued: *For years I had wanted to be part of a big musical from the first days of production. Having joined My Fair Lady when it was already two years old, I had missed all the original creativity and stress. Now my opportunity had come. The theatre world had been awaiting the new Lerner musical for two years; it was said that Louis Jourdan and Barbara Harris had been under contract for many months. New York was agog with rumors and gossip.*

I was sent the script and couldn't put it down. It had a very good story line, was romantic and unusual and full of delightful characters. The dialog was satirical and witty: in fact, pure Alan Jay Lerner, with no dependence of George Bernard Shaw.

Being primarily a present-day story with seventeenth century flashbacks, it afforded great opportunities to both Scenic and Costume Designers. The director Robert Lewis was also a noted acting teacher from Yale University, and his rehearsals were sometimes affectionately known as 'Bobby's Acting Classes' and I, for one, learnt a lot of useful stuff to pass on to my own acting students. Burton Lane's music was as delightful and memorable as the script and the brilliant choreographer Herb Ross was responsible for the staging of all musical scenes.

Needless to say, this led to some tense confrontations, especially at the first dress rehearsal when our creative author decided that the play must be cut.

When one of Bobby's scenes 'got the knife' he insisted that something balletic should also be 'cut'. Out went the 17th Century Royal Academy Ballet, one that was lovely to look at and full of humor.

Rehearsals had started in the Mark Hellinger Theatre in New York in a very hot July. Then we moved to the Colonial Theatre in Boston, where the lighting designer Abe Feder was much in evidence. Once, after a bombardment of expletives, I asked him "why?"

"I had a dead man in the booth," he grunted.

"A dead man?"

"Yes...dead drunk...You can't sack 'em...Union."

Having an elegant, but small, role opposite that Neil Fitzgerald, I was able to watch the developments which went on around us. Our young female 'star' Barbara Harris was a natural comedienne and full of invention. If only she had been audible! Actors playing opposite her could barely hear their cues. Likewise, her charming co-star Louis Jourdan was also inaudible. It was a problem. What a relief when the Greek actor Titos Vandis bounced on with his show-stopping number "When I Will Be Born Again.!" All of Alan's amusing lyrics could be heard.

On the first night of On A Clear Day... in Boston, the curtain was due to rise at 7 p.m. Everyone, from the orchestra in the pit to the 'fly-men' over our heads, was at the ready; Bobby Lewis, flapping like a free-range hen; Alan Jay Lerner, quiet behind his dark glasses, at the back of the stalls; and the performers, each alone with his or her own set of nerves, waiting to spring into action. The biggest musical of the coming New York season was about to be unveiled.

The curtain did indeed rise at seven p.m., but it came down well after midnight. Commuters, dependent on trains, either missed them or miss the last act. It was a sober 'morning after'. Alan, with a solemn face, assembled us all in the front-of-house lobby. He thanked us for a 'good show,' then came to the point:

"I'm sorry," he said, "but we have to 'cut'...It's a bladder hazard."

For a moment there was silence, then we all laughed. Then we all listened intently as characters, dialogue, costumes and scenery came under the guillotine.

Most actors understand that 'the good of the show' is paramount; but for each individual affected it is heartbreaking. With all the good grace we could muster, a few of us went quietly back to New York – but not to Broadway.

Some months later, I sat through a pretty, but boring, musical, and thought of the excitement of its inception. What had started as a witty, innovative production had ended up as another romantic show. And, in a few hectic months, a fortune had been spent. But, I for one had had one hell of a lesson — perhaps the best technical lesson of my career. And I'd loved every minute of it. For now, though, it was back to New York, then on to Cape Cod for the very end of our Summer Theatre season.

The Broadway production opened at the Mark Hellinger Theatre on October 17, 1965 and closed on June 11, 1966 after 280 performances and 3 previews. The show was not well received. Ben Brantley of the <u>New York Times</u> recalled:

"The book was strained and muddled; most critics agreed; its big production numbers were simply cumbersome. But it did have a lushly melodic score."

Meanwhile, Colgate and I were enjoying our little son, and I had joined the group of mothers in Riverside Park. Like us, many of them were connected either to journalism or the arts. We were a microcosm for the birth of *Sesame Street*. Tom Whedon, Jon Stone, Sam Pottle and Joe Raposo often gathered at the Whedon's apartment, one block away from ours, and Lee Whedon with her red-headed Joey (now known as Joss Whedon) and Sue Raposo's little Joe were part of Riverside Park's stroller Moms. Colgate and I, along with Ralph and Genie Ellis, often joined in the creative merriment — and it *was* merriment at the Whedons.

It was through Ralph Ellis that Colgate started working in Soap Operas – the actor's bread and butter. Ralph was a writer for several soaps: *Dark Shadows, As the World Turns, Another World* and *Search for Tomorrow*. Colgate was to have roles in the last three. He was kept busy working on television in Soap Operas, which paid well but were not artistically satisfying. He got a lot of fan mail.

A few months after Corin's birth I was pregnant again. On October 27th 1965, I gave birth to Abigail at New York Lying-In Hospital. I had changed both gynecologist and hospital, as my memories of Columbia

Presbyterian were painful. My mother-in-law took Corin to her home in Hartford for a week.

Again, Mother did not come to the hospital to see her grand-daughter. She had taken the measure of what was happening on Cape Cod and cut her losses. Certainly, Bob Grose had moved out of the Dorilton around this time, because when Mother was out of town, she would have a "lodger."

In the fall of 1965, Mother was in *Major Barbara* at the Charles Playhouse in Boston. In early 1966, she went to Mexico and obtained a "quickie" divorce. In the program for the 1966 season for the Yarmouth Playhouse, the producers are listed as Robert Paine Grose and William Shepard — no mention of Mother at all.

She rose above that, too.

Returning to New York, Mother was engaged to replace the actress playing Mrs. Hitchcock in Stuart Burge's production of *Sergeant Musgrave's Dance*. Considered one of John Arden's most important plays, it had opened at The Theatre de Lys on March 8.

Mother must have taken over the role a few weeks after it opened, because I know she was in rehearsal on March 23rd.

On March 23rd our son Corin had a terrible accident! The window cleaner had come the day before, and made funny faces at Corin, while he worked. Mimicking the window cleaner, Corin had pushed a chair over to the window, stood on the radiator and pushed the window up. (We didn't know the sash cord was broken causing the window to open easily). He fell. I was in the other room changing the baby. The radio was on. I heard nothing. The window had silently closed after him. I searched for him in the apartment and as I was calling his name in the hall, someone shouted to me that something was happening in the courtyard five floors below. He was wearing his little red shirt and yellow overalls when I looked (which I wish I hadn't). I hurriedly handed five-month-old Abby to our upstairs neighbor and went in the police car, following the ambulance, to the Emergency Room at St. Luke's Hospital. My mother-in-law arriving at our apartment to take us to see Hal Halbrook in *Mark Twain Tonight*, was told by Lucius the doorman where I was. Meanwhile my pediatrician, Leo Wilking, ran every traffic light to the hospital and was there with me while they operated on Corin, trying to save his little life.

They said he had a fifty-fifty chance. Never believe that!

Leo asked where Colgate was.

I said, "*He's in Brooklyn. They're filming* Another World *live. He can't possibly come.*"

Leo said, "*Judy, you have to call him.*"

I dialed the number on the hospital phone and was making apologetic sounds.

Leo snatched the phone out of my hand and said, "*Colgate, get here as fast as you can.*"

My mother-in-law arrived. Colgate arrived.

Corin died.

He died at St. Luke's Hospital two hours later — the worst two hours of my life. He was just eighteen months old when Colgate and I said goodbye to him.

I heard the window cleaner wept when he was told.

We went back to the apartment. Colgate went upstairs to get Abby.

Edie ran a hot bath for me, handed me a brandy and said,

"*Judy dear, you must call your mother.*"

"*I can't,*" I whispered. "*I can't tell her. I don't want her here.*"

Edie said, "*She has to know. I will call her. What is the number?*"

She dialed the number and I heard her say,

"*I must speak to Joan White. This is a family emergency.*"

Then there was more talking. Edie returned to the bathroom. She sat on the toilet seat and said, "*Judy dear, you've told me about your childhood and your mother. I've met her. I always thought you were exaggerating... until now. Now I understand.*"

"*What did she say?*" I asked.

"*She said she could come after rehearsal this evening.*"

It was two in the afternoon.

Many years later, I was having dinner with my old friend Chuck Maryan. He had been Production Stage Manager on *Sergeant Musgrave's Dance*. I asked him if he remembered that day. He told me,

> "*I have never forgotten it. I answered the phone at rehearsal when your mother-in-law called and I got Joan to the phone. I was standing nearby when I heard her say, "Corin died? Oh, dear. Well, I can't come now I'm in rehearsal. I'll come this evening."*"

And she hung up.

I said to her, "Joan, you can go now. We'll manage without you. I'm so sorry."

She replied, "Oh, there is nothing I can do now. He has died. Besides Colgate's mother is there."

Chuck said to me, "*I didn't understand how she could be that way. And you and I were friends. I tell you, I never forgot that day. It changed how I thought about people."* Sergeant Musgrave's Dance got very mixed reviews and closed on July 3, 1966 after 135 performances. The critics were not kind.

Sometime after her play closed in July, Mother took me to see *Mame*, saying it would cheer me up. I came to love the show and the music, but that day, when Angela Lansbury sang,

"Where's that boy with the bugle,
My little love was always my big romance."

I burst into tears and had to leave the theatre.

Mother was very upset with me and firmly said, "*You really must buck up.*"

My little boy had just died. I had a baby daughter to care for. My husband had left us and was using his grief to justify an affair with our upstairs neighbor.

Bucking up wasn't in the cards.

That summer, Mother was cast in the Hallmark Hall of Fame production of Noel Coward's Blithe Spirit starring Dirk Bogarde, Rosemary Harris, Ruth Gordon and Rachel Roberts. Mother played the small role of Mrs. Bradman, but it was quite a coup to be in such company in a popular television series. It aired on December 7th, just before she left for England.

On December 15, in a letter to my mother-in-law, she wrote,

All this year I have felt that Judy might need me, but now I have you there for her, it is lovely for me to go to England and see my other daughter and her family.

She had seen me perhaps twice since *Mame*. I really think that my Mother was totally self-involved, just incredibly insensitive and wrapped up with her own world. She never forgave our father for being court martialed. She saw it as compromising *her* career. She never understood my sister Susannah's long, hard search for some man to replace the Father she had adored; marrying four times with no success. She only understood that because Bob preferred men, it made a mess of *her life*; even though Bob was very good to her. She thought her sister Audrey a fool for deeply loving a man she couldn't marry. And me, well she never ever understood me…she didn't know me, and she never really tried.

She meant well though, in her way.

Chapter Fourteen

ACTING HERE, THERE
AND EVERYWHERE

Back from England, in May she went to play Lady Bracknell in Cincinnati Playhouse in the Park's production of *The Importance of Being Earnest*, followed by Mrs. Tarleton in *Misalliance*. By the middle of summer, she was back in New York to play Mrs. Dedalus, the hero's mother, in *Stephen D*, It opened at the East 74th Street Theatre on September 24, 1967 and closed, after 56 performances.

> *It was while I was playing James Joyce's mother in Stephen D. that I received a play from Norman Holland, The Years of the Locust, about Oscar Wilde's two years in prison. On the advice of Tony Guthrie, I took it to Adrian Hall, who wanted it to be presented in tandem with The Importance of Being Earnest at his theatre, Trinity Square Playhouse in Providence Rhode Island. So, I played that Edwardian monster Lady Bracknell, again.*

After several weeks of rehearsal, Mother was unable to join Gate's family in Hartford for Christmas. His architect father and his writer mother lived in a style to which I was learning to adapt. Oblivious to the kind of family I had married into, she mailed us a package. Opening it on Christmas morning, I was mortified to find three books of Green Stamps and a note saying Gate and I could exchange these for a nice bath mat. This made Gate so angry, that once in our room, he threw an ornament at the wall exclaiming, "*Your bloody mother!*"

The Importance of Being Earnest opened on December 28th for a two and a half week run. *Years of the Locust*, opened as a world premiere on February 8th 1968 with Richard Kneeland as Oscar Wilde. Scottish Arts Administrator Peter Diamand went to see the new play and invited

Trinity Rep to perform at the Edinburgh International Festival, the first American theater company to do so. *Years of the Locust* by Norman Holland was chosen to represent the Company, with Mother proudly acting as producer.

Mother's diary again:

> *That August 1968, Years of the Locust was so well received at The Church Hill Theatre in Edinburgh, there was talk of transfer to London; but Equity rules regarding American casts precluded a transfer. The same rules apply in reverse for British casts wishing to play in the U.S.*
>
> *However, my guardian angel 'came up trumps' once again. There was a phone call from my British agent. Stuart Burge and Jonathan Miller were taking over the Nottingham Playhouse and wanted me for their Company.*
>
> *We opened with Barry Foster as Shakespeare's King John and I, who had once been his instructor at RADA, as his mother Queen Elinor of Aquitaine.*

> The Stage wrote *"Directed by the inventive Jonathan Miller, the production had elements of pantomime, circus, satire and Lewis Carroll."* and *"Joan White was a bristling Queen Elinor..."*

Jonathan Miller also directed the next production, *The School for Scandal* by Richard Brinsley Sheridan. Mother was to play that nasty old gossip, Mrs. Candour.

Lorna Heilbrun, who I knew at Shakespeare & Company many years on, was fresh out of LAMDA then, and according to *The Stage* was a *"charming"* Maria.

> Lorna wrote this memory, *"Jonathan Miller, who directed it, decided to have all the costumes 'broken down' or unglamourized so we would look as dirty and smelly as people of that period would have appeared in real time. Joan took to it and seemed to relish the experience, unlike some of us who had imagined looking pretty and shiny as period productions were in those days. It was a great success and I remember Joan getting some mentions in the press*

and being a huge favorite with some of the young actors in the company – Nick Clay, my late husband – being one of them, I seem to remember! I have a memory of Joan being kind to me as I was very inexperienced and lacking confidence."

In her obituary, Alan Strachan wrote, about her Nottingham season.

"She was Mrs. Candour dripping cloaked venom, like prussic acid on sugar cubes, in Jonathan Miller's pox-and-all reappraisal of The School For Scandal." and "She was a stoically careworn Paulina in Stuart Burge's production of The Seagull."

Mother said: *It was a joyful time for me. But the Nottingham damp was so insidious, (Moira Redmond and I ate and slept in our fur coats) and my bank manager so insistent, there was general rejoicing when I accepted a position on the Drama Faculty of the University of Washington in Seattle. Back I went to the U.S.A. and was engaged in Seattle for one year. I remained for five.*

Mother gave up her lease on the Dorilton apartment, packed her bags and flew out to Seattle not to return until 1975.

Meanwhile the rest of the 1960s were busy for Gate and me and our little family.

After Corin's death and the following upheavals, things quieted down. I was pregnant again by the fall of 1966. The cloak of sadness had hung over our apartment on 105th Street and West End and we looked in earnest for a new apartment.

As well as the soap operas, he also made a few commercials, the most memorable was the first Scope commercial:

"Boss, you could fire me for this but...you have bad breath."

Gate was constantly assailed by cabbies and truck drivers, who would lean out and yell that line at him. Ah, the price of fame!! But that commercial paid for all the medical and hospital bills in May of 1967 when our second daughter, Sherrod Louise, was born. Screen Actors Guild had the best health insurance plan for those lucky enough to belong. A month before Sherrod was born, Gate's father, Charles Salsbury died suddenly at only 59. Shortly after, we found the apartment of our dreams at 801 West

End Avenue between 99th and 100th street. A wonderful, old building, our apartment had eight rooms and was on the fifth floor overlooking West End.

When he wasn't making commercials and in soap operas, Gate was acting in several off-Broadway plays. In June of 1966, he was Paul in Arnold Wesker's *The Kitchen* directed by Jack Gelber (author of *The Connection)* at the 81st Street theatre. He later took over the leading role of Peter, after Rip Torn left the cast. *Fireworks* was three one-act plays. Gate was in two of them: *Football*, and *Fireworks For a Hot Fourth. Fireworks* fizzled out quite quickly. In 1967, he understudied Alec McCowen in *After The Rain* at the John Golden Theatre on Broadway.

1967 and 1968 were rich with roles on WNET-TV, New York City's Public Television. He read Jewish poetry wearing a yarmulke, and Russian poetry bareheaded. Director Barry Boys created The Actors Company hoping to produce the entire Shakespearean Canon for public television, but he ran out of money after three productions. Gate was Leontes in *The Winter's Tale* with Stacy Keach as Autolycus, and Macduff to Earle Hyman's chilling *Macbeth*. In the third production, *Twelfth Night*, Gate played Antonio the sea captain. It was an exciting and ambitious idea, while it lasted. Some of the company would come to our apartment and play poker into the night. (I had learned to play poker on the road with *A Man For All Seasons.)* Between hearing Gate's lines, watching him on soap operas and playing poker, I got my theatre kicks vicariously in those days, and once for real.

Steve Aaron, who had been our Best Man, was teaching Directing at Julliard and had been invited to SUNY Purchase to teach *Hamlet*. He brought four actors with him to illustrate key scenes: Colgate as Hamlet, James Earl Jones as Claudius, Marian Seldes as Gertrude, and myself as Ophelia. A time to remember.

We went to Center Stage in Baltimore for six months in September 1968, We rented half a house in Ruxton, Maryland and I learned to drive. It was not a happy time for me.

Gate was gone at the theatre all day and most of the night and, I suspected, he was dallying. Our mothers both visited; mine briefly, before she left for Seattle for five years and Edie Salsbury came, before she learned she had the cancer that would kill her in 1971.

We returned to New York in early 1969 and I was happy to get home to my friends and join my fellow shadow puppeteers. Puppetry was something I had begun doing to use my theatre skills, and to which I could also bring the children. Five of us, all women with small children, went from playgroups to day care centers with our collapsible theatre and our back-lit puppets. Asian puppets are fanciful and made of stiff pierced leather, creating silhouettes on the screen. Our puppets were simple, but colorful, thanks to cellophane and other colored material.

In 1970, Gate was cast in *The Trial of the Catonsville Nine*, Daniel Berrigan's free verse play about the trial of the Vietnam War protesters who poured napalm on Draft records. The play opened at the Good Shepherd Faith Church on 66th Street. Ed Flanders played Daniel Berrigan originally. When it moved to The Lyceum Theatre, Flanders left the cast and Gate, as his understudy, took over the role, getting the Broadway credit.

While the play was in production at the Good Shepherd Faith Church that winter, an arrest warrant was out for Daniel Berrigan. He was a fugitive for several months before he was finally caught and sent to Danbury Federal Correctional Institution. I went to see the play as often as I could, it was the beginning of my political activism. Both Dan and Sister Elizabeth were wanted by the FBI, and the agents were out in full-force. They came to watch every audience. So easy to spot; they all wore black suits, white shirts, black ties, and spoke to their top left pockets. What a joke! The house manager and I would count them, sometimes as many as eight, each evening. Dan and Sister Elizabeth did come to see the play a couple of times, but they were never apprehended. Dan wore a loud check suit and a false beard and Sister Elizabeth, a purple polyester pants-suit; those FBI guys had no imagination.

Abby, now five, had started kindergarten at P.S. 95 and we realized we had to think about the children's education. We loved our big apartment, very convenient for Gate's work in the city, but we had both grown up in the country. Friends in our building had a weekend house in Millerton, New York and their children were the same age as ours. They invited us up for a weekend. Reading the Sunday Times, we spotted a small listing in the real estate section: *'Carriage House. Housatonic MA. $10*,000' and a phone number.

"Let's go take a look," we said, and we all piled into our cars.

Half an hour up Route 7, just north of Great Barrington, we found it and fell in love. It was an ornate 1880 carriage house, badly in need of attention. No road frontage, a long skinny acre of land, just a short walk to the shop and the school. It was perfect. We bought it, with a gift from Gate's mother Edie, and we closed on the house at the end of December, 1970.

It needed a lot of time and money, but we worked hard, meeting new people, especially plumbers, electricians and heating specialists. We learned new skills every day. By spring, I had moved up from the city full time. The girls were enrolled in school. While Gate was still in *Catonsville*, he came up on Sunday, his day off. Once the play closed, he decided that he wanted to give up New York City.

So, at the start of the 1970s, Gate and I, with our growing daughters, had left New York to begin a new life in Housatonic, Massachusetts. My beloved mother-in-law, Edie Salsbury, due to aggressive cancer, was sadly entering the last year of hers. She was the closest thing to a real mother that I had ever known, and one of my greatest regrets has been that she never saw her granddaughters grow up. She would have been so proud of them.

Chapter Fifteen

TEACHING IN SEATTLE
1970 – 1974

"The only way to become an actor is to act." Joan White

My own mother, the indefatigable Joan White, left New York City in 1969 to embark on a new phase of her career; teaching American college students at the University of Washington. Not that she gave up acting. Ever.

In Seattle, she taught speech and drama in the theatre department, headed by Duncan Ross. For her first production in 1969, she directed the students in Chekhov's *The Seagull;*

Writing in *The Seattle Post-Intelligencer* Patrick MacDonald wrote:

> "When the curtain rises on the University of Washington's production of The Seagull at the Showboat, a blue light fills the upstage so that the first thing that strikes the eye is the silhouette of a man in the act of building something, pounding nails into a board. It is a stark, effective and very stylish beginning. And the same sense of style prevails to the final curtain. Director Joan White hasn't tampered with Chekhov's masterpiece in achieving this style but she has done much to enhance it.
>
> "This is a very exciting production of a particularly important play. The students involved are to be congratulated for it. And people who value theater should make every effort to see it."

As a teacher and director, she was off to a good start. As an actress, she was invited that year to appear in *A Day in the Death of Joe Egg* at Seattle Repertory Company. Other roles in Seattle would follow over the next few years.

At the Rep, she was Frosine in Moliere's *The Miser* in 1970 and Aunt Penniman in *The Heiress* at ACT a year later. The late Gregory Falls, who was head of the University's School of Drama and founder of A Contemporary Theater, (ACT) directed her there as Meg in Pinter's *The Birthday Party* in June of 1970. The following year, she played Mrs. Crowe in Peter Luke's *Hadrian VII*.

She directed ten plays with the students, primarily Shakespeare and Chekhov including

> *The Seagull,* Federico Garcia Lorca's *The House of Bernarda Alba, The Merry Wives of Windsor* and a modern version of *Love's Labours Lost.*

It was during her stay in Seattle (she never did have tenure, but was reappointed each year for five years) that she founded The English Summer Theatre School with the blessing of Greg Falls and Duncan Ross. Under the aegis of the University of Washington's School of Drama, Mother introduced this program for the first time, to run from July 20th through August 30th, 1970.

> *"In association with the Adeline Genee Theatre of East Grinstead, I taught the first English Summer Program for students. The following year we became affiliated with the Thorndike Theatre in Leatherhead. We played each summer at the Edinburgh Festival Fringe and we crossed the U.S. and the Atlantic each year from 1970-74"*

The University's School of Drama listed the following information in their prospectus:

> *"Students will travel to England and will be working with a professional English acting company in order to study the styles of English acting. In addition to classes and lectures, students will perform in short plays and scenes from an exclusively English repertoire with English teacher and directors.*
>
> *The Adeline Genee Theatre will also be available for private performances. Students will be the guests of the professional resident company and are free to attend their rehearsals and possibly*

perform with the group. There will also be field trips to other the-
atres, museums and professional rehearsals.

The total cost is $600.00 that included travel and room and
board. The program is limited to twenty students. Each student
will gain nine credits."

In an interview with Sue Lockett in *the Seattle Post Intelligencer*,
Mother is quoted:

"Students must go to the fountainhead. To learn British drama,
go to Britain, live at the source of the plays and work closely with
British actors.

"There are other summer programs in England for American
drama students, but they involve only viewing and discussing
plays, not acting. The only way to become an actor is to act. The
emphasis will be everything English, including the dialects."

As well as publicizing the project among University of Washington
students, Mother sent notices to 90 other drama schools in the US. She
was determined to make it successful.

In England, she received great publicity for her program. Her students were popular and welcomed, and the reviews for the first production, *Every Number Wins* by Michael Almaz, were very favorable.

The Stage and TV Today wrote, *"A seventy-minute satirical piece that bit
raw into life"* The play was listed as one of the Best Short Plays of 1968.
Harvy Blanks, one of Mother's students this first year, played a leading
role in this production. Blanks went on to perform in all ten of August
Wilson's ten-play Century Cycle, and was a recipient of the Drama Desk
Award for the Off-Broadway hit *Tabletop*. Other students that year went
on to careers in the Arts. This first program was a success and, in the
ensuing years, students from other colleges enrolled, with sometimes as
many as thirty students travelling to England in future summers.

Elizabeth Pursey, RADA teacher of dialects and speech, also taught
each summer at The School for the fifteen years it was in existence. Speaking at Mother' Memorial Service in 1999, she talked about Mother's ide-
alism and love of the theatre, and also of her sometimes rather quixotic
behavior. She remembered,

"Her colleagues were often plunged into unforgettable adventures and I will give two personal examples; on a trip to Oyster Bay, south of British Columbia, at a camping lodge, Joan produced a champagne breakfast with oysters. Now, she did this while I was at Mass. The oysters had been secretly bought the night before and put under the car to keep cool. Joan had tried several in the early morning to be sure they were fresh. This was confessed only after the triumphant breakfast.

She then said, 'You know we are quite near one of the two remaining rain forests in the world. You must experience that! We'll tie plastic bags over our shoes.' Well, one must seize the moment! Surely that was education of the highest order… unforgettable education. Years later, Joan wrote on a postcard of the Olympic Mountain, "Once you and I walked in the rainforest at the foot of these mountains."

Lucky Elizabeth Pursey to experience a side of Mother quite unknown to me!

In 1971, having transferred her program to the Thorndike Theatre in Leatherhead, she and eighteen students presented *Salute to Sir Walter*, a miscellany of writings to celebrate the 200th anniversary of the birth of Sir Walter Scott. This curtain raiser was juxtaposed with a new play by Gertrude Samuels, an American journalist, called *The Corrupters*.

In 1972, *The Stage* wrote,

"Now, for the third year running, Joan White, Lecturer in Drama at the University of Washington in Seattle, has come to the Thorndike to run what is now a well-established Foreign Study Course for American drama students.

This year, she has with her 25 students from seven states — California, Illinois, Minnesota, New Jersey, New York, Connecticut and Washington — who are studying under Elizabeth Pursey for Speech and British Dialects; Bert Stimmel for Movement; James Cairncross for Shakespeare; Madame Fedro for Period Styles; Giles Havergal for Directing; and Joan White herself, as well as having lectures from many distinguished theatre personalities."

Mother used all her contacts to make this program a success: Hazel Vincent Wallace at the Thorndike, and Giles Havergal in Glasgow were old friends and so were many of the actors, teachers and choreographers she persuaded to join her program.

She also used her connections with the Edinburgh Festival director Peter Diamand. Soon her students were performing in the Fringe Festival every August. In 1972, they presented *Tobias and the Angel* by Scotland's own James Bridie in Edinburgh.

She chose plays that would suit her company. In addition to the first year's *Every Number Wins* and *The Corrupters* in 1971, *Tobias and the Angel* got rave reviews in 1972 and additional publicity when they auditioned a dog. Mother was good at getting as much publicity as possible for her students. Local newspapers picked up on the following:

> "Members of the cast of the original production of James Bridie's Tobias and the Angel will be at the Thorndike Theatre tonight and they are coming at the invitation of the play's producer, Joan White, who was herself in the original production about 40 years ago."

Another twenty-five students crossed the Atlantic in 1973 to present another James Bridie play, *Jonah and the Whale*, again to much praise. Mother directed and Bert Stimmel choreographed. Having just returned from working with the Caracas Dance Company in Beirut, Stimmel introduced sounds and music from the East for this updated version of the play. *Jonah and the Whale* played in Leatherhead in early August, before going to the Edinburgh Festival, where it played for three weeks at the Viewforth Centre.

In the summer of 1974, the English Summer Theatre School faculty added Dr. Richard Lorenzen to direct Augustin Daly's 1867 melodrama, *Under the Gaslight*. In its suspense scene, an actor is tied to railroad tracks as a train approaches, only to be saved from death. Mother opened the evening with a Victorian one act farce, *My Friend from Leatherhead*. She had found the battered script in a second-hand bookstore.

Laudatory comments were written throughout the Seattle Summer Theatre School.:

"My husband and I thought your students made a wonderful job of Tobias and the Angel — *we voted it the best of many shows we saw at the Festival."*   Grace Franklin, Glasgow

"This is to thank you for the delightfully gay evening you gave two elderly persons. It was a charming gesture to come and speak with the audience later." Isabel Stirling

"We did want to let you know how much we enjoyed Tobias and to thank you for all you made possible for Sally this past summer. You perfected a splendid program."   Mrs. Mollie Palchik

On March 12, 1975 *The Seattle Post Intelligencer* wrote about her again, bracketing her five years at the University of Washington. This time from journalist Maggie Hawthorn:

> "The School of Drama is losing one of its special personalities this June when Joan White, for six years a lecturer and director, leaves Seattle for more benevolent pastures.
>
> "Short, invincible, sharp-tongued and witty, Miss White came to the University from the Nottingham Playhouse in 1969, invited to the local faculty by Dr. Gregory A. Falls during his chairmanship of the School of Drama...
>
> "Her pet project has been the English Summer Theater School, which she organized in 1970 and which has benefited over 90 students during its few seasons, almost a third of them on scholarships generated by Miss White and some dedicated friends.
>
> "This year, for reasons cited as "budgetary primarily" by present department chairman, Paul Hostetler, the University declined further sponsorship of the English summer program. And so, Joan White is leaving and taking her program with her. It's our loss."

So ended her time in Seattle. But she was unbowed. She rose above it.

Chapter Sixteen

THE JOAN WHITE
ENGLISH THEATRE SCHOOL
1975 – 1984

With interruptions for family matters

She moved back to New York City and bought a small co-op apartment at 54 Riverside Drive with glorious Hudson River views. (I watched the tall ships sail up the river celebrating the 200th anniversary of Independence in 1976). What the University of Washington no longer wanted, she found that the City University of New York did. They accredited the program through their Study Abroad Program and extended both the time period and the number of credits offered. Her new associate director was Bertram L. Joseph, PhD, chairman of the Department of Drama and Theatre at Queens College of CUNY. Before establishing that department in 1970, Dr. Joseph had been a fellow at the University of Wales in Cardiff, a lecturer at the University of Bristol in England and professor of drama at the University of Washington, Seattle, where he met Mother. Dr. Joseph had also taught Shakespearean acting at the London Academy of Music and Dramatic Art and at the Bristol Old Vic School, both establishments well known to her.

The new program was now called *The Joan White English Theatre School* (hereafter The School*)*. It would thrive from its base in New York City and, later, from her new home in London until 1989.

Meanwhile, when Mother was still in Seattle, Susannah had been back in England for several years. Her first husband, Jim Walker, had left her in 1963 and taken their wee son, Jamie, to be raised by Jim's mother Ina in Aberdeen, Scotland. Sue did not contest this. She was now with

Ron Horton and they had three children: Ronnie in 1964, Sarah in 1965 and Gayle in 1967. Our Aunt Audrey, had given her the money to buy a house on Braemar Avenue in Thornton Heath (South London). Ron was working as a manager for Sainsbury's Supermarkets and the children had entered school. In late 1970, Sue got itchy feet and persuaded her husband that they should try Australia where Ron's brother Peter lived. So, while my husband, daughters and I had moved from New York City to the country, Sue and Ron Horton sold Braemar Avenue. They bought tickets on a P&O liner, packed up the children and left for the new and exciting world of New South Wales.

Peter had found them a house in Adamstown, Newcastle in New South Wales, and had lined up a job for Ron.

As Sue said in a letter to Mother in September, 1970,

"So, we feel as though the future is rosy. See you in Canada."

They steamed out of Southampton. The outward-bound leg included Bermuda, Port Everglades, Panama, Acapulco, Los Angeles, San Francisco, Vancouver, Hawaii, Fiji, Auckland, and Sydney. They would be forty-seven days at sea before seeing Mother in Vancouver during the Christmas holidays. It would be another thirty days to Sydney. It must have been exciting, especially for Ronnie and Sarah at 6 and 5, to be on that big, comfortable liner with all the things to do on a ship that size.

But the adventure didn't last. Sometime in 1971 the family returned by air to London. Sue and Ron had disliked Australia and the ways of Australians and within the year they were back, now renting a house on Dumbarton Road, Brixton and, I expect, having to start from scratch. Ron, not an adventurous man, had been particularly unhappy in Australia, missing his mates and his regular pub, and was unwilling to try it any longer. He got his job back at Sainsbury's. The children went back to school.

It was in April 1972 that Colgate and I decided to take our children to England, travelling on to Norway, Sweden and Denmark. Gate's play *The Trial of the Catonsville Nine* had closed and his mother, my beloved mother-in-law, Edie Salsbury, had died the previous September. We went first to London, staying in a small flat in Sloane Gardens and visiting old friends. We also saw Sue and her brood, now back in Brixton. All had seemed well with Susannah's family then, aside from her negative remarks about Australia and how many poisonous bugs and animals lived there. The cousins loved meeting each other. Ronnie was almost eight, Abby and Sarah would be seven in the autumn, Sherrod had just turned five and little Gayle was four and a half. Little did we know what was to come?

We four meandered slowly north to Newcastle stopping at various castles and National Heritage sites along the way. We took the boat to Bergen, the train to Oslo, rented a car to Gothenburg and Copenhagen and then home.

Within a year, all went topsy-turvy (or as my Aunt Audrey would say *'Arse over teakettle'*). We were to learn from Mother that Susannah had left her family and disappeared. She left a note on the kitchen table,

"I can't do it anymore. Love Mum"

On returning from school, young Ronnie read that note. It has affected him deeply ever since.

I was furious at this news! How could she, after our childhood without a mother? Was she following in Mother's **and** her great-grandmother Emma Lee's footsteps? Was this an inherited family trait? I don't think I could ever forgive her for this — for not staying with her children. If her life with Ron was, as she later said, boring; then file for divorce, but, for God's sake, take the children. She'd already lost Jamie to his father and now she would lose these three precious, bright children. But "no", she left and took up with other men. They were probably exciting at first and not 'boring' like Ron, but they were no-good bounders. It is many years later and I am still angry about her attitude about her children. You don't just give birth to babies and leave them as soon as they can walk — like kittens or baby birds. Children need guidance and love forever. Ronnie said to me, years later, that he would have nothing more to do with that *"cuckoo's nest."*

Our mother was also very upset. She flew home to England, on a break from her classes in Seattle, and tried to sort things out as best she could. She did find Susannah and that is all I will say. That marriage was over and Ron took his children to live with his elderly mother and father, Vera and Jack Horton, in Brixton. Things would never be the same for those children, but they have survived and found lasting partners. Both Gayle and Sarah have children. Ronnie is happily married and is a promising writer. Susannah did stay in touch with them, off and on, over the years, but it always came to naught because she couldn't see that what she did was unforgivable. They have since kept their distance.

Sue said to me recently,

"I always remember their birthdays with a card. Never forget them."

But I don't think she understands that a card just doesn't do it.

Mother *was* a good grandmother. Since that day in 1972, she always kept Sue's children foremost in her mind, seeing them whenever she went to England each summer with her American students. She also helped Jack and Vera Horton financially, as much as she could. Sarah wrote to me,

"On the odd occasion, when we were young, Granny would come to the UK. She would sometimes take us three up to London to have lunch in a very posh hotel, something we never did, or knew anything about. It was like Royalty visiting and we all had to be on our best behavior and try to speak nicely. Our South London accents were very strong (and still are!). We were like three vaga-bonds from Fagin's gang in Oliver Twist."

She was good to my children too while she was in New York City and on her frequent trips to the U.S. after she had moved back to England in 1983. My girls, Abby and Sherrod, have happy memories of her visits to Housatonic and visits to see her in the city.

My Abby remembers:

"During my Sophomore/Junior year in college (1986), Granny was back staying with friends, across the hall from her old apart-ment. She and I slept together in a pull-out couch bed under the windows. I remember lying in bed with her with the lights off, facing each other, and seeing the way the city lights, outside these windows, hit her face. Our conversation was partly me asking her about relationships. I'm not sure if it was about Dean, (her future husband) and I don't remember her answer, but I remember the tone being comforting. My friend Mandy came to get me on the Saturday, during my stay. We had tickets to the Blue Note to see Bobby MacFarren. Mandy drove into the city, picked me up at Gran's and we went to the club from there. When Mandy came up

out of the elevator, Granny immediately opened the door to greet her in her pants and bra. Mandy used to tell that story for years.

"I remember staying with her in her own apartment quite a few times by myself, when I was younger, before she moved back to London: going through her front door; chatting with her doorman; being in her small, tight elevator. I also remember walking out her door with Riverside Drive to your left or straight up hill to the right. I can still see her marching, pretty steadily up that city street incline, in her fur collared fall/winter coat, to get us a cab. I loved that apartment. It was big for a New York apartment, but cozy at the same time. I liked the lighting too — lots of lamps, low light and dark furniture with a big rug in the center room. My bed was along the windows looking over Riverside Drive and I loved the city light. It always took me time to get used to the city noise, coming from the country, and then to go back to the country noise from the city.

"I remember going to a gathering of her students in a loft-like apartment — lots of angled, low ceilings. I don't remember why we were there or what anyone said but I do remember the general energy in the room being busy, chatty and excited. I also remember meeting Drew Eliot on one of these excursions — the memory is mostly looking at him (and being impressed by his strong features) in a cab with the city rushing behind him."

Reading these vivid descriptions, I can see why she became an artist.

To my sometime chagrin, Mother never seemed to worry about me. *"Judy is so sensible,"* she told my friend Val Evans, *"I never have to worry about her."* So, she never did. Since I had never ever known her to worry about me, I have just carried on with my life. I too, Rose Above It. Actually, I probably just swallowed my anger and stuffed it down, as I had all my life. Here I am, after she is gone, still trying to understand her.

Without pausing for even one summer, Mother left Seattle and, under the aegis of CUNY, she continued gathering interested students from all over the US and Canada, and signing them on for an immersion in English theatre, classes and performances in the Summer of 1975. That first summer, under her own steam, working with Bert Joseph and

CUNY, the students travelled to England, once more to the Thorndike Theatre in Leatherhead. They took in lots of British Theatre and put on their own production of Dias Gomez's *Journey to Bahia*, translation by Stanley Richards, and choreographed by Bert Stimmel. Mother had presented this play before at The Berkshire Playhouse with my first husband, Colgate, playing the pivotal role of Joe. Reviews of this new production in England were much more complimentary. Michael Parva played Joe.

When the production moved to the Fringe in Edinburgh, Carry O'Connor in *The Financial Times* on August 30th wrote:

> "Joan White's production is sharp, combining satire and charm…and generally speaking, an excellent spirit emanates from the company."

And this from *The Daily Telegraph:*

> "An absorbing play. We have every reason to be grateful to Joan White for drawing our attention to this play by Brazilian Dias Gomes."

And on September 2nd, *The Glasgow Herald* describing the play said:

> "The American drama students gathered together in Joan White's English Theatre School – an enterprise which offers the students varied theatrical experience during a visit to Britain of several months — are contributing to the Fringe for the fourth year in succession. This time they bring to the Viewforth Centre, *Journey to Bahia*, a prize-winning piece by the Brazilian playwright Dias Gomes, hitherto not seen in Britain. It is a simple and moving parable of the stony path of faith in the modern world. 'A peasant, to save the life of his donkey, fulfills a vow to the local saint (also identified with a deity of voodoo). He carries a heavy wooden cross to the saint's church; but when he arrives all the forces of society, from organized crime and the law (in close collaboration), commerce and the Press, to the ecclesiastical hierarchy itself, combine to deny, deride and exploit, and finally destroy him. He ends, inevitably, laid out on his own cross.

The play is performed by the students – some 20 of them, exchanging parts among themselves — with a guileless directness, which suits the tale."

The Western Mail was equally complimentary.

In 1976, Mother set up her office, with the invaluable Zelda Englander, in New York and proceeded to enroll American students for another intensive summer course of British Theatre. This year in addition to her affiliation with CUNY she added accreditation from Webster College, Missouri, which offered 25 academic credits to be earned in the twenty-two-week program.

The production for this year was to be *Once Upon a Mattress*, Mary Rodgers' musical. Joining Mother's production team once again was Bert Stimmel, choreographer and a stalwart of the School for many years.

The musical was a smash hit, playing to sold out houses both in Leatherhead and on a tour of Scotland, as well as at The Fringe. It was so successful they were invited to stay on in the UK and tour the production through November. The School was invited back to tour Scotland the next year. *The Croydon Advertiser* headlines boldly led with "*Shear Delight*" referring to Claudia Shear, playing the role of Princess Winifred. Shear went on to become a Broadway star with her play *Dirty Blonde*, which she both wrote and starred in. Many of Mother's students went on to successful careers.

The following year, in association again with CUNY-Queens, New York and Webster College, Missouri, they presented two plays by Henri Ghéon: *St Anne and the Gouty Rector* and *The Sausage Maker's Interlude* at the Thorndike Theatre in Leatherhead. Ghéon was a French playwright and physician who wrote many plays with a religious theme. A program note says: *These plays, were written for performance anywhere and for all people.* The Sausage Maker's Interlude *is particularly applicable to all eras, so we have costumed it in many periods. Please join us in singing and dancing at the end of the performance.*

The faculty for the School that year added Michael Macowen, former principal of LAMDA, and Stuart Hopps, British dancer, teacher, and choreographer.

A Press Release from the Thorndike Theatre tells a sweet story:

Joan White has brought her students to Leatherhead to present Henri Ghéon's two light comedies at the Thorndike on Tuesday, August 8th and then for three weeks at the Edinburgh Festival. In the autumn they will play other dates in the provinces.

The plays call for some child actors and this could have caused a problem with all the travelling involved – but suddenly the problem has been solved simply. The three ragamuffins in The Sausage Maker's Interlude are being played by Joan White's own grandchildren: Ronnie, Sarah and Gayle Horton.

Sarah Horton Kennedy:

"Gayle and I both remember Granny getting the three of us to perform in The Sausage Maker's Interlude *at the Leatherhead Theatre in 1977. I can't remember how we got there and back, but I can remember our line...'Oh, what a Fair! Oh, what a Fair!'... then we were put in the sausage machine and had to scream at the top of our voices. I remember those rehearsals but not the actual performance."*

The Horton children played only the Thorndike performance; Scottish children were hired for the longer run in Edinburgh. This was a way Mother found to stay in touch with her young grandchildren, abandoned by their mother, my sister.

Sarah added,

"Also, I thank Granny for my straight teeth. My teeth were very overcrowded and must have been very noticeable to Granny (I don't think Nan, Dad or myself at 10 had taken much notice). She arranged for me to attend the Royal Dental School in London. I think braces weren't the norm at regular dentists! I hated the full mouth of metal as I had the permanent braces cemented onto my teeth and it was very unsightly. I went through a lot of pain and discomfort, but now I am so pleased I stuck it out. It was a bind having to go all that way for monthly dental appointments, but they sorted me out and — I did get the morning off school."

1977 was the school's sixth year at the Thorndike Theatre, and the forecast was looking a little dim. The alliance with the Thorndike would end in a year or two, but Hazel Vincent Wallace continued to champion Mother and The School. They would return to the Thorndike in 1980 for one more summer, before moving on.

> **Author's Note: For the years 1978 and 1979, in spite of a hefty press book, various brochures and much searching of the Newspaper Archives and the Internet, I can find no information on the productions or the affiliated colleges.**

However, back in New York City, she was still available for acting roles.

She was engaged by The Meadow Brook Theatre near Detroit, Michigan to play Old Mrs. Dudgeon in Shaw's *The Devil's Disciple* in October 1968. A local paper, *The Oakland Sail*, singled her out, "Joan White, as Richard Dudgeon's puritanical and unforgiving mother, literally commands the stage every moment she is on."

In 1979, she was Joan Hickson's standby in the National Theatre/Robert Whitehead production of Alan Ayckbourn's *Bedroom Farce*. Most of the original company had crossed the Atlantic for a Canadian/American tour of the play. It opened in Toronto in January 1979 for four weeks, and then to Washington for five weeks before opening at the Brooks Atkinson Theatre, New York, where it would run for 276 performances, closing Thanksgiving week in 1979. Mother left the production in June, in order to continue her Summer School. This was now in its tenth year. One of the joys of being standby, was that it gave her plenty of time to organize the coming summer from her home on Riverside Drive, all the while getting her Broadway Equity salary.

During the run of *Bedroom Farce,* she took the job of dialect coach for an upcoming Broadway musical, *The Utter Glory of Morrissey Hall.* Its premise: British students at a girls' boarding school playing endless pranks on the staff. It was as ill-fated as it sounds. After seven previews, it closed after one performance. Mother got paid though and, as always, every penny counted.

That autumn, she took a holiday with a friend and went to Ireland, spending time in Dublin to see the theatres there, especially the Abbey and the Gate. While there, she met with the Trinity College Drama Department and encouraged them to become an associate of The School. They did and, for the next five years, Mother spent part of her summers in Ireland. The nineteen eighties were to prove busier than ever for Mother, both personally and professionally.

In 1980, The School with its new affiliation with Trinity College Dublin, offered an intensive nine-week study of theatre techniques in England and Ireland. Five weeks at Trinity with daily classes in movement, speech, Irish dialects, acting and visits to Dublin theatres. Having cemented an agreement with Trinity to bring American students to Dublin, followed by four more weeks in England at the Thorndike Theatre, Mother set to work to enroll students from all over America and Canada. By the time The School was winding down nine years later, credit for courses had been granted by the following American universities: Adelphi, Columbia, University of Southern Illinois, University of Minnesota, University of Puget Sound, East Washington State College of Cheny, University of Washington, SUNY at Buffalo and SUNY at Stonybrook, CUNY at Baruch College, Sam Houston State University, Oakland University, Michigan University and Cornish College of the Arts.

And I probably missed a few.

The four weeks spent rehearsing at the Thorndike Theatre would end with a week of performances for a paying audience and theatre critics.

For this first Anglo-Irish program, the school presented *From Ireland With Love:* three Irish Plays – *Cathleen Ni Houlihan* by W.B.Yeats, *Riders to the Sea* by J.M. Synge, and *Bedtime Story* by Sean O'Casey.

> *The News and Mail* wrote, "their Irish dialect was faithful, fluent and sustained." and continued with "Long may they continue to visit Leatherhead! Their freshness and enthusiasm come like breaths of fresh air."

Alas, this was to be their last visit to the Thorndike.

> And *The Advertiser* said, "It was a rare chance to see drama which – through practical difficulties or nationalistic indifference – is not performed often in England."

Her School was doing its bit towards understanding the Irish Peace process.

It was in the early 1980s that I began receiving regular letters from Mother, and she visited our house in Housatonic several times. They were very fond letters, full of how she was, and not so much on what she was doing. Going through them now, I find the occasional nugget to use about her professional life. I suspect she was beginning to feel her mortality and, what with the upset with my sister's family, wanted to stay close to us, her American family. I had recently begun working in Public Relations and Marketing for the very new Shakespeare & Company at Edith Wharton's home, The Mount in Lenox, Massachusetts. I was enjoying it very much, even as Colgate and I were drifting apart.

1981 was a busy year for Mother in other ways. The School flourished again that summer both at Trinity and in England. That September, her good friend and colleague Bert Joseph died, and her affiliation with CUNY ended, but the academic credits offered continued.

> As an actress, there was more work: In his tribute to Mother in *Canadian Equity Magazine* (after she died), Vernon Chapman wrote: "In 1981, when I was Artistic Director of the Gryphon Theatre in Barrie, Ontario, I was delighted to bring her (Joan White) back to Canada to play Delia in Bedroom Farce, a role she had understudied and played several times during a pre-Broadway North American tour of that comedy."

Then in October she played Marjorie in *Just Between Ourselves*, another Ayckbourn comedy at The McCarter Theater in Princeton, New Jersey. In a review by Louis Cooke in *The Trentonian*,

> "Joan White portrays the mother-in-law for broad laughs and there are many of them. Ms White is a real pro; her portrayal is the classically malevolent mother who understands her son's needs as no wife can. She is hysterical in her robe and old boots."

That December, she was asked to understudy Eva LeGallienne on the tour of *To Grandmother's House We Go*. The previous December, the play, after 19 previews, had opened at the Biltmore Theatre on January 15, only to close on March 8, 1981 even though LeGallienne had received glowing reviews from the New York critics.

That summer, LeGallienne wanted to give the play another try-out. They remounted it at the Cape Playhouse in Dennis, Massachusetts, moving on to the Westport Country Playhouse, Connecticut during August and September (both part of the old Straw Hat Circuit). Later in the fall, the producers asked Mother to again understudy LeGallienne, because of their concern about the star's age. Dates were booked at the Morris A. Mechanic Theatre in Baltimore in December and then the play would travel on to Palm Beach, Florida for the New Year.

In Robert A. Schanke's biography of *Eva LeGallienne, Shattered Applause*, he writes that in Palm Beach, against LeGallienne's will, the producers secretly miked her, as audiences frequently complained that they could not hear her. LeGallienne was by now eighty-two and simply didn't have the stamina or projection, but she abhorred the thought of using a microphone.

I am guessing here, simply because most of the players are deceased, that Mother, who was ten years younger and a well-known speech teacher, was hired to standby.

It was early that November that I received a call from Spain saying that my aunt Audrey was in a coma in a hospital in Malaga and would I come at once. Audrey had named me as her next of kin. I went immediately, leaving Gate with the girls, and was gone for almost a month. Arriving in Malaga, I went to the British Consulate, where the Consul informed me that Audrey was in the *Loca* ward of Malaga *Ospital Civil*. He said he was so pleased that I had come and if I needed any help etc., etc. He clearly wanted to wash his hands of my aunt, this crazy English lady.

I booked into a hotel for an indeterminate stay, and went to the *Ospital Civil's Loca* ward. I found her jaundiced, in a coma and surrounded by six screaming *loca senoras*. A crazy ward it was! The doctor on duty told me that she was dying of acute alcoholism; all her systems were shutting down.

"How long I asked? Quanto tiempo?"

"Horas! Dias! Hours, Days"

"Does she need to be in here?" I asked.

"*Senora,*" the doctor said kindly, "*She does not know where she is and here a doctor is on duty all the time.*"

"*Would you please call me at my hotel if she comes around?*" I asked.

"*Of course!*" He replied.

I crossed to her bed where she lay, her breathing shallow, an intravenous drip in her arm. This was my only aunt. She had always been there for me when, as a teenager, she had stood in for my absent mother. She was gruff and tough but I knew she had loved me. With tears streaming down my face, I said,

"*Adios, mi tia. I love you.*"

Taking her personal belongings with me, I went to the hotel and, poring through her address book and the telephone directory, found the numbers of her Bank manager, friends in Nerja (the nearby town where she had lived), a funeral director and other necessary information. Suffice it to say that during the days before she died and for a few days after, I managed to pay her bills, arrange her funeral and bury her decently. I talked to my sister in London, who insisted on coming down, and Sue told Mother in America, much to her relief, not to come.

"*I can manage.*" I remember saying. "*I know you can.*" She replied.

Having inquired several times, "*Is she dead yet?*" Susannah arrived for the funeral.

The bank manager in England had by then told me the provisions of Audrey's will. He asked me to act for the bank, as her executor *in locus,* since I seemed to get by with my own brand of peculiar Spanish and he felt I was trustworthy.

Audrey's money was to be divided four ways: to my mother, her only sister; to myself; to her great-nephew Ronnie Horton to help pay for his education; and to her cousin in New Zealand, Roy Beach, with whom she had once stayed. She noted in the will that her niece, Susannah, had already been given five thousand pounds to buy a house and had squandered it on a trip to Australia. She left her bits and pieces for the bank, as executor, to divide up, and requested that her good fur coat go to Vera Horton.

Needless to say, on hearing about the will, Susannah was furious and called Audrey all manner of names. But I pointed out that Audrey *had* given her the money, and anyway she should make the most of this trip to Spain, since the estate was paying for it. This made Sue mad at me and, when it was time to leave Spain, she was suddenly unable to put me up while I was in London dealing with the bank. That was okay by me, I still had many friends from the Orphanage in London and could easily get a couch to sleep on.

And I did.

By the time I returned to America, Mother was away, standing-by for LeGallienne, and then, on her return, busy in New York preparing for her Irish/English Summer School. I went back to Shakespeare & Company and all seemed normal.

After her trip to Florida as LeGallienne's standby, Mother returned to New York City and began preparing for the coming summer in Dublin and London. Promotional materials were mailed out to the various colleges and applications were received and processed by Zelda Englander. Ten students from America were accepted this year and several more Irish students joined The School from Trinity College.

Mother and Bert Stimmel, along with Elizabeth Pursey and teachers from Trinity, concentrated on movement, speech, period, dialects, both Irish and Cockney, and rehearsed a program called *The Naughty 18th Century*. Written and directed by the Bert Stimmel, the students worked on the original material. After four weeks at Trinity College, they travelled to England to a new venue this year: The Bellairs Playhouse in Guildford, Surrey.

> "With a minimum of props and costumes they created the fun and games of an 18th century London Theatre, backstage and in front of the footlights. They showed the haphazard way stars were made in those days.
>
> "Joan White's group left the audience in no doubt of their many talents. They belted out their lively numbers in fine traditional style and appeared to move effortlessly. Their visits are a delight to anybody interested in the future of the theatre. I wish them every success."

So wrote June Wood of *The News and Mail* on August 26th, 1982.

When the Americans in the company returned to New York, they showed off their talents and presented this to the American public:

The New York Public Library at Lincoln Center.
Bruno Walter Auditorium
JOAN WHITE ENGLISH THEATRE SCHOOL LTD.
a Reader's Theatre Entertainment
written and directed by Joan White
SALUTE TO WALTER SCOTT
September 9, 1982 at 4 p.m. Admission is free.

Chapter Seventeen

LITERALLY RISING ABOVE IT
1982 – 1984

"But she said a great deal more than that.
Oh, everso much more than that!" – the White Queen

Later that autumn, Mother received a call from her agent. Eva LeGallienne would, once more, like Mother to understudy her in the forthcoming production of *Alice in Wonderland*. This new production was to be the fifty-year revival of the original.

Robert A. Schanke, again, in his biography "Shattered Applause": *"Le Gallienne, with Florida Friebus, had originally adapted the play from Lewis Carroll's texts of both* Alice in Wonderland *and* Through the Looking Glass *into an acting version, back in 1932. They adhered faithfully to Carroll's text, costuming the characters exactly as they were dressed in the popular John Tenniel drawings. Assuming the role of the White Chess Queen, Eva used her previous experience as Peter Pan and actually flew onto and off the stage. Whenever she got angry, the White Queen rose into the air."* Back in 1932, the critics had hailed the production as a triumph.

LeGallienne would take her original role of the White Queen and, against the wishes of the producers Sabra Jones and Anthony D. Marshall, also direct the production. She got her way. Mother was needed as both understudy and "alternate" for the production: when LeGallienne was directing from the stalls, Mother would be "on stage."

The cast was large, the set was very complicated and the production went way over budget. LeGallienne, at almost 83, had taken on both performing as the White Queen and directing. Jones and Marshall insisted on Kate Burton for Alice; as Richard Burton's daughter, she would be a draw. Once again, the costumes were designed to re-create the original Tenniel drawings and Sabra Jones was constantly making changes.

More and more problems piled up. For Mother, who had never flown before, it must have been a challenge.

Writing this biography, I have come across things I didn't know about which, when discovered, have proved to be like finding jewels in Aladdin's cave.

My friend Susan Davies told me that her brother-in-law, Chic Silber, had flown my Mother across the stage in *Alice in Wonderland* on Broadway. Susan gave me Chic's phone number. He and I had a wonderful conversation about his memories of working on that elaborate historical production.

Here's Chic from my notes of our chat in Spring 2019:

"I have fond memories of that production, even though it was thirty-seven years ago, Your mother was a dear woman to work with, and most agreeable to challenges.

"I recall the amazing tremendous twin vertical scrolls, one for each act, designed by John Lee Beatty, that unrolled horizontally upstage as a traveling cyclorama with the line drawings replicating the original Tenniel illustrations. And The Puppet People, who operated the larger than life-sized Walrus and the Carpenter from a platform high above the stage, along with, what seemed like, hundreds of little oyster puppets. Oh, so many special effects! It was all very expensive. It's a shame it ran for such a short time and lost all that money. Kate Burton was both stiff and charmless as Alice – the critics all said so, — and the producers were quick to blame Le Gallienne, who was magic as far as I was concerned.

"She was a tiny waif-like little person and yet she was like a firefly when she flew. When we started production, she came to me with this tiny hand-made harness she had used fifty years ago. I made a new one by hand with the same details exactly but of modern materials for safety. She loved to fly. But she needed your Mother as alternate on account of her age — and the fact that she was also directing.

"Your Mother was a real trouper and had great stamina. Flying was not really her thing, but she did it with grace. As I recall, she was a full-figured lady, so her harness had to be quite different from LeGallienne's. I had to hand-sew it to her dimensions, while maintaining her shape and softness, and make it as comfortable as possible for her. I created a stable twin lifting cable design to help her maintain balance. Each time she was lifted off the ground she always made a little groan.

Sometimes, during rehearsal, Alan Hall, our Production Stage Manager would say,

'Miss LeGallienne, we need to bring Joan down for a rest. She's been hanging up there for quite a while.'

She never complained. Like I said, she was a real trouper, your Mother."

Chic Silber has done special effects and special props for numerous Broadway productions. He has also been affiliated with Ringling Bros. and Barnum & Bailey Circus for many years, and he had been Production Coordinator for the John F. Kennedy Center in Washington, D.C. It was a special delight talking to him.

Mother is listed in the Playbill as both understudy and alternate. It also states that: *"At Tuesday evening and Wednesday matinee performances, the role of the White Queen will be played by Joan White."* Somehow, I vaguely knew she had been involved. So, why didn't I see my mother fly on a wire across the stage on Broadway?

> I have accumulated boxes of letters, reviews, articles and photographs of her at different stages of her career in the theatre. Sorting all the pertinent papers to do with the 1980s, I came across Martha Swope's photograph of her in costume as the White Queen in Eva LeGallienne's production of *Alice in Wonderland* at the Virginia Theatre. It was on Broadway from December 23, 1982 to January 9, 1983; a short run of 21 performances following 18 previews.

Looking at that photo, I wondered why I never went to New York to see her perform this flight of fancy and, even more, why I had not taken my girls with me – something they would surely have loved.

I thought back to that time and it all came rushing back to me. In September of 1981, while I was in Spain, my husband Colgate had chosen this time to have yet another affair.

I had returned to a distant, but unforthcoming, husband. I knew something was not right. Ever the peacemaker, I kept my mouth shut and carried on, with my job at Shakespeare & Company and as mother to our children. In September of 1982, one year later, Mother was visiting from New York. She never told us what she was doing, only that she was very busy and how lovely it was to come to the country for a day or two.

On the night of September 19, Gate and I had a major row. Mother and the girls were sleeping, so it was a whispered row, but no less unpleasant. He admitted he had been seeing someone. She was 'the one.' They all were!

My anger, bottled up over the years, spewed forth and I lost my temper. I threw a bag of frozen peas at him and I remember saying,

> *"This isn't the first time, is it? By my count, it's the third time. I don't want to hear about any others. We have two teenage daughters. What kind of example are you setting them? As far as I'm concerned, three strikes and you're out."*

He had never seen me blow my stack like this. He walked outside to his car and left.

I was in shock. I was shaking. I had no idea I had that in me. I don't remember much of the night. When the girls came down in the morning, I was silently fixing breakfast.

"What's wrong, Mum?" said Sherrod.

"Where's Daddy?" said Abby.

"He had to go out." I said, *"Go on off to school. I'll talk to you later."*

With much persuasion they left.

Mother came down shortly after they left. She rambled on about how wonderful the country air was and the peace and quiet. How lucky I was. But she had to catch the nine o'clock bus and get on with her life in the theatre.

I was silent. She did not seem to be aware of my distress. I drove her to the bus in Great Barrington. As she stepped up onto the bus, she leaned forward to peck me on the cheek,

"Don't work so hard, dear." And totally unaware, as usual, she was off.

I went home. I wept, screamed and cried for a while. Then I pulled myself together and called Fran Lippmann, my friend, who is also a psychotherapist.

She helped me a lot. Gate came back for his things and we told the girls that we were separating. My friends took me in and held me and let me talk. My daughters came home from school each day and did the same. They were upset in their different ways.

My colleagues at Shakespeare & Company rallied around. My good friend Joel, the Company stage manager, even moved in and helped out, moving logs, coercing the girls to do chores and homework, and rolling me the odd joint. Once again, I survived and moved on.

A week after Gate left, Mother called to thank us for

"Such a lovely weekend in the Country, Darlings."

I said abruptly,

"It's over, Mother. Gate has left. I have asked him to leave after he admitted to having yet another affair."

She said,

"Oh, you silly girl! Men do these things. You should not have thrown him out. He was so good-looking and such a good actor."

"Mother," I screamed into the phone, *"What the hell would you know about men. And as for being good looking, when I was ten, I overheard you casually say to someone that while Susannah was so pretty and talented, I would be good-looking when I was forty! Well, I want you to know that I will be forty in a few weeks and I'm a fucking knockout. I never want to speak to you again."* And I slammed down the phone.

And that is why I never took the girls to see their grandmother fly across the stage on a wire!

I should note here that bridges were mended in 1984 when my oldest, Abby, wanted her grandmother to attend her High School graduation before she left for Philadelphia College of Art.

After *Alice* closed, Mother put her charming little Riverside Drive co-op on the market and sold it within the year for a very tidy sum. The real estate market in Manhattan was booming and her apartment was very saleable indeed. I suspect she more than quadrupled what she had paid for it. In a letter to me in January 1985 she wrote,

> *I have sold 74 Riverside Drive. My Merrill Lynch broker has already built me a nice portfolio with the proceeds. It's a joy to feel solvent and not worry about work; of which I have plenty as I am preparing to direct Christopher Fry's* The Boy With a Cart *with a cast of RADA graduates, to be done on March 24th in Saint Luke's Chelsea (where you were baptized); and maybe in more churches.*"

So, after eight happy years on Riverside Drive, she had decided to return to London, where she felt the pace was slower. She had already found a flat at Tryon House, 17 Mallord Street in Chelsea, just off the Kings Road and minutes away from Paulton's Square where Sue and I had been babies. Her flat, number 16, was on the third floor "*Climbing stairs is good for my heart.*" Even so, buying a flat in Chelsea, one of London's more desirable neighborhoods back then, was expensive. She must have done well indeed selling her New York co-op.

In 1983, before decamping completely for England, once *Alice in Wonderland* had closed after its unexpectedly brief run, Mother still had the 1983 summer of her English Theatre School to organize. Applications from all over America came in and plans were set for another summer, first at Trinity College in Dublin and then again at Bellairs Playhouse in Guildford.

Mother had long been interested in the plays of Dion Boucicault; a nineteenth century Irish actor/playwright known for his melodramas.

With the Irish connection and an abundance of Boucicault plays to choose from, Mother decided upon a program for that season called *An Evening of Melodrama from the works of Dion Boucicault: The Romantic*, featuring selected scenes from *The Old Guard, Used Up, The Octoroon* and *Robert Emmett*, with an edited version of *Formosa or! The Road to Ruin*. The Irish and American students would study the plays and the dialects needed and the final performance would be held at The Bellairs Playhouse in Guildford, Surrey on August 6th.

Also, that year *Sister Clare,* one of Laurence Housman's *Little Plays of St. Francis,* was staged on the altar steps at St. Nicholas Church, Guildford. It followed the Sunday evensong service. As with all The School's performances, admission was free, however a collection was taken for the church's roof and organ repair appeal.

> *The Guildford Advertiser* noted, "For Miss White, drama in general, and her school in particular, forms an altruistic rather than profitable way of life. 'I consider acting very much a service — it's certainly no livelihood for me. The School is my principal interest, especially bringing students to England each summer.'"

When she finally moved back to London, she got back on stage twice in 1985.

Tennessee Williams' *Slapstick Tragedy* was presented for three performances in May. The cast included her good friend, Rosemary Dunham. Then, in September, after her Summer Theatre School was finished, the same cast and management staged scenes from *Macbeth,* for one performance only. After years of bringing American and Irish students to perform in England, she could now stretch her London theatre legs and enjoy acting with fellow British actors.

In April 1985, Constance Cummings CBE, Christopher Fry, Greer Garson, Julie Harris, George Rose, Donald Sinden CBE and Jessica Tandy were advisors and Lord (Bernard) Miles was President of The Joan White English Theatre School, now in its fifteenth year.

That summer, the sixth at Trinity College in Dublin, The School was undergoing some changes. They would no longer perform at Bellairs Playhouse and stay in Guildford, but would be housed in greater London after their stay in Dublin, and would present their traditional final production in a London venue.

In August,1985 they presented a one-act play, *A Marriage Proposal by Anton Chekov,* a favorite of Mother's, coupled with the summer's production of *These Men, These Men,* directed by Laura Livingston. This time the venue was Kensington Library Theatre.

On January 18, 1985 Mother wrote to me,

"Sue and Jon (Slater) are now in a ground floor flat at Tryon House, which I have bought for them, to get them out of unsavory lodgings in Fulham. My flat is on the third floor, which you and yours will inherit one day." (I didn't count on it!)

She continued, *"My New York students are doing Shakespeare at the Donnell Library on January 24th. Dear Lorna Heilbron's husband Nicky Clay is on the RADA committee for The Next Stage.*

(The first time I heard of this new venture – The Next Stage)

"I am now working toward our 8 weeks summer program helped by a splendid Irish student, Isolde O'Neill."

Isolde had been a student with The Joan White English Theatre School in the early 1980s, shortly after the merger with Dublin. Leaving home at twenty-one, she moved to London to "become an actress." She wrote to me recently:

"That is when I reconnected with your mother. She hired me as her secretary to help write her autobiography and help run the school. I worked with your mother before I went to drama college in England, (Manchester Polytechnic School of Theatre), around 1987/8. After drama college, I didn't work with Joan anymore. We remained friends though."

I had managed to find Isolde in Canada through my correspondence with Jason Mullen. He had spoken at Mother's Memorial Service about her work with The Next Stage. I wrote to Isolde and she wrote back, several times.

When I first contacted Isolde in May 2019, I asked her if she knew about Susannah and me. She e-mailed me back,

"It's funny...funny in not so nice a way, I guess...but I do know about you. I never met you, but because of my work with your Mom, I know about you because I worked with her on her autobiography. She wrote and I typed it up. (I do not know if you have a copy of this, but it has a lot of information you might need.)"

(Susannah found a copy among her papers, and it has been very helpful).

"Anyway, I remember when she handed me the pages about her life during the war, that is when I learnt she had two daughters. I eventually met Susannah, but I never met you! I remember my shock. My shock that she had put you both in an orphanage! My own mother and I didn't have much of a relationship — she pretty much ignored me. I have pieced together as to why my mother didn't bond with me and put it down to post-partum depression. I left home at twenty-one from Dublin and never returned.

"So, sitting in your Mom's flat, reading and then typing that she gave up her children was shocking to me – beyond belief. I thought about how I was with your Mom, who was being a Mom to me, and it did upset me and changed how I saw her.

"Your mother was so good to me – it was very hard to reconcile our relationship with the facts I was typing. But I was alone in London and your Mom was all the family I had and we had a great time. She spoke about you, Judy. Her shame over how she had failed you; what she had done; how she had been so self-absorbed and selfish. She accepted your need to be separate, she felt she deserved it. She told me she never should have been a mother at that time, that she didn't know herself, gave men all the power and sacrificed her children because of her career. I know this will sound odd, but I have thought about you – because I struggled with my own mother and how your mother was the best mother I had, and how she had failed as a mother to her own daughters. I am glad we are in touch now."

More than anything I have read relating to Mother, Isolde's letter has hit me in the gut. I had no idea that Mother felt any guilt about Sue and me at all, or that she was sensitive enough to know of my need to stand back from her. That she was even aware of what she had done to Sue and me, emotionally. She always seemed too busy and otherwise engaged. Emotionally she was remote to us but not to her friends. I guess it was her shame taking over when she brushed aside any questions about Father. As she got older, she *was* more in touch with me, but she never apologized or tried in any way to make up for everything. I was just supposed to "Buck Up!" "Get on with it!" or "Rise Above It." Hearing from

Isolde was seeing another, more human side of my mother. I wished she had been that way with me when I was twenty-one.

Isolde wrote some more of her thoughts and memories of those days in London with Mother:

"Your Mom liberated me. That sounds crazy but she had such a sense of fun and adventure and would always encourage me to explore and take risks. I remember one day when I was at her flat. We were chatting about life and she said, "When I die. I would like to die young." I blinked, looked at her and said, "But Joan, that can't happen!"

She turned to me and asked why. I replied, "Because you are already in your 80's. You've kind of missed the "young thing." She said nothing, took a breath and said, "OH" and burst out laughing. It had never occurred to her that she was already old.

"We did a show one time – in an old folks' home. We did excerpts from plays – just the two of us. But I most remember your mother choosing a piece from Alice Through the Looking Glass. I played Alice and she was the Queen. We had such a hoot doing it. She taught me a lot about comic timing and how to use it properly. Advice I have kept always and often used to my advantage in Canada.

"I have so many memories…we spent a lot of time together drinking tea or coffee and chatting about all kinds of things. Theatre was definitely her life, but when we talked, we talked about life, love, men, and London. She loved the City and loved where she lived. She had a rather naughty sense of humor. She also made great cheese on toast sandwiches. They were so good! But most of all she was very strict about her teaching of acting – in a good way. She wanted everyone to respect the art, the process and all the talent behind the stage. One day in Dublin, I had showed up late for rehearsal and she recast me!! It was a lesson well learned. I would never be late or ungrateful ever again. She honestly loved teaching young people but in a manner that was about the craft, the legacy. She saw life in the theatre as a vocation. She wanted to pass the torch and teach in a way that made her students less selfish and "me, me, me".

I asked Isolde if she could tell me anything about the people who had worked with Mother, like Bert Stimmel.

Isolde: *"I loved Bert. He was American and he worked with the Caracalla Dance Theatre in Beirut, Lebanon as their movement/choreographer. He was a very special man — like a tiny Buddha. He gave me a ring, which I wore for years. He was a wise soul; completely authentic.*

Judy: *"How about Elizabeth Pursey, Alan Sleath, anyone else of importance?"*

Isolde: *"Christopher Fry was important to your Mom. They were friends and had worked together. Personally, I thought he was a bit odd and "old school" but your Mom loved him."*

Judy: *"Did you work at all with The Next Stage Company?"*

Isolde: *"Some. After I left Drama School, I worked out a sort of barter system with your Mom. She'd help me with acting and auditioning, and I'd help her with more typing, mostly for The Next Stage. In 1993, I was offered a part in Christopher Fry's* One Thing More, *directed by your mother and Christopher Fry. That was the last thing I did with her".*

Isolde stayed on in London for a few years, while pursuing her own career and presenting her own one woman play *Lady with a Hammer* about Florence Nightingale. In November of 1992, Isolde presented *Lady with a Hammer* and Mother did her monologue, *Alive to Tell the Tale,* as a fundraiser for The Next Stage.

Lady with a Hammer won the Duke of Westminster Award. She performed it at the Florence Nightingale Museum. She eventually took it to Canada, when she settled in Toronto. She showed me a different side of Mother; one I am coming to terms with.

Chapter Eighteen

ENTER THE NEXT STAGE COMPANY
1985 – 1994

"To give RADA students the opportunity to perform for the general public."

It was early in 1985 that, along with her continuing work with her successful summer school, Mother started yet another venture, this time with Alan Sleath, a highly respected former BBC producer in the early days of television who, in his retirement, became Chairman of the Associates of the Royal Academy of Dramatic Art. Mother was an Associate of RADA and had known Alan for years.

The company was named The Next Stage and, over the next ten years, it gave young RADA graduates an opportunity to perform in front of the general public, gain some press coverage and hopefully attract an agent or producer. It earned the ringing endorsements of theatre professionals. Richard Attenborough, then President of the RADA Board, heartily encouraged her; Christopher Fry, who was to see many of his own plays produced by the Company, said,

> *It is wonderful work The Next Stage is doing. It has been a delight to be part of their success.*

and Paul Scofield, her friend and fellow actor, wrote;

> *The opportunity for showcase performance has been sadly lacking. The Next Stage Company fills a gap, which has been blank for some time.*

Equity Library Theatre, where I had worked and performed years before, was formed with the same ideals as The Next Stage: to provide actors with an opportunity to perform for agents and producers.

The following description of The Next Stage is by Jason Mullen, another of Mother's invaluable assistants. Jason had joined the company in 1989. He spoke these words at her memorial service in 1999, and since he knew The Next Stage so well first hand, I asked if I could use them:

> "*I first met Joan White over ten years ago through a mutual friend, Tony Hyland. Some costumes needed collecting and I was drafted in because I had transport. I didn't know then how much a part of my life both Joan and The Next Stage Company would become. Over the next few years, I was to serve on the committee of the Company, eventually becoming Business Manager. In that time, I observed at close hand Joan's dedication to young actors.*
>
> "*The Company was founded in 1985 upon her return to England. Originally set up with Alan Sleath, it was launched under the auspices of RADA and was to have been called "Off Stage Left." This however was deemed by some to be too political, so under a new name The Next Stage was launched.*
>
> "*The aims of the Company from the outset were to give young drama school graduates a chance to continue practicing their craft by providing an arena for them to work in, alongside established performers: over the years, this was achieved with great success. The first play produced was Christopher Fry's* The Boy with a Cart *in March of that year followed by that same author's* A Phoenix Too Frequent *in June. It was to be the start of a special relationship with the plays of Christopher Fry.*
>
> "*Over the next nine years the Company would present the London premieres of* One Thing More *at Chelsea's St Luke's Church and* A Sleep of Prisoners *at Holy Trinity Sloane Street plus a revival of* The Boy with a Cart *for the 1994 Chelsea Festival.*
>
> "*The main purpose of The Next Stage for Joan however, above any other, was the students and young people who performed in the many productions. When most people would have been happy to retire and take a back seat, she devoted boundless energy to them because she cared and had never forgotten her early days as an unknown actress. She was also concerned that in these days of television and increas-*

ingly amplified theatres, the skills of live performing were being lost. Students who were directed by Joan would get a taste of the discipline and skill that made her such a great actress and director.

"Behind the scenes she was just as active. With as little as one phone call, leading members of the profession were persuaded to come and work for the Company in freezing churches or cramped fringe venues for very little or sometimes no money at all. They performed alongside young people, many of whom were making their debuts in professional theatre...and it wasn't just actors who got their first engagements with The Next Stage. New directors were also given a chance: Tony Hyland was asked to direct Godspell; *Chris Bridgeman directed* The Provoked Wife *and later* Breezeblock Park *at the Chelsea Centre Theatre at World's End Place; and in keeping with the Company's ideals, Joan also called on established directors such as Vere Lorrimer, Ken Parrot and Leonard White to give young performers the value of their experience.*

"The technical side of the business wasn't forgotten either. Graduates from the stage management course at RADA were drafted in regularly to assist with lighting and sound, while design students from the Wimbledon School of Art were responsible for many of our sets.

"Once the play *was selected, Joan, with tremendous energy, set about the task of producing it. There was, of course, the committee of The Next Stage Company who met once a month. All of us who served on it played our parts, but I think they would agree that it was Joan who was very much in the driver's seat.*

"In selecting plays she had the chance to pick some of her own favorites, which saw playwrights such as James Bridie and Ian Hay being interpreted by a new generation of actors.

"In 1990, when The Next Stage decided to do a Sunday performance for the Charity Crusade at the Garrick Theatre, As You Like It *was chosen, Joan having played Phoebe in the 1936 film with Laurence Olivier. Only Joan could book a West End venue with such ease.*

"Of course, contemporary plays were produced and included Seasons Greetings *by Alan Ayckbourn and* Abigail's Party *by Mike Leigh, the latter being directed by Joan. But the Company was most associated with the plays of Christopher Fry. In 1990,*

a revival of A Phoenix Too Frequent *was produced with Joan taking the role of Doto which she had played in the West End production with Paul Scofield forty-four years earlier.*

Cast alongside her were two other Next Stage regulars Terry Diab and Nic d'Avirro. "Over the nine years of its existence, many young actors worked for The Next Stage before embarking on successful careers. Joan was always pleased to be told of their progress. Judy Damas, choreographer and composer for The Boy with a Cart *and a regular Next Stage performer went on to work at the National Theatre. Susannah Doyle, who played in* The Good Doctor, *found fame in* Drop the Dead Donkey *for Channel 4, and David Kershaw, also in* The Boy with a Cart, *had a regular role in* Bergerac. *Isolde O'Neill, a talented Irish actress and former Next Stage committee member, regularly performed her acclaimed one-woman show about Florence Nightingale,* The Lady with a Hammer.

"Every one of the students who worked with Joan will remember her for her kindness, patience and sense of humour. It was a unique time I for one will never forget. If I have one memory in particular of her it is the advice, borrowed from Sir Tyrone Guthrie that she would give, when in the course of our work things sometimes got a little stressful. 'Rise above it, Darling!' It has held us all in good stead."

Jason Mullen now lives in Scarborough, North Yorkshire and still works in and around the theatre! He wrote to me in a later correspondence:

"Your book is not just a theatre biography; Joan was so much more than that. I always feel very lucky that our paths crossed and we became friends. I consider her one of the people who influenced me enormously in my 20's and 30's."

It was in the summer of 1985, immediately following her graduation from Monument Mountain Regional High School, that my younger daughter Sherrod went to England to sign on for a year with Community Service Volunteers — Great Britain's answer to VISTA. Sherrod's job during her high school years had been working for women with intellectual and developmental disabilities at Riverbrook School in Stockbridge,

Massachusetts and, at that time, she was interested in pursuing a career in human services.

Arriving in the summertime, she went first to her grandmother's flat on Mallord Street. She spent time with her, going to rehearsals for The School's production of *These Men, These Men,* and meeting the students. She also met up with her Horton cousins Ronnie, Sarah and Gayle, going to nightclubs with them, before reporting to Community Service Volunteers for her assignments. After a short time working with a critically ill child, she requested a less-emotional posting and was soon in Yorkshire as aide to a quadriplegic man named Mick; learning to care for his needs: bill paying, meals and even some more personal things. She enjoyed Yorkshire and Mick. Her favorite story was driving in Mick's handicapped van to Manchester United games. On her days off, usually three every two weeks, she would take the train to London and Mother's flat, and discover London.

Sherrod's cousin Sarah wrote that, *"Visiting Granny once she had moved to Chelsea was always a pleasure. Visits never had to be too long as she was always busy, but she was always pleased to see us and would put together an unusual lunch of bits and pieces."*

Once while Sherrod was visiting, Mother fell in the bathroom. She told me it was pretty scary but somehow, she managed to get her grandmother to the emergency room. I think Mother was *finally* beginning to feel her age.

That Christmas, 1985, my other daughter, Abby and I both came to London. Abby and Sherrod planned to go to Paris for Christmas. My sister, Susannah and I were spending Christmas with our Mother.

I was newly single and was visiting England, partly on business for the Massachusetts Division of Tourism and, partly to be with my family. It was the first time my sister and I spent with Mother at Christmas since I was three, just a few days before she placed us in care of the Actors' Orphanage and we went to live at Silverlands.

Sue and I had often tried to get information from Mother about our father, but to no avail. She would invariably burst in to tears and in full Drama Queen mode say,

"I did love Paddy so…but I can't, I simply can't talk about it!"

It was forty-five years ago!

Sherrod and Abby returned from Paris. Abby returned to Philadelphia, where she was in Art School. Sherrod went back to Yorkshire and Mick for a few more months, and I returned to Salsbury/Ziglar, my new Marketing and Public Relations agency in Lenox, having left Shakespeare & Company after seven eventful years.

In 1986, The School's July training sessions at Trinity College took place and culminated on Friday July 25 in the Edmund Burke Hall at Trinity with a Victorian Pantomime of *Beauty and the Beast*. Nine students appeared in the production directed by clever Bert Stimmel.

Pantomime provided the cast with opportunities for broad comedy, singing and dancing with glorious costumes designed by the talented Tadgh O'Neill. As usual, admission was free, but any donations went towards the Irish Scholarship Fund. The production was a great hit.

Greer Garson, a longtime friend of Mother's from the 1930s when both were young, auditioning actresses, wrote the following for The Joan White English Theatre School promotional materials:

> *"The Joan White English Theatre School is a unique and valuable enterprise. Lovers of theatre must rejoice over all the efforts towards exchanges between the countries, keeping in mind also that artists, like athletes, are some of our finest ambassadors of good will and understanding everywhere they go."*

And this from Meghan Dean, a former student:

> *"Teacher, director, actress, producer, committed hard worker, Joan White is the sort of living proof drama students need while staking their initial professional lives."*

The Joan White English Theatre School was to run in tandem with The Next Stage for four years when in 1989, Mother decided she could no longer keep it going; not for want of trying. Those last years continued with four weeks in Dublin in July followed by five weeks in London, but with fewer and fewer students.

Social activities for the students varied from year to year and typically included: a Fourth of July party in Dublin provided by Guinness; tea in Hurd Hatfield's lovely country house; a students' birthday party to see the Player's Club Victorian Music Hall in London; sitting on the floor of Donald Sinden's dressing room, and hearing him describe how he prepared a character; lunch with Constance Cummings in her Chelsea apartment; sandwiches and wine with Judi Dench backstage; meeting Christopher Fry and the season's stars at Chichester; a tour of the National Theatre complex led by a well-known actor.

It sounds wonderful, doesn't it? And activities like these happened every year. She would also arrange events later for The Next Stage. Jason Mullin was amazed at how often Mother could call her old friends and get them to agree to all kinds of perks for her young actors.

Following the success of *Beauty and the Beast*, the 1987 London session presented a program called *From Will to Noel*, four centuries of British comedy at St. Augustine's Hall in Queen's Gate. It was devised and directed by Bert Stimmel and Joan White, and included scenes from *Beauty and the Beast; Henry V; Merry Wives of Windsor; Romeo and Juliet; The True Born Irishman; The Rivals; The Old Guard* and *The Importance of Being Earnest*. The second half was a selection of Noel Coward's songs called *Mr. Coward's Party*.

Her own acting roles never stopped., Mother was cast in Dennis Potter's *The Singing Detective*. A detective, Michael Gambon, is riddled with dark memories of his past while lying in a hospital bed covered in painful psoriatic sores. George Adams is consigned to the hospital bed next to Gambon, and upon arrival is readied roughly for bed by his wife, (Mother as old Mrs. Adams)sc. While undressing her elderly husband she says:

> *"Shut your mouth, George. Mind yer Ps and Qs. Now, George stop mucking me about."* She slaps him.
> *"Give 'im one. Only way to deal with 'im. I know, I've 'ad years and years of it. He's not strong enough to give you one back. Not now he ain't"*

George Adams, played by Charles Simon, would later be cast into another *Bed* with Mother at the National Theatre in 1988.

The BBC4 production won acting awards for Gambon, and received good notices on both sides of the Atlantic. *The Guardian* said, on its release in the UK in 1986,

> "It breaks every TV convention. Michael Gambon is a podgy middle-aged man raddled with skin disease, battling hallucina-

tions and dark memories of childhood abuse. And yet the tempo is upbeat – even merry – and the tale is hypnotic and addictive."

The New York Times in1988, "*The Singing Detective* is strong stuff, not just another serving of television escapism. Stuffed with a memorable collection of characters, The Singing Detective has recruited a cast to do them full justice."

The 1986 School season ended with a performance of *From Will to Noel* at the Bruno Walter Auditorium at Lincoln Center for three performances in September re-directed by one of Mother's former students Michael Parva, now an established New York director.

In 1987 she continued with Trinity College in July followed by four weeks of performances in Chelsea and Kensington and later a performance in New York City again in September. In February 1988 she was in New York City to give a performance of her one-woman show *Alive to Tell the Tale* at Lincoln Center, and to drum up funds and students for that year's School.

Back in London in 1988 she wrote to me, "*Sue and Jon have gone to Mojaca*" and later "*Daniel Horton has been born to Gayle*" Her second great-grandchild after grandson Jamie Walker's Jody!

Two months later I had a letter,

> "*Sue and Jon have sold Tryon House. Off to Spain! They are pack-ing cases ready to move, just waiting for completion of the sale. I hope it all works out for them and not be another Australian fiasco! Thank God for you and your sensible girls. As my cousin Adrian Beach used to say to me in my past miseries, 'Give all to your work — your work never lets you down.'*"

I could say, that if you gave all to your children, **they** will not let you down!

Later that July, with her summer School still going strong, she wrote to me that

> "*In Dublin, this year's company is nice and talented. It is our tenth year with Trinity so they gave us a 10ᵗʰ anniversary cake, which we enjoyed. I love the Irish generally, but the crowds on Grafton*

*and O'Connell Streets are as bad as Oxford Street, and teeming
with all nationalities. I shall tell our president, Constance Cummings, who takes a real interest in our work, that this Dublin
season has been a success and they would like us back next year!"*

But, alas, it was not to be. With only six students signed on for the
next year, Mother decided to wrap up The Joan White English Theatre
School after almost twenty years.

So, 1988 was the last full year of The Joan White English Theatre School.

In Dublin and London and, later, in New York City, the students
presented three one-acts, the choice of plays required that they be acted
in three different dialects:

A Millenium Surprise, subtitled *To Dublin with Love*, devised and
directed by Bert Stimmel; *Laundry and Bourbon* by James McLure is
set in Texas and directed by Vincent Scott, who had been a student in
the School and was now a director living in New York City; and *Family
Album*, a Victorian comedy with music from *Tonight at 8:30* by Noel
Coward, directed by Joan White.

The Next Stage Company had already presented Christopher Fry's
play *One Thing More or Caedmon Construed* at Chelsea Old Church in
November of the previous year. Now, Mother and Christopher were invited to present it, in the magnificent ruins of Whitby Abbey in Yorkshire where the story takes place, for one week in June of 1989 as part of
Whitby Heritage Week. Caedmon was an early seventh century farm-
hand who sheltered lost animals in Whitby Cathedral. As a poet, he is
known as 'the father of English song'.

Mother wrote to me later about the production:

*"We opened at Whitby Abbey on June 24ᵗʰ. It was spectacular and
all 300 people sat rapt. John Farquhar Smith did a marvelous
job with the lighting and the weather was perfect. Alas, owing
to quarrels between English Heritage, the Whitby Council and
Scarborough Borough Council, further performances were played
in a local school theatre! Not at all the same, and all because the
bureaucrats couldn't get it together. But the poetry of Kit's writing
and the acting was actually more moving in the school building."*

On the last page of her monologue, *Alive to Tell the Tale*, Mother wrote:

> *"On a sunny afternoon, just before our Next Stage Company played Christopher Fry's One Thing More in Whitby Abbey, I wandered into the peace and quiet of that magnificent ruin. All was serene, the only sound the low voices of a few visitors and, in the distance, children happily playing. And I suddenly realized that, despite all my travels and a life mainly spent 'on the road', here I was, back home again, a small, still active survivor of an England that had almost vanished. Not entirely, though. I was still here. I was still alive to tell the tale."*

Chapter Nineteen

AND ON SHE WENT
1988 – 1997

Future Plans and Family Matters

To give the reader an idea of how busy my mother was in the last years of her life, here is the schedule of plays she was directing and producing, in churches and community centers, all around London for The Next Stage. All the while teaching at her Joan White English Theatre School, **and** acting on stage and television.

THE NEXT STAGE COMPANY PRODUCTIONS

1985
The Boy with a Cart	*March*	Christopher Fry
A Phoenix Too Frequent	*June*	Christopher Fry

1986
A Village Wooing	*April*	GB Shaw
and The Proposal		Anton Chekov
Abigail's Party	*June*	Mike Leigh

1987
This Happy Breed	*January*	Noel Coward
Tobias and the Angel	*May*	James Bridie
A Sleep of Prisoners	*November*	Christopher Fry

1988
The Good Doctor	*May*	Neil Simon
The Provoked Wife	*October*	Sir John Vanbrugh
One Thing More	*November*	Christopher Fry

1989

The Children's Hour	*Spring*	Lillian Hellman
One Thing More	(Whitby Abbey)	Christopher Fry
Godspell	*October*	Tebelak & Schwartz

1990

As You Like It	*April*	Shakespeare
Alive to Tell the Tale	*October*	Joan White
and A Phoenix Too Frequent		Christopher Fry

1991

Season's Greetings	*January*	Alan Ayckbourn
Breezeblock Park	*April*	Willy Russell
Thor with Angels	*October*	Christopher Fry

1992

Shadow of a Gunman	*May*	Sean O'Casey
Lady with Hammer	*November*	Isolde O'Neill
and Alive to tell the Tale		Joan White

1993

One Thing More	*June*	Christopher Fry
The Old Guard & Used Up	*October*	Dion Boucicault

1994

Formosa or The Road to Ruin	*March*	Dion
Boucicault A Boy with a Car	*June*	Christopher Fry
Housemaster final show	*June*	Ian Hay

JOAN WHITE ENGLISH THEATRE SCHOOL

1985

"These Men These Men"	*January, July*	Trinity College
"These Men"	*August*	
and "A Marriage Proposal"	*August*	

1986

"Beauty and the Beast" Panto	*July*	Dublin
"From Will to Noel"	*August*	London

1986 (cont.)
"From Will to Noel"   *September*   NYC

1987
                             July – September   Trinity College, Dublin
                                                  Chelsea and Kensington,
                                                  London
                                                  New York City

1988
Alive to Tell the Tale   *February*   NYC
Millenium Surprise   *July*   (Stimmel)
Laundry and Bourbon   (McLure)
Family Album   (Noel Coward)
                                                  Dublin and London
Shakespeare and Friends   *August*   London

JOAN WHITE'S ACTING ENGAGEMENTS

1986
"The Singing Detective" (Mrs. Adams)   BBC-TV

1988
"Bed" (one of The Couple)   National Theatre
Heinz Baked Bean commercial

1989
"One Way Out" (Mary)   Screen One TV

1990
"Some Lie and Some Die" (Granny Peckham)   ITV
"Jeeves and Wooster" (old woman)   for Granada TV

1992
"Kinsey" (Mrs Craig)   BBC-TV

1993
"The Wimbledon Poisoner" (Vera Loomis)   BBC-TV

Late in 1988, she took on two very different acting jobs. (A scrawled addendum to her journal),

> *"I nearly drowned myself rowing a dinghy across a lake in glorious Devon, bringing Heinz Baked Beans to David Bellamy. That paid very well. Then, in my eightieth year, I was climbing nightmare furniture in Jim Cartwright's lovely play,* Bed *at The National Theatre."*

Bed opened March 8ᵗʰ 1989, after some energetic rehearsals for the eight elderly cast members. Mother, partnered with Donald Bissett, received some lovely reviews:

> Paul Taylor in *The Guardian* wrote: "This pair, captured in all their dosily symbiosis by Joan White and Donald Bissett, by contrast have slept happily side by side for so long that they have almost merged affectionately into the one person. Here, Cartwright touches unexpected areas of tenderness."

The Independent added:

> "Joan White and Donald Bissett, as the couple wandering slightly out of their minds, create memorable snapshots of old age."

Michael Coveney in *The Financial Times* said:

> "In 90 rather wonderful minutes, Jim Cartwright conjured a world of dreams." And, "this is an evening of elegant disturbing loveliness, with never a chance of 40 winks."

In a later letter, Mother wrote:

> *"Don Bissett and I were on "Kaleidoscope" doing one of our little scenes. I wish you could see* Bed. *He (Cartwright) is a remarkable writer and one of my scenes is quite lovely. I could do without the physical gyrations…going down trapdoors, playing a love scene on a window ledge etc. etc., is not exactly eighty-year-old exercise. And here I am back with Charles Simon, who played my husband in* The Singing Detective."

She added:

"Keep well and busy, it is the best cure for all ills and better than any shrink!"

I guess that was her credo about everything — that and "Rise Above It."

On the family front: in 1989 Mother wrote saying she had wept reading my poetry! Thinking about my poetry back then, I wondered what had made her weep. Was it the one about Philip Larkin? Or perhaps *Sorrel: Metaphor for a Marriage* about my divorce? Or was it *Weather?* Questioning her absence in my life? She went on to say she was happy to know I now had a so nice-sounding man. (My future husband John Staber)

"He sounds very interesting. You are wise not to rush things. All my life I have rushed into relationships and so has Susannah."

She continued to be engaged with her grandchildren. From a later letter,

"I am absolutely overjoyed with the nicest letter from Ronnie: 'Just to say how glad I am to have you as a Grandma and a friend. Your consistency and energy have been a real enlightenment to me these past few months and I just wanted to say that I love, respect and admire you. Hopefully I can gain some respect from you in time. This is not written hastily but to show you how much you mean to me.'"

Ronnie, Susannah's son, had been through some rough sailing in his teens. Mother was very moved by this letter. In May that year she wrote again,

"After the summer, I shall possibly go to Spain where Sue is happy in her surroundings, but she's having an awful time with Jon. Another separation? But perhaps you know."

I did know. I had returned from my year in Boston as Cultural Tourism Director for the Commonwealth, — way too much bureaucracy for me — and resumed my life promoting the arts in the Berkshires of Western Massachusetts. I had moved into a sweet little house in Stockbridge, adopted a puppy and was happy to be home.

One spring evening, sitting and reading in front of the woodstove, my phone rang.

It was Susannah calling from Spain. (It must have been three in the morning there.) She sounded panicked.

"Judy," she sobbed, *"it's me, your sister, and I don't know what to do."*

"Why, what's wrong?" I asked, *"You sound awful. What is going on?"*

I could hear sounds of crashing and banging in the background.

"It's Jon. He's gone mad. I think he's drunk or on something. I've barricaded myself in the bedroom. I can hear him smashing everything."

"Can't you call a neighbor?"

"I'm scared Judy. Very scared. And I'm afraid he'll disconnect the phone."

"Can you give me the number of the local police and I'll try and reach them."

"I don't know the number for Bedar police or even Andalusia. And I'm afraid there's no time. He's beating on the door." She sounded desperate.

"Sue. Listen to me. Is there a window you can climb out of and get to a neighbor?"

"I might be able to get out of this window. There's about a twenty-foot drop but I could try that and get to my neighbors across the way."

"Try that while I try information. Be careful. Remember to roll with the fall. And call me when you get to the neighbors."

The phone suddenly went dead. I waited — helpless. I tried *Informacion Espanol* and was having a hell of a time getting anywhere. I hung up and, I have to say, I prayed.

What felt like hours later the phone rang. She was safe at the neighbors. They had called the police and Jon had been arrested. Thank God she was safe!

The next day, she went into her house, the home she had bought with the proceeds of selling the London flat, and found that Jon had smashed her china and pictures, and generally torn the house apart. The police had taken him away and told him he was not to go near Bedar. He didn't, at least I never heard he did.

Poor Sue! She really did pick the wrong men.

I called Mother and gave her a watered-down version of that night's happening. She was very distressed and glad that Sue was safe and Jon was gone. She said to me,

"I never liked Jon, he was much too slick and there was something a little off about him. She's well rid of him. I wish she'd stay single now."

Despite family dramas, through it all, her focus was always on her work.

Between 1989 and 1994, along with her work for The Next Stage Company and writing down her memories (and constantly adding to her monologue *Alive to Tell the Tale*), Mother managed to appear in no less than five television programs.

In 1989, she had the small role of Mary, an elderly seventy-year-old in *One Way Out*, for Screen One TV, starring Denis Lawson. In 1990, she was featured as the cantankerous, boiled-sweet-sucking Granny Peckham in one of TVs popular Ruth Rendell mysteries, *Some Lie and Some Die*. It starred George Baker as Inspector Wexford and Peter Capaldi as a rock star returning to his roots. That same year, as an old woman, she shouted a few words from a window at Hugh Laurie in Granada TV's first season of *Jeeves and Wooster*. (I discovered this one when my friend Susan gave me the DVD set. I was watching the first episode and exclaimed, "That's my mother!")

That December she decided to visit Denville Hall for a few days' rest, and wrote

> *"To see if I like it for my retirement home. Susannah and my pet driver, Bob Desmond (whose father was stage manager on Little Ladyship) brought me down yesterday and I think Sue was impressed with the whole place. It is so comfortably furnished and there is such warmth from the staff and one's contemporaries.*
>
> *Bernard Miles (now in a wheelchair) has just joined. Bernard, or Sir Bernard as he now is, was the first 'M' in those very popular James Bond films. I sat with Diana Churchill and her husband Mervyn Johns (Glynis's Pa) and we had great gossips and giggles. I have just had breakfast in bed in my little room (temporary). It is so snug here. I am so glad you approve of my plan! My Chelsea flat has had four people to view it in four months — the market is very bad as yet, but my accountant says I could afford to live at Denville without selling number 16.*
>
> *"Susannah, who has been working at Bella Vista in Spain near Bedar, for very little money, has decided to let her house now*

*that her divorce from Jon Slater has come through and has come to
stay with me. She has been looking after me and keeping the place
very clean. She is marvelous at anything to do with "Home" —
cooking, cleaning and mad about laundry. She IRONS everything,
unlike you and me who excuse ironing whenever possible. I don't
notice dust unless I can write my name in it! And I certainly do not
iron sheets or panties. She is much too generous with presents and
then works like a dog to pay for her extravagances. She tells me she
doesn't want anyone to know she is in town, but then she will no
doubt call a hundred people and I will get no rest. However, that
is a small grouch.*

*"She works very hard and is very concerned for me. (A condi-
tion I am not used to, having been by myself for so many years.)
But I am not good at being ordered about!"*

Meanwhile, Mother was winding up her School; going to her cousin
Macklin's for Christmas; and planning her trip to the States for my
daughter Abby's wedding the following September — coupled, of course,
with a showing or two of *Alive to Tell the Tale* in New York City. Mother
always made a point of securing a talk or speaking engagement when she
traveled abroad, so she could count the cost as a business expense.

She made no plans to come for John's and my wedding in July. Ah well.

That trip to the USA, for Abby's wedding to Dean Pulver in September 1991, came not long after her English grandson Ron Horton's
wedding to his Petra in London; which she also attended.

On December 14, 1991, her oldest and dearest friend Robert Eddison died. He had taken ill in November with bronchial pneumonia.
Mother and he had been fast friends ever since they were apprentices in
Tyrone Guthrie's Cambridge Festival Company. Robert was her sounding board. Whenever she was in need of someone to talk things over
with – be it her daughters, her plans for her students or anything else, no
matter how trivial, she would telephone him or simply walk down the
Kings Road to his narrow little house on Burnsall Street for a chat.

**I was very fond of Robert. I had seen him play Oberon in *A Mid-
summer Night's Dream* in Regent's Park when I was an impres-
sionable ten-year-old and became hooked on Shakespeare that**

day. I later knew him and came to love him, when I was a young mother in New York City and he was performing on Broadway in New York. He often joined my little ones and me in Riverside Park, spending quality time with us, for which Mother never had time. Later on, he encouraged me when I began writing poetry. (In spite of his distinguished career, he is probably best remembered as the Grail Knight in *Indiana Jones and The Last Crusade.*)

I wrote to Mother when she told me how ill he was and enclosed a note to tell him to, *"Hurry up and get better. Hospital is no place to be"* Mother wrote, in her uncompleted memoir,

> *"I gave him my Judy's note. This he treasured and made quite sure it was safe beside him. My closest and dearest friend for sixty years was not 'Rising Above It' as Guthrie would say. That night he died. He was eighty-three."*

Throughout her letters over the next few years, she mentions how much she misses him.

In 1992 she had a nice little cameo, Mrs. Craig, in *Conflict of Interest*, an episode of the *Kinsey* BBC-TV series. She wrote she had

> *"a goodish scene with the excellent lead actor Leigh Lawson. I hope I won't end up on the cutting room floor and that the USA will see it eventually. I am lucky to get it, as work is nil here right now."*

Susannah had returned to her house in Bedar. Her daughter Sarah called to tell Mother that she and husband Stuart and baby Sonny had returned from a good week with Susannah and relations seemed mended. Sarah reported that Sue was very busy and had lodgers. Sarah also brought back a cross letter from Sue because Mother had said,

> *"No, I can't let you have another five hundred pounds."*

But then Susannah's birthday was coming up on July 12th, so Sue would get some money then, no doubt. Mother was generous to a fault, as she got older; writing checks for wedding and birthday presents.

For her final TV appearance, she was Vera Loomis in two episodes of another BBC-TV series *The Wimbledon Poisoner*. It aired in December

1994 as she was turning eighty-five. She told me that she loved doing the "tellies" as they paid so well, and the producers always sent a car for her to and from the studio, gave her a good lunch, and she had only a few lines to learn.

"Those dear drivers always help me up the stairs and see me to my door. It's nice to have the luxury of old-age sometimes."

With time-out for her television appearances, Mother was still very involved with The Next Stage, even as she was feeling her age. She had already looked into retirement homes, pretty much settling on Denville Hall, the Actors Retirement Home in Northwood, just north of London, so she could be among her fellow thespians. She wrote to me about her health,

"I am bent on getting my ticker right, and lowering my blood pressure."

She had recently acquired a *Help I've Fallen and I Can't Get Up* necklace for emergencies. She kept it hanging on the wall in her bedroom! How she thought she'd reach it when she needed it, I don't know? Also, lately, she had started having her groceries delivered.

But her work with The Next Stage must go on!

Sunday May 13 1990, The Next Stage Company had presented Shakespeare's *As You Like It* directed by Valeria Boulton at The Garrick Theatre no less! One of the West End's finest. This performance was in aid of the Lighthouse of London and Crusaid charities to help the victims of AIDS. Jason Mullen said only Mother could obtain the use of theatres, large and small, for their productions.

"A good production but I missed your delightful Phoebe at the Berkshire Playhouse," she wrote that month. I had never heard her praise my acting before. It was nice to hear even after so many years.

In October, The Next Stage presented a double bill at the Chelsea Centre Theatre for five performances. Mother did her monologue *Joan White: Alive to Tell the Tale* and then, with Terry Diab and Nic D'Avirro, she revived her role of Doto in Fry's *A Phoenix Too Frequent*, telling me how lovely it was to be working on Doto again.

Showing her affection for the plays of Alan Ayckbourn, she selected *Seasons Greetings* for The Next Stage to start the 1991 New Year, opening January 3rd for eight performances at the Chelsea Centre Theatre. A black, often farcical, comedy about four days in the life of a dysfunctional family starting on Christmas Eve, it is set in an average English suburban house. The Royal Borough of Kensington and the Chelsea Arts Council now supported the Company.

The next production was Willy Russell's *Breezeblock Park* directed by Chris Bridgeman from April 15th through 27th, again at the Chelsea Centre Theatre in collaboration with OXFAM.

The end of that year was another Christopher Fry play, this time *Thor with Angels* about the return of Christianity to England. Directed by Brian Spink, Fry had written this originally on a commission from the Canterbury Festival. Each year a poet was asked to write a play with an ecclesiastical theme. T.S. Eliot's *Murder in the Cathedral* had been commissioned a few years before.

Mother's friendship with Fry had begun in 1946 with *A Phoenix Too Frequent* and loving his work, she was now able to revive his lovely poetic plays, now gone out of fashion. The company was to produce ten productions of Fry's plays with their spiritual, religious and humanistic topics over the years.

The twelve actors did a mini-tour of London churches with *Thor with Angels*: St. Paul's Church, Hammersmith; St, John's Church, Ladbroke Grove; and Holy Trinity in Sloane Square. Mother received the following letter from Desmond Harney, Deputy Mayor of the Royal Borough of Kensington and Chelsea:

> *Thank you for inviting me to Thor With Angels at St. John's.*
> *Wonderful language. Marvelously expressed. I admire the purpose behind the work of The Next Stage and praise the dedication of the players, not least the seasoned ones helping the new wood.*
> *Well done,   Desmond Harney.*

The Next Stage Company received several such encouraging letters from local dignitaries. They went from strength to strength and continued to cast plays with known actors along with those fresh out of RADA.

The 21st production of the Company was *The Shadow of a Gunman* by Sean O'Casey and opened on Tuesday May 26, 1992 at the Rose Theatre Club on the Fulham Road for a run of three weeks. The Press was good:

"Members of The Next Stage Company contribute sensitively to Sylvia Denning's production. Derek Mann was outstanding." said Wendy Trewin in *The Lady*.

In Mother's newsletter for the Autumn of 1992, she congratulates those from the production who have gone on to further success, something she did every year, as well as listing her actors' subsequent successes in each newsletter.

In July, she had gone to Ireland to Ballentogher near Sligo to visit old friends from Seattle, Bob and Sally Heyman. The village, close to Sligo, is near the fabled *Lake Isle of Innisfree*, made famous by Yeats. She had a wonderful restful time there and sent me a postcard saying, "*Your father was reputedly born in Sligo, or so I was led to believe!*"

A few years ago, in writing a book about Father, necessarily partly ficticious, I had learned that it was his grandfather Tom Moore, a sailor from Sligo, who had emigrated to England during the potato famine. My father and his father were born in Lambeth, South London; but Mother never knew that.

Then she was back in England at Christopher Fry's house, *The Toft* in Sussex, where she was a frequent, pampered guest, staying there even when Christopher was away on a lecture tour.

Flying back to the USA in November of 1992, she attended her other American granddaughter Sherrod's wedding to her Ed. There she danced with her two-year-old great-grandson Daniel Patrick Bailey.

Mother wrote to me later,

"*I am so glad it's Patrick — you see I did love A.P. very deeply and he did give me two lovely daughters — in their so very different ways.*"

On December 4th, a Sagittarian party/fundraiser was held at the Cadogan Arms on the Kings Road. An appreciative audience, including many Sagittarians, attended.

Sagittarian Christopher Fry cut the cake and Sagittarian Hazel Vincent Wallace drew the raffle prizes. The entertainment was two one-woman shows that evening! Former Irish student Isolde O'Neill presented her portrait of Florence Nightingale in *The Lady With a Hammer*, and my Sagittarian mother did a condensed version of *Alive to Tell the Tale*. The party was a great success. She then went to Spain to spend Christmas with Sue and give a performance of her monologue for Sue's friends and neighbors.

Thus ended the year 1992.

In the spring of 1993 she was off again, back to Bedar, where she had promised Susannah, she would do *Alive to Tell the Tale* again and Carol Dance, another Bedar resident and expat, would give a performance of her *Jhelum Journey*. Thanks to Sue's organization and the after-the-show Tapas Party, they made money for local charities.

Mother sent me her schedule for the year — not as hectic as in the past — wanting to come to the States and "*dandle my smallest great-grandson.*" Kyle Stuart Bailey had been born on Valentine's Day.

> *"In May, we start rehearsing for the Chelsea Festival production of Fry's One Thing More with performances in two churches.*

One Thing More this time featured Constance Cummings as Abbess Hilda and Hugh Manning as the Venerable Bede. Isolde O'Neill played the novice nun. This was followed by the Tower scene from *A Man For All Seasons* with John Casson as Sir Thomas More and Judy Campbell as Lady Alice. They performed at Chelsea Old Church and at Holy Trinity, Sloane Street.

Around this time an article appeared in Tabard's column of *The Stage*: The headline: **Don't write White off yet, there's a lot of life left!**

> *Those of us inclined to marvel at veteran actress Joan White's energy don't know the half of it. Not only has the founder of the Next Stage Company defied the years but also, if one newspaper is to be believed, she has even defied the Grim Reaper himself.*
>
> *According to the publication, which I will not name (but whose offices are close to the City Road), Joan is, in fact, dead. Unfortunately, as is so often the case when one becomes a corpse, the person directly affected is the last to know. So ignorant was the actress of her supposed departure from this world that, in complete defiance of natural law, she has been busy producing another play. (One Thing More).*

The Next Stage Company publicity and promotions spokes-woman Liz Marsh tells me that Joan remains, like Mark Twain, unconvinced by the report of her demise. This, in spite of the article's inclusion in a broadsheet paper renowned both for its fondness for reporting the truth and ignoring the worst excesses of the tabloids.

To add further insult, the piece, which not only refers to her as Joan White (now dead) is based on an interview with Beryl Bainbridge the author (still alive) recalling the performer's problems in learning her lines many years ago.

I hope for the sake of all concerned that there is truth in that allegation, otherwise the lawyers can look forward to a field day.

Warns Marsh, 'She's very much alive and well and she might look like a sweet little old lady but don't be deceived.' Mother was most amused.

She continued with her schedule:

June 20-27 recovering while housesitting for Christopher Fry. July FREE. Could come and see you!

She did and stayed for several weeks. While with us, my pilot husband John took her for a flight in his early Lake Amphibian. She loved it and exclaimed,

"Everyone should have one of these!" She was 84.

She visited her two American great-grandsons, Kyle, just a baby and his brother Daniel aged three. She wrote that she had had "a splendid time" with us Americans and returned to London. There she saw Sarah, Ronnie and Gayle's families, who had all been out to visit Sue in Spain.

Another entry: *"A week ago, I tried to go out with dear Bert Stimmel, but my legs would not go beyond the end of the road, so have had to obey the Quack and go slow…not my style at all, but everyone is very kind and do the odd bit of shopping for me. I am wearing those medical support hose today and the legs have not ached at all and I went for quite a good walk…with a stick of course."*

The stick brought to mind the following memories of Mother from Kate Peake, who was her stage manager in 1993 and 1994. I've edited them slightly:

"I think I was only 19 or 20 when I first met Joan and she invited me to her flat in Chelsea. (April 1993). She gave me a big hug on greeting me and said, 'Darling do come in, there's a pot of tea and A Man For All Seasons is on the telly, so let's watch that before we discuss anything.'

"So, we sat watching the TV in silence for about two hours before we even spoke again. I realized at that moment what a character she was.

"We were rehearsing a Christopher Fry play (One Thing More) above a pub in Chelsea, I was deputy Stage Manager. The director she had hired wasn't working out, so Joan took over about halfway through. She was directing one scene and we started from the top. Joan suddenly shouted at one of the actresses,

'What are you doing standing there? I didn't direct you to stand on the foreskin!'

Everyone just froze and then started laughing. Joan didn't realize what she had said. I said — 'I think you meant to say the forestage, Joan.'

"During this same play, I spent one Saturday morning with her, going around Chelsea dropping off leaflets about the show. We got to the library and she said, 'I have already been here but we'll just see if they want some more.' There was no sign of any leaflets so we offered some more to the librarian on duty. The librarian explained that because the production was out of the borough the library didn't want them. Realizing that the previous bunch of leaflets had been thrown away, Joan became quite angry. The conversation became quite heated and Joan started banging her shillelagh on the counter and shouting,

'I don't know what you're talking about, I am the borough!'

At which point the librarian called security and I felt it was best that we both left. "I remember how generous she was and how much she valued all the folk that worked behind the scenes. She paid me £25 a week and would often take me out for dinner at a little restaurant, Le Gourmet, down the Kings Road because I think she knew I wasn't eating well. She was the theatrical mother to so many young people.

"I remember her shillelagh, her laugh, her smile and her energy. I also seem to remember she was very partial to a pint of Guinness at lunchtime.

"She called me once and asked me to do some typing for her. When I got to her flat, she answered the door in just her underwear, complaining it was just too hot. She then asked me if I would like a drink — thinking she meant tea, I said yes. She poured me the biggest and strongest vodka and tonic I have ever had (to this day)! "I did three shows for her One Thing More (1993), Formosa (1994) and The Boy with A Cart (1994), which was by far the best. Constance Cummings played Mother Abbess in One Thing More. There was also the Tower Scene from a Man for all Seasons, performed after One Thing More, by members of the cast. I can't remember why; I think Joan just liked it. She directed that bit herself. One Thing More was directed by Ken Parrot. We performed at Old Church Chelsea then did one performance a week later at St Mary's Church just up the road.

"I met Joan for dinner in the West End not long after the run of A Boy With A Cart. We went to a little Italian place where they knew Joan and kept giving us free drinks. At the end of the evening, I walked Joan to her bus stop and saw her on to the bus. I remember waving 'Goodbye'. I never saw or heard from her again."

I never did see that shillelagh, which is a short, Irish blackthorn walking stick with a knob of wood on the top. She probably purchased it in Ireland to use as a cane. (She could, she was only five foot one).

Kate did not work on the final production of 1993: two Boucicault one acts, *The Old Guard* and *Used Up*, but was back for 1994.

Vere Lorrimer had directed the Boucicaults. He was one of the many established professionals who gave their time to The Next Stage. A British television producer and director, Lorrimer's work included many BBC dramas: *Compact, Dixon of Dock Green, Doomwatch* and *Blake's.*

The one-acts were presented at Baron's Court Theatre at Baron's Ale House on Comeragh Road for three weeks and one performance at The Player's Theatre — off The Strand.

Helen Fry, writing in *The Gazette*, kindly said, 'the evening offered gentle laughs.' Mother wrote, "*There is no business, even though the production is very good.*" I suspect that audiences were not as tuned into Mr. Boucicault as she was.

She said she would spend Christmas with her cousins Mack and Joan in Ottershaw.

The first production of 1994, *Formosa, the most beautiful or The Railroad to Ruin*, yet another Dion Boucicault, opened at the Players Theatre in Villiers Street for three performances in March.

> "*Wildly successful and controversial when it was first produced at the Drury Lane Theatre in 1869 with Henry Irving as the Villain, this wonderful Victorian melodrama has not been performed for many years. Joan White unearthed a dingy script in a second-hand bookstore in New York City. We think is it quite a find, and are sure it will be a great success.*" So stated the program flyer for the production.

The play was adapted, for the Next Stage Company's production, from said 'dingy script' by Richard Fawkes. In his program notes he says:

> *The original production at The Drury Lane Theatre was met by a storm of protest. It was a typically well-constructed, effective Boucicault sensation drama, culminating in the Oxford and Cambridge Boat Race, for which the Times predicted a long run.*

In the 1994 reincarnation, the play didn't fare so well, in spite of a cast of several well-seasoned players mingled with recent RADA graduates.

Mother may have appreciated Boucicault, but the audiences did not.

> Her journal, Good Friday, 1994, "*This elderly lady is now resting at her cousins in Ottershaw until Tuesday after overdoing it (of course!) with our production of Formosa for three good performances at The Players Theatre. It was all well worth it, but I do think merely acting is much easier than producing which involves*

TACT, INTELLIGENCE, ARITHMATIC, ENERGY and CHARM — and pretending you know who you are talking to when mingling with the people who have paid to see your show."

The Company participated in the Chelsea Festival again that June. Christopher Fry's *A Boy With a Cart*, the play that launched The Next Stage Company nine years before, was performed at the Kings Road Methodist Church.

She sent congratulations to my artist daughter Abby for her print show 'Press On." And said *"I am still pressing on."*

Chapter Twenty

HER LAST ACT
1997 – 1999

"The wheel is come full circle." Back where she began.

Mother had been torn about moving right away to Denville Hall on Duck's Hill Road in Northwood, for retired members of the Theatrical profession. She decided on Denville Hall at this time because, as she said,

> *"Denville is for the gregarious (me!) And everything is done for one and the cooking is very good. Anywhere else, I would still have to cook and shop." Her fellow residents at Denville were theatre folk, many of whom she knew:*

Ronnie Waters, who'd been in *Jonah and the Whale* and became a well-known agent; Eileen Carey (Mrs. Sean O'Casey); and Robert Harris, who had played Sir Thomas More in my United States tour of *A Man For All Seasons*. It was the perfect place for her to end her days.

She would sell her flat at Tryon House, put her affairs in order and, with her grandson Ronnie's help, move into Denville Hall later that year.

But there was one more Next Stage production to do: *Housemaster,* the 1937 Ian Hay comedy in which Mother played Button, one of her many popular teenage roles. An abbreviated version of *Housemaster* was produced in the summer of 1994, at a hall in Pimlico, shortly after *The Boy With a Cart* closed. Charles Stapely played the Housemaster. Mother did not reprise her role as twelve-year old Button!

On November 30, 1995 a brief notice in *The Stage* read

NEXT STAGE — CLOSURE

Underfunding has been blamed as the Next Stage Theatre Company announced it is to close at the end of the year. Founded under the auspices of RADA ten years ago, the company aimed to give opportunities to young acting graduates, staging twenty-five productions.

Announcing the company's closure, Next Stage's Jason Mullen said, "In these increasingly competitive times, the directors feel they can no longer obtain the necessary funding to produce productions of the desired quality.

Jason emailed me,

"I remember the article in The Stage quoting me. I think Joan and I met in late 1995 and decided that with her moving to Denville Hall, we would wind the Company up. Housemaster had been the last production, I briefly considered doing other stuff or at least using the name, but never did. My new career in theatre management took over. We saw the accountant in Covent Garden and closed it down. End of an era."

Mother had begun to sort out her flat at Tryon House. She labeled her pictures and books with the names of family members she wished to have them. I am happy to now own almost all of Christopher Fry's plays as well as several other plays and books about the theatre, including Tony Guthrie's writings. I also have some of her posters and many family photographs to remind myself of where I come from. I have kept most of her letters —I admit to being a pack rat, but that is the writer and archivist in me.

Without them I wouldn't have been able to tackle her amazing career. Sadly, there hadn't been many letters to me until the 1980s.

Her work was now finished, effectively, and she could relax with her peers; although she never really stopped! My sister was planning a party and there would be other events.

In December 1994, my husband John and I crossed the Atlantic (he for the first time) to visit Mother and take her to celebrate her eighty-fifth birthday at my sister's home in Bedar, Andalucia, Spain. We were headed for Denville Hall, her new residence.

A former actor turned car-for-hire driver acquaintance of Mother's met us at London's Heathrow Airport in the early hours of a gray Tuesday morning. He drove us, at rather frightening speeds, through the house-packed suburbs of London, on our wrong side of the road. After an interminable time, and the passing of several recognizable roundabouts more than once, I who was not a stranger to the far western reaches of London, suspected he was deliberately taking us the long way around to Northwood, probably on Mother's instructions, so that we didn't arrive *too* early. We were to spend the night at Denville Hall on our return, after we had taken Mother to Spain and my sister's village. There, two days later, her birthday would be celebrated in true Joan White style, with plenty of laughter, drama, attention and liquid libation.

The car finally pulled in to a charming old house with a circular driveway and surrounded by spacious lawns. Our driver got out and pushed the front door bell. We staggered after him, exhausted by our flight and the early dawn ride through London's drearier side. The door opened. As we crossed the threshold, my early life flashed before me.

Mother bustled forward to greet us with a loud *"Here you are, Darlings,"* and as I kissed her cheek, I noticed over her plump shoulder, three large, framed publicity photographs lined up on an ornately inlaid credenza in the lobby.

There they were, the three Doges of my childhood: Sir Nöel Coward, Lord Olivier and, as he had been dubbed, Baron of Richmond Hill, but as he always will be to me — simply Dickie Attenborough.

> *"Well, of course,"* I said to myself. *"I mean after all this place is run by The Actors' Charitable Trust now, just as Silverlands, my childhood home had been then. These peers of the theatre's nobility had all been Presidents of the Trust at one time over the years."*

We exchanged some greetings with various retired ladies and gentlemen of the stage who would be spending the rest of their lives with my Mother. I was sorry not to see Robert Harris, who was away. We were served tea and biscuits in a drawing room decorated with theatrical posters of bygone hits and flops. We went upstairs to see Mother's room. Mother took the elevator, and it being too small for three, John and I elected to walk up the stairs. Over the landing hung a large oil portrait of a handsome gent in Elizabethan costume.

"Who's that?" asked John.

"I dunno, probably Olivier," I muttered, climbing on up.

Then I stopped. No, it wasn't. It bloody well wasn't Olivier! That portrait had hung in the front hall at Silverlands on Holloway Hill near Chertsey in Surrey for all my childhood.

That man had watched us sneak downstairs on our way to raiding the larder; he had seen us gather to hang tattletales on the sneak's chair over the front hall stairway's highest balustrade; he had been there when someone played Father Christmas and handed out empty gift-wrapped packages to us, for publicity photos, on Christmas Day; he had observed the showy arrivals and departures of our theatrical relatives on Visiting Sundays, and the disappointment of those children whose parents never came; and he had witnessed some of us lined up from time to time on "adoption parade." Susannah and I were spared that humiliation, but my friend Terry Mac remembered being paraded out with great regularity — yet never chosen. Poor Terry. How awful that must have made him feel. If that portrait could talk, what stories he could tell.

My curiosity was piqued. We dutifully inspected Mother's new abode and deposited our hand luggage in the guest room, which was equipped with several "Positively No Smoking" signs and some fine examples of wonderfully complex English plumbing.

Later that day, while John rested and experimented with the plumbing, I met with the director of Denville Hall, Mrs. Moira Miller and, after discussing Mother's needs and well-being, I asked what she knew of the portrait on the stairs. She became quite animated and told me she had it researched as it had interested her, too. It was of an actor named William Terriss and had been painted about 1890. He was wearing his costume for *Hamlet*.

"But where did it come from?"

"Oh," she said, *"well, you see the Actor's Charitable Trust ran an Orphanage somewhere in Surrey, for the destitute children of actors and actresses. When they closed the Orphanage in 1959, they had some of the rather nicer furnishings put into storage. Then, when*

they decided in the 1960's to take over Denville Hall, this home for
the elderly members of the profession, they brought these furnish-
ings out of storage and put them into this house. That portrait came
from there."

"Yes, I know," I said. "I went there. I was sure I knew that por-
trait. I lived at the Actor's Orphanage from 1947 until 1959. In
fact, I was boarded with a family in Staines, after the Orphanage
closed at the very end of 1958, to finished my O levels at Sir Wil-
liam Perkins School. After school one day, I sat in a beech tree and
watched the movers take everything out of the house."

Her jaw dropped. I could see that she assumed that the children at
the Actors' Orphanage were all truly orphans. They couldn't possibly be
children of respectable, fairly well to do, educated members of the profession like *my* mother.

Her curiosity piqued now, Mrs. Miller asked if I would like to walk
around the ground floor rooms and see if I recognized any pieces of furniture. I said I would, and so we did. The grand piano in the drawing
room was the same one on which Janet had practiced *"The Moonlight
Sonata"* endlessly, forty years ago. On the wall hung a photograph of Princess Elizabeth in her wedding dress, its train artfully arranged down some
steps. That used to hang in the room where the big wooden wireless set
was kept and where, for years every Christmas Day, we gathered to listen
to the King's, and later the Queen's, Speech. In another sitting room was
a portrait of that same lady, now Queen of the Realm, with her Corgis.
That had pride of place over the front hall fireplace at Silverlands, just
across from the portrait of Mr. Terriss.

Along the passage, in the residents' library, against two of the walls,
were the same glass-fronted bookcases that had stood in the long downstairs hallway outside the dining room. Our sweet rations, doled out one
at a time for good behavior after church on Sundays, were kept in one.
In the other there had been books; the only titles I remembered were
a set of Hugh Lofting's *The Adventures of Doctor Doolittle.* Those books
were not used to improve our minds, but to improve our posture and to
imprint upon our souls, our transgressions; for following the too-frequent
punishments of bare-bottom caning, we were ordered to fill a box with a

dozen or so of these books and stand, holding them on our heads, outside the headmaster's office until he said "*Enough.*"

I asked Mrs. Miller if there was a bust of Sir Gerald du Maurier. She hadn't seen one but it might be in the attic, would I like to look.

"*No,*" I said, "*I just wondered. Janet and I had to dust Sir Gerald every Saturday morning, and knew him rather too well.*"

I didn't tell her that we used to pick our noses and stuff our snot up Sir Gerald's nasal cavities; that would have been rude. As we walked around, I spotted furniture and pictures that rang familiar bells. We chatted about life and its twists and turns. For my mother "*The wheel is come full circle,*" she would spend her last years now amongst those furnishings of my childhood, with which she was not familiar.

Moira Miller had met my mother on a number of occasions before Mother actually moved in. She probably could not conceive how such a charming, little old lady could have put her children in an orphanage! But she did.

After my tour of the house, John and I collected Mother and went downstairs for a very good lunch. We met some more of Mother's new neighbors. Betty Marsden had been in *Junior Miss.* I knew this because she, indeed the whole cast, had signed my baby pillowcase and Mother's dresser had carefully embroidered each signature. I have it now, framed in my home. We also met Gerald Savory, an elderly playwright who was now in a wheelchair. When introduced to him, he said to Mother,

> "*Joan, I asked you to marry me back in the thirties. If you had married me then, your lovely daughters would have had a father.*"

Mother replied,

> "*Gerald, I didn't want to marry you then and I don't want to marry you now!*"

I have to admit that, though he *was* rather unprepossessing, — dare I say unsavory. I felt sorry for him after her rebuff and chided her for it.

After lunch, with Mother's luggage loaded in the car to join ours, our driver drove us into London to spend the night with dear Rosie at her Cheval Place flat near Harrods. Rosemary Dunham had been a good friend to Mother for many years, acting with her, and later adding her considerable talents in the casts of several Next Stage productions. Her flat was cluttered with theatrical memorabilia: statuettes, photographs, cards and ribbons took up every available space. John and I were immediately put to bed in the guest room for a long nap, before dinner. The next day we got up very early, to catch the Thursday flight to Almeria. In 1994, only one plane a week! Sue had arranged to meet us and had planned grand festivities for the Saturday, December 3rd – Mother's 85th birthday.

The flight was short and since we had slept very well in Rosie's comfortable bed, we enjoyed the flight over France, the Pyrenees and most of Spain before landing in Almeria. I remember that wonderful holiday in the little village of Bedar; perfect weather, great food, trips to other villages, tapas bars, street markets and colorful, friendly people. Susannah threw a marvelous party for Mother, who got very tiddley; but then so did we all.

The week was over too quickly and I found myself envying my sister living in this wonderful, sunny place. The following Thursday, we returned to Gatwick and took Mother back to Denville Hall. We were, again, given the guest suite complete with "No Smoking" signs and the many emergency cords to pull, in case we fell over and couldn't get up.

After dinner, John and I walked up the road to a cozy pub to be alone. The next morning, we went into Northwood to do some last-minute *English* shopping: Ribena, Marmite, LemSips, Crunchie bars, etc. (all of which one can now get On-line.) Then it was off to London. Mother took us to her club (everyone who is anyone has a club in London). Hers was The Green Room Club, popular with actors: rather dingy and with treacherous stairs. There we were to meet with her solicitor, Vivien. While Mother showed John around the Club and the photographs of the many actors who had been members, I managed to have a quiet chat with Vivien about Mother's finances and her will, etc. I felt that she was in good hands.

John and I managed to get a quick visit alone with my nephew Ronnie and his Petra at a nearby pub, and then we all took Mother back to her Mallord Street flat, where Sarah and her family along with Gayle and her little Daniel were waiting. We all went to The Stockpot on the Kings Road and had a "getting to know you," dinner, and then it was back to Northwood in a taxi with a very exhausted Joan White, pleased with her week away.

Saturday morning, John and I packed our suitcases and went to say goodbye to Mrs. Miller and to tell her how pleased we were with everything. I gave her my phone number for emergencies. She thinks Mother is wonderful and will help to keep up the spirits of the other old bods. She also said Mother may still work if she wants to; several residents do. We hugged Mother 'goodbye' and she told us her lawyer had said the sale of her flat was going to go through. (Once she had said that flat was to be mine. I guess not!)

Another car ride through West London to Heathrow, this time so much shorter than before, and we were on our way home…exhausted but glad to have seen my family.

Sue and her children seemed to be reconciled.

That Christmas, Rosie stayed at Denville Hall as Mother's guest. Ronnie and Petra went off to Spain to stay with Susannah. They ended up putting down roots there for a while but, like Sue, in a few years were unable to stay when financial bubbles began bursting in Europe. Eventually, like many ex-pats, they left Spain and went home to the UK.

Mother was content at Denville Hall and so glad she had made the choice to go there. Her grand-daughter Sarah made several trips with her children and wrote,

"Granny was very happy and loved being around her fellow thespians. Always a lovely afternoon had on those visits."

Gayle and son Danny visited Granny at Denville Hall for lunch with *"the old people."* Young Danny enchanted them. They had come on public transportation, all the way from Streatham, taking buses, tubes and a train to Northwood, a long trip with a small child.

They returned home the way they had come. (Surely Mother could have paid for a taxi!)

The following year, after our trip to Bedar, Mother organized, along with Susannah, "A Celebratory Party of The Next Stage Company Limited" on Sunday, December 3 from 3 – 6 p. m. to be held at Denville Hall, 62 Ducks Hill Road, Northwood, Middlesex, this to be on her 86th birthday. One hundred invitations were sent and fifty said they would be pleased to come. The invitation read:

Joan White and the late Alan Sleath founded the Company ten years ago, both were Associates of The Royal Academy of Dramatic Art. In ten years, it has successfully staged twenty-five productions, giving many young actors and directors the experience and opportunity of working before live audiences and playing with distinguished professional players. Regrettably despite all these achievements, the party will be to wind up The Next Stage Company's Activities.

DO COME...

Susannah and Peggy Cummins, Mother's co-star from *Junior Miss*, and many staff members pitched in to help decorate and prepare the food. Denville Hall provided a lovely big cake.

A week later on December 10th, Mother reported,

"Last Sunday was terrific. It has taken me a week to regain my senses and my physical energy. The party was a huge success with fifty guests and, of course, the residents. Susannah was, as usual, invaluable and looked lovely. Christopher Fry toasted me and cut the cake. And with that we wound up The Next Stage Company.

Now we are covered in snow. My room is cozy and the view quite beautiful with the tall bare trees looking like a pencil drawing. It's really home here and it was wise of me to do it".

On December 29th, her strength recovered, she took Sarah and Sonny with Gayle and Daniel to see a "*wonderful*" production of *The Wind in the Willows* at the London Palladium, a real Christmas treat.

Then she was off again!

Her printers, David and Liz McGill, had given her the printing of the invitations for the party as a gift in thanks for all the business she had given them over the years. When she went to pick them up, they said,

"We're going up the Nile, why don't you come too."

She jumped at the idea! Why not? Long ago, she had hoped to go with her father, but her life, busy as usual, got in the way and then her beloved father was gone. She had always wanted to see the land of her birth; after all, she was an Egyptian according to US Customs. This was to be a luxury cruise but priced very reasonably. She could afford it.

They left on January 15th from Gatwick and flew to Luxor. There they travelled to Aswan and boarded a comfortable river steamer. They cruised slowly down the Nile to Luxor, through the Valley of Kings. On the way, they were able to get off the boat and visit the tombs or climb pyramids, or even sit on a camel. Mother mostly remained on deck in comfort, only going ashore a couple of times. The weather in January was ideal, 60 degrees at night and during the day the temperatures ranged between 70 and 80. The cruise operators promised virtually no rain and little chance of *khamsins,* the infamous desert sandstorms that begin in mid-to late March.

At the grand old age of eighty-six, she visited Egypt, intrepid as ever. By all accounts, she had a wonderful time.

> Mother wrote in 1996, *"I am writing away at my biography, now to be called "Miss White, Dear". I was called that by Tony Guthrie and Robert Eddison those major influences in my life. I love Denville Hall. It is so quiet and I can find places to write."*
> She added, *"Susannah is back."*

I asked Mother *'What happened to that lovely house in Bedar?'*

But I never did get an answer. As usual, she wrote how helpful, caring and in touch Susannah is, and how hard she works. It seems that my sister was now back in London — for a while. But I was glad that she was nearby and could bring Mother some comfort in her old age. Sue's children also visited regularly and cheered up Mother and her friends.

That June, she was asked to speak at Greer Garson's Memorial Service on Sunday, July 4th in the Actors Church in Covent Garden. It was mentioned in both *The Telegraph* and *The Times,* even though Greer had died in Texas in April, where she had lived for many years. Mother was very flattered.

> *"I was chosen, as I am one of the few early friends of hers left. In 1934, Greer spent a lot of time in my Long Acre flat. I was honored to have known and loved Greer. I wrote and spoke most of the enclosed, which you may keep or destroy. Susannah seems to horde*

"efforts by her Mother" — but I shan't be offended if you don't. I was so nervous, I shook!"

Little did we know that in just over three years, I would be speaking at *her* Memorial Service at that same Church? *I* was nervous then, too. Part of Mother's speech remembering Greer Garson:

> *"Imagine if you will that it is 1934 and that you are in the top flat of number 118 Long Acre in the heart of the theatre district. The flat is small but cozy and convenient to actors who are on their way to auditions or meeting with agents.*
>
> *A beautiful young redhead used to visit me. She was not well known at the time but was very striking in her large black hat, black cloak and a red rose, looking like an ad for Sandeman Port. Greer Garson, for it was she, was playing small parts in small theatres at the time. Her visits to me (and there were many) was to find out "How to get on in the theatrical profession and become a star." But why ask me? True, I was playing on the West End, but I didn't have her looks or her education. Greer went on, up and up and eventually Hollywood snapped her up and the world knows her as Mrs. Minerva.*
>
> *Years later, we met up again in Hallmark Hall of Fame's The Invincible Mr. Disraeli. Greer played Mrs. Disraeli with Trevor Howard, and I played Mrs. Gladstone with Geoffrey Keene. We enjoyed our short reunion, remembering when we were both young actresses together. Then she went back to Texas and her beloved husband Buddy Fogelson, and I eventually returned to England, the richer for having known her."*

In the spring of 1996, I was appointed Director of The Spencertown Academy, a job I loved and held for almost nine years. The Academy was a 150-year-old former Schoolhouse, first for the training of teachers and later, as a two-room schoolhouse, to serve the children of Spencertown before they went on to high school in nearby Chatham. Located in the village of Spencertown in Columbia County, New York, my challenge was to continue to create an Arts Center for the community. During my tenure, I worked with my colleague and friend Susan Davies and a wonderfully supportive Board of Directors. One classroom became an Art Gallery capable of exhibiting art, thanks to a grant from the internationally known artist, Ellsworth Kelly, who with his husband, photographer Jack Shear, were generous supporters of the community. The second classroom became half showroom for craft artists, half an art classroom for all ages. A large auditorium took up the whole second floor. We added a sound and light booth, got new chairs for our audiences (the old ones had been contributed by a funeral parlor and showed the sloping evidence of many seated mourners). We put on concerts: classical, folk, rock and jazz. We offered ballet, yoga, tai chi and other movement classes. We showed films. We hosted The Actors Ensemble and their productions. We had puppet shows and other programs for children. And to my everlasting joy, we introduced our area to British Pantomimes... well, British-American that rather quickly became American-British.

I wrote, produced and acted along with a corps de crazies, gleaned from our area. We did five Pantos, one a year, and then when I left the Academy in 2004, we took them on to a little playhouse in nearby Ghent. In all, fifteen Pantos, each one original. All in the spirit of those British ones I had grown up with, but much more intimate. We called ourselves the PantoLoons.

It was a wonderful job. I met and made many friends. And I ended my career of Arts publicist, which had kept that wolf from my door for more than thirty years.

Mother had written to say she was thrilled, *"Your new job sounds absolutely YOU!!"* And so, it was.

Trying to keep my sister's jobs straight was another matter entirely. She had given up Bedar, returned to London, and been kind and attentive to Mother. That September, Mother wrote to say,

> *"I hope I get news from Bermuda. But Sue is silent. No news is good news."*

Sue had, apparently, taken a job in Bermuda which did not last. Mother's letter is hard to read, she says,

> *"This is painful for I seem to have lost the use of my handwriting, and I can't type anyway. Writing is very difficult for me and I am*

*a fool on the phone." She adds, "I am so proud of you and Susan-
nah. You are a credit to all of us who somehow managed to help
educate... (illegible)!"*

I have noted before, that the frequency of her letters to me began in the 1980s which, I suspect, was when she began to feel her mortality and be concerned about Sue and me, and about her grandchildren. She wanted to be remembered kindly, who doesn't, and to make amends where she could. Her own memoir, which various people have had a hand in typing, has proved invaluable.

Mother improved slightly, thanks to a course of some miracle procedure to de-clog her veins along with some physiotherapy. In June 1997, she wrote,

*Great joy here as Sue has landed a very good job as deputy warden
in a 'posh sounding' rest home in Sutton, not far from the River
and Kingston upon Thames — only a five-minute walk from her
family which is very very good. She has had excellent references,
and so she should. Just hope she sells Bedar.*

A later letter was full of the goings-on at Denville Hall, and how she was trying to fix people up with her contacts. She never stopped thinking about theatrical opportunities, but I expect, having done that all her life, it was hard to drop the habit. This was the last letter I had from Mother. Communication was then done by phone.

I did make a quick trip to England in 1998. I stayed with Sue in Sutton and we visited an old Orphanage friend, Pauline, who lived nearby. Sue and I went up to Northwood for the day; by this time Mother was pretty much bedridden, although she did get up and come down to lunch. Once again, I was introduced to new residents. My old friend Bobby Harris had died since I last visited.

After lunch, we went back to Mother's room and had a look at her few remaining possessions. We had fun entertaining her, singing Cockney songs while trying on her many hats. We ended up taking a hat each, as a memento. Very forties they were! Sue went off to talk to Moira Miller, the director, and Mother took the opportunity to tell me about her change of plans.

She said it had all been cleared with her solicitor Vivien, but she wanted me to know that originally, she had left her estate to be divided evenly between Susannah and myself. But she had had a change of heart and had now decided to leave her money eight ways; so that each daughter and grandchild would get an equal portion. She wanted to make sure I was all right with that since my family would get less: Sue having four children and I having only two. She just felt that if she left it to Sue and me alone, Sue's children would get nothing, knowing how money seemed to slip through Sue's fingers.

What could I say? Of course, I said it was fine. I reassured her that this was sound thinking and anyway it was her money to do with as she liked. She had made wise investments, and with her pensions (both British and American) she was comfortably off. She said she had not shared this information with my sister. When Sue returned, I kept mum – no pun intended. Later, I returned to the States, my husband and my job.

One year later, Sue called me on June 8th 1999 to say Mother had died. She had been in the nursing unit at Denville for a few days with pneumonia. Sue had gone up to see her several times. On this day, she was sitting quietly by Mother's bed, thinking she was sound asleep, her breathing very shallow. Suddenly, Mother opened her eyes, looked straight at Sue and said, "*I did it all wrong with you!*"

Sue went into a panic and protested, "*No! I'm just fine. Really I am.*"

The nurse came in and leaned over the bed, closing Mother's eyes, and said, "*She's gone, dear.*"

How's that for last words?

Sue told me this on the phone and sort of shrugged it off. She said she and Denville Hall would make arrangements for cremation and funeral, as Mother had wished. She would get back to me.

A few days later, I was sitting at work when my ex-husband, Colgate called. He had been fighting cancer for a couple of years and had recently stopped all treatments.

"*Judy, I am so sorry about Joan.*"

Abby must have told him; she and Sherrod were visiting him at the time.

"*Thank you, Gate. But I am worried about you! How are you?*"

"*There's nothing more they can do.*"

We said a sad goodbye and within a week, he too was gone.

I did not go to Mother's funeral. My daughters needed to be at their father's in Baltimore, so John and I said we would take the grand-boys. There was no one else. Besides it was a happy choice to have.

The Berkshire Playhouse

STOCKBRIDGE, MASSACHUSETTS 1960 -1964

The Waltz of the Toreadors *1960*
Joan with Paul Ballantine

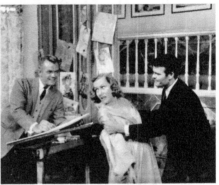

Between Seasons *1961*
with Gloria Swanson

The Happiest Days of Your Life
Judy White, Paul Ballantine,
David Vaughan, George Vogel

Also -- Avis Lennard, Drew Eliot
and Margaret Hamilton, 1960

Playhouse production photos by Louis Hansen Courtesy of Berkshire Theatre Archives

Joan White in 1962

with Gertrude Robinson-Smith, Ruth St. Denis and Ted Shawn at Jacob's Pillow 1962 opening Photograph: John Lindquist ©Harvard Theatre Collection

Charlie Davisson and Joan White In Ten Little Indians *1961*

William Swan and Sylvia Sidney in The Silver Cord *1964*

Anna Russell and Geoffrey Webb in Lady Audley's Secret *1963*

Playhouse production photos: Louis Hansen courtesy of Berkshire Theatre Archives

*Anne Wakefield as Eliza with Joan
in* My Fair Lady *1964*

with Jim Oyster in
The Corn is Green, *1963*

[ABOVE] *Angela Wood, Anne Wakefield, Judy
White, Dan Walker, and Colgate Salsbury in*
Night Must Fall, *1964*

[AT RIGHT] *Judy as Phoebe and William
Shepard as Silvius in* As You Like It, *1964*

[ABOVE] *Mrs. Tarleton in* Misalliance
Cincinnati Playhouse in the Park 1967

[AT LEFT] *Lady Insdale in* On a Clear Day…
In Boston 1965 (her role cut before NYC)

Mrs. Candour with Lorna Heilbrun
as Maria in The School for Scandal
Nottingham Playhouse UK 1968

Mrs. Dudgeon in The Devil's
Disciple *with Patricia Reilly as Essie*
Meadowbrook Theatre, Michigan 1978

[ABOVE] *as Frosine in* The Miser *with Michael O'Sullivan Seattle Rep. 1970*

Photo; Camera Craft, Seattle

[AT LEFT] *Teaching in Seattle 1970– 74*

English Summer Theatre School at University of Washington, the first summer 1970

Joan White English Theatre School.

[LEFT] *1980 students at Trinity College, Dublin* [RIGHT] *1985 Elizabeth Pursey and students.*

Above three photos from Joan White's scrapbooks

Cast and directors of One Thing More *at Whitby Abbey, June 1989*

Isolde O'Neill and Judy Campbell in
One Thing More, *London 1993*

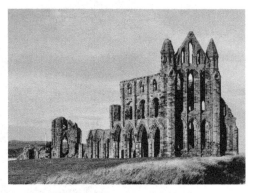

Whitby Abbey North Yorkshire

Director Joan White and author Christopher Fry 1990s
50 years after they met with A Phoenix Too Frequent

Heinz Baked Beans commercial Oct. 1988

The Next Stage Company
Joan White and Elizabeth Pursey center, Bert Stimmel at left.

BED *by Jim Cartwright*
National Theatre 1988
[L-R] *Joan White and Donald Bissett as the Couple, John Boswall as the Captain, Margery Withers as Marjorie, Charles Simon as Charles, Ruth Kettlewell as the Bosom Lady and Vivienne Burgess as the Spinster.*

Photograph by Simon Annand
Courtesy of National Theatre Archives.

Dancing with great–grandson Dan Bailey.
Watching are son–in–law John Staber and grand–daughter Sherrod Bailey 1992

After the Memorial Service, her descendants gathered for a family football game.
[L-R] Sonny Kennedy, Abby Salsbury, Sarah Kennedy, Dan Bailey, Sherrod Bailey,
Dan Horton, Edward Bailey, Susannah Slater, Jamie Walker, Gayle Horton
and Kyle Bailey. Seated Stuart and Scott Kennedy. September 1999.
(not shown Ronnie Horton and Jody Walker)

After Words

The British press did her proud with her obituaries.

Alan Strachan in both *The Observer* and *The Independent*, was succinct and the most complete about her long career. With his permission, I quote the obituary in its entirety:

"JOAN WHITE, stylish and versatile, and an especially gifted exponent of the vanishing art of high comedy, would surely have had an even more prestigious career had she had fewer strings to her bow – she produced, directed and taught besides – and had she at the height of her career based herself more in the British theatre.

Born in Alexandria in 1909 but educated in Britain at St. Helen's School in Northwood, Middlesex, she had early theatrical leanings and after RADA had a vital first chance in 1929 at the then highly adventurous Festival Theatre, Cambridge, under Tyrone Guthrie, as Azorah in James Bridie's "Tobias and the Angel" (Bridie was to remain a favourite writer – she appeared later in his Burke and Hare play "The Anatomist" in Guthrie's flickeringly atmospheric production, and in the title role of "Susannah and the Elders").

Much of her work was in the more adventurous theatre of the time; a challenging 1933 Westminster Theatre season included an early British production of Pirandello's "Six Characters in Search of an Author," in which she played the Assistant Stage Manager. Exciting experimental theatre was in much smaller supply at a time when London had little to compare with the scale of the modern fringe and White also served her time in the more genteel world of 1930s commercial theatre, much of it catchpenny work but with occasional showy roles such as the winsome Bella in Rudolf Besier's 1930s blockbuster "The Barretts of Wimpole Street" (Piccadilly, 1935). She also played Phoebe in the over-decorative Paul Czinner movie of "As You Like It" (1936), starring Elisabeth Bergner and Laurence Olivier.

She retired from the stage following her second marriage and the births of two daughters for a period during the Second World War, returning in a piece of mindless Broadway froth, "Junior Miss" (Saville, 1943). A better role followed in Walter Greenwood's loving and sturdy Lancashire comedy "The Cure For Love" (Westminster, 1945.)

The post-war years developed into a golden era for the British repertory system, led by a generation of energetic younger talent prior to the rise of television. At the Birmingham Rep in 1949 White had a superb run of parts, ranging from a majestic Duchess of York in "Richard III" to a gloriously batty Madame Maniefa in Rodney Ackland's Gogol adaption "The Diary of a Scoundrel."

Even more impressive was her work at the Bristol Old Vic in the 1950-51 season, the first under its new director Denis Carey; its company then included John Neville, Donald Pleasence, Lally Bowers, Stuart Burge and Donald Sinden. During this outstanding season, White's appearances included a delightfully garrulous Mistress Quickly in "The Merry Wives of Windsor", one of the first repertory productions of Christopher Fry's "The Lady's Not for Burning" (the relatively small but telling role of Margaret Devize, in which she handled the spring-morning music of Fry's verse beautifully) and a brilliant farce performance in Pinero's "The Magistrate", as Agatha Posket, married to the pillar of respectability of the title and trapped in a lie about her age. Donald Sinden, matching her in comedic invention, as the more-than-adolescent stepson forced to pretend he is only 14.

At Bristol she also played Mrs Candour in "The School for Scandal", her voice curdling from assumed concern to acidulated malice within a sentence, and perhaps most memorably, a finely etched Julia Shuttlewaite, out of T.S.Eliot's Furies, in "The Cocktail Party", with Donald Pleasence as the Unidentified Guest in Carey's compelling production in a setting disturbingly evocative of a birdcage.

Her subsequent British work included one of her outstanding roles – the faded but irrepressibly gallant Lady Kitty in Maugham's best comedy of manners, "The Circle" (Manchester, 1953) and, in the West End, Miss Marcy in the surprisingly unsuccessful version of Dodie Smith's "I Capture the Castle" (Aldwych, 1954).

The focus of her career shifted to North America thereafter – encouraged by Guthrie, always a champion of pastures new and of regional theatre – initially in 1956 with her appointment as Director of the Trans-Canada Theatre Company. Her work for the Company for the next two years was based in London, Ontario, and included the direction of many plays, mostly popular comedies, with occasional acting appearances including the flustered society wife in "The Reluctant Debutante" (1957.

She made her US debut taking over Mrs. Higgins in the touring company of "My Fair Lady" (1958).

Throughout the 1960s she was phenomenally busy, mostly in American regional and stock theatres. With her third husband, the director and designer Robert Grose, she co-presented over 50 productions between 1960 and 1964 at the Berkshire Playhouse (including a musical version of "Lady Audley's Secret" which she co-authored with the diseuse Anna Russell), fitting in sporadic New York performances including an off-Broadway "Trelawny of the Wells" as the ageing actress Mrs Telfer (Master Theatre, New York, 1961) and the Broadway production of "A Passage to India" (Ambassador, New York 1962). She also appeared on US television in several Hallmark Hall of Fame productions.

A welcome return to the UK saw her back in British repertory, at Nottingham Playhouse in 1968, then at a high point under Stuart Burge. Her parts included Eleanor in "King John", a stoically careworn Paulina in "The Seagull" and another Mrs Candour, again dripping cloaked venom, like prussic acid on sugar cubes, in Jonathan Miller's pox-and-all reappraisal of "The School for Scandal." Back in the US, she joined the faculty of the Drama School of the University of Washington in 1969 for a six-year period, during which time she also directed and acted for various Seattle companies. She made a redoubtable landlady to the deluded Rolfe in "Hadrian VII" and a touching Aunt Penniman in Ruth Goetz's "The Heiress", adapted from Henry James's "Washington Square" (both at Seattle Rep, 1970).

Approaching old age, she concentrated her still formidable energies on the acting school she formed in 1975, initially in Seattle and then, after she returned to London in 1982, at her Chelsea flat. She proved to be as incisive and inspiring a teacher as she had been actor and director, impressing students with her passionate sense of discipline and her always stylish aplomb. She was still on occasion acting on television into her eighties, most memorably in 1986 with a vivid cameo role in Dennis Potter's "The Singing Detective".

Joan White, actress: born Alexandria, Egypt 3 December 1909; married first J.V. Beanes (marriage dissolved), second A.P. Moore (two daughters; marriage dissolved), third Robert Grose (marriage dissolved); died London 8 June 1999."

Alan Strachan told me she had a reputation as "an actor's actor." She was also given a lot of ink in:

The Daily Telegraph "...one of the most vivacious and versatile West End Players of the Thirties and Forties, with a particular line in precocious schoolgirls."

The Guardian, "Among her adventurous exploits were flying across the stage on a high wire in Eva LeGallienne's Alice in Wonderland, and riding side-saddle in a Canadian TV version of The Last of the Mohicans,"

The Times of London. "A familiar face on the London stage from the 1930s onward."

and *The Stage* added to its copy with the following on Sept 16 1999. **Last Orders for Joan** *"Joan White, the actress aged 89, in June got her last wish and had her ashes scattered on the stage of the Duke of York's. The venue is currently the site for "The Weir," so there could only be one resting place for Joan – behind the bar."*

The Berkshire Eagle in western Massachusetts, where she had directed The Berkshire Playhouse for five years, ran a nice story by the late Mary Jane Tichenor, who had known her. I, her daughter, wrote her obituary in *The (Columbia County) Independent* for which, at the time, I was Theatre reviewer. *Variety,* the entertainment news for the States, also covered her passing.

After the London funeral, attended by Susannah and her children and several close friends, Sue began to organize a Memorial Service for Mother at St. Paul's, the Actors Church in Covent Garden. It was to be held on September 9, 1999 (9/9/99) three months shy of what would have been her 90th birthday.

The day before our mother Joan White's memorial service, my sister Susannah and I, along with our family friend Rosemary Dunham, went to the Duke of York's Theatre on St. Martin's Lane in London's West End. We each carried a small plastic bag containing a tablespoon or two of Mother's ashes that we planned to scatter backstage. (Sue had obtained permission from the Ambassador Theatre Group, the current tenants of the Duke of York's).

At about ten-thirty in the morning, we passed through the lobby and entered the darkened theatre. We groped our way down the aisle towards the single work-light standing in the center of the stage — the only illumination. In the gloom we could just make out, high above the proscenium, the shield on which had once been emblazoned the letters "VM," the initials of Violet Melnotte — grande dame, founder and former owner of the Duke of York's. She was part of the reason we were here. In the early 1930s Violet had hired our father, A.P. Moore, to manage her theatre. She had later asked him to marry her, but because she was fifty years older than he, there was an ensuing scandal.

Violet, always mindful of negative publicity, changed her mind and said she was going to adopt him instead, but she died before that could come about. After Violet's passing, Father met our mother who was appearing in a play at this theatre, now under his sole management. Their wedding reception, in January 1937, was held on this very stage.

Much sadness had come from their marriage.

It was rumored among actors that Violet's ghost haunted the theatre. Had she cursed our parents' union from beyond the grave? Our hope was, by scattering our mother's ashes here, they would counteract Violet's malevolent spirit, lift any remaining vestiges of the rumored curse and, at the same time give Mother a theatre to haunt — if she needed one.

Reaching the apron, Sue opened the house door to backstage, and we walked through the wings and onto the set for Conor McPherson's play, *The Weir* — an Irish pub. Our father's forebears came from Ireland.

Rosie took stage right, dribbling ashes around the prompt desk and the props table. Sue took center stage, sprinkling ashes liberally behind the bar. I had stage left. My portion of the gritty ashes fell around the hundred-year-old fly ropes and sandbagged counterweights in the stage house. There was the dust of ages back there. The cobwebs seemed to have been woven before the First World War. Mother's ashes, caught in the webs, made a delicate pattern.

We were quickly finished and thanking the stage doorman, the only living soul in the theatre beside ourselves that morning, we exited through the lobby and into the weak sunshine of that September day. Feeling just a little ghoulish, and since it was now past eleven o'clock, we walked up St. Martin's Lane to a nearby pub. Raising her glass of the best bitter to the dear departed, Sue said she swore she had seen the ghost of Violet out in the orchestra seats while she was ash-scattering.

"Not possible, Sue," said Rosie, *"Violet only shows up at ten o'clock at night to slam doors during performances. I know, I was in a play there a couple of years ago."*

We were happy to have left a little bit of Mother at the Duke of York's, where she had been young and carefree, before we were born and Father had gone. Her life had changed so dramatically afterwards. She had immersed herself in her career, setting aside her children for her theatrical responsibilities.

Later, Sue and I would each take a small amount of her ashes home with us. Mine are planted under a Rosa Rugosa, in my New York State garden — a tiny part of her forever in North America where her career flourished for almost thirty years. Sue took hers to Gibraltar to be scattered over our grandparents' grave, because Mother had grown up in Portugal and Gibraltar before she left for boarding school in England and later sought her fortune on the stage. The rest of her ashes are buried in the corner of a family plot in a country churchyard within sight of Salisbury Cathedral, where her maternal ancestors had worshipped for centuries. After almost ninety years on this earth, her remains are now laid to rest in the lands where she had lived her long life.

The day after our visit to The Duke of York's, dressed in our best clothes, we held a memorial service for this actress, Joan White, at St. Paul's the Actors' Church in Covent Garden. Sue and Rosie had arranged the event, sent out the notices, ordered the flowers and notified friends, colleagues and students. Some were invited to remember Mother with short speeches. Richard Syms, an actor and a priest, would lead the religious portion of the service. Appropriate music was selected, played and sung by former students. Her family was seated in the front row: two daughters, five of her living grandchildren, and five great grandchildren. I, her American daughter, was to give the eulogy.

My daughters, Abby and Sherrod, my son-in-law Ed Bailey, her American great grandchildren, Kyle and Daniel Bailey and I flew over from America. Three of Susannah's children, Jamie Walker, Sarah Kennedy and Gayle Horton, along with Mother's three British great-grandsons Danny Horton, Sonny and Scott Kennedy came into London.

The Church was filled with flowers and a photograph of Mother placed near the front door. Programs had been printed with the order of service.

The Reverend Richard Syms would officiate. He was a member of the Church's clergy and was an actor himself. The family was seated in the front row, with the other participants near the front. Friends of Susannah's and students of Mother's were ushers. Organist Michael Broadway contributed accompaniment. Once the guests had arrived and filled the pews, Reverend Syms greeted the congregation and Susannah welcomed everyone, wearing one of Mother's little hats.

Then it was my turn. I was rather nervous having such an august professional crowd before me.

What did I say about a mother who wasn't maternal or motherly, but was a highly respected actor, director and teacher? About this woman, who could and did set aside her children, but who would never have put aside her students or fellow actors. About this woman who had had three husbands, two daughters, seven grandchildren, and seven great-grandchildren, all of whom knew her slightly, yet she had many great and close friends.

Former students, musicians and actors, including her former co-star Paul Scofield, all read, sang or praised her life to a packed church. She'd worked with many well-known actors over the years: Paul Scofield, Robert Donat, Lilli Palmer, Laurence Olivier, Eric Portman, Flora Robson, Googie Withers, Eva LeGallienne and Gladys Cooper, to name just a few. She'd had plays written for her and numbered many playwrights among her closest friends. But it was I who was to write her eulogy. I, who knew her only as 'Mother,' the one role at which she had not excelled and in which she was least comfortable.

Did I chastise her for her maternal omissions? Did I say that Sue and I had been put aside, placing us in care of The Actors Orphanage at a very early age, in order that she might continue her career and eventually be worthy of being eulogized here in the Actors' Church with this gathering of her peers? No, I didn't. My Granny always said, "*One must not speak ill of the dead, Ducky.*" Our mother did what she did because she was, first and foremost above all else, a woman of the theatre, and that she did well. For that, I am proud of her.

I had decided to speak of her accomplishments as an actress and woman of the theatre, inserting our entrances into the world as if motherhood was a role she had signed on to play.

I took my place at the lectern, wearing one of her jaunty little 1940s hats, I looked out at the sea of faces and said:

"It's a full house, Mother," and then I began:

"She forgot to mention the hats. They were Mother's. Rather jaunty aren't they." Laughter. (Oh good, they're listening).

"My mother, Joan White, was cast as Phoebe in the 1936 film of *As You Like It,* which starred Elisabeth Bergner and Laurence Olivier, when she was just 26 years old. George Bernard Shaw had spotted her in a performance of *The Black Eye* at The Shaftsbury Theatre and said to Bergner, 'There's your Phoebe.' As Phoebe, she is now immortalized on film:

Think not I love him though I ask for him

'Tis but a peevish boy, yet he talks well;

But what care I for words? Yet words do well, When he that speaks them pleases those that hear.

Good lines for a lady who later became a teacher of speech and drama and taught Susannah and I the importance of enunciation. Shakespeare also wrote 'One man in his time plays many parts.' Our mother was a woman of many, many parts. As well as a mother, grandmother and great-grandmother, she has been a wife — several times — a director, a producer, a teacher to scores, no hundreds of students, and an actor in more roles than I can name.

"For the first fifteen years of her long career she mostly played teenagers: *Little Ladyship* with Lilli Palmer (while pregnant with my sister); *Susannah and the Elders* (from which my sister got her name); *Housemaster* with her classic line '*Do you mean funny peculiar or funny ha-ha?*' and as thirteen-year-old Judy Graves in *Junior Miss* when, at thirty-four, she had just given birth to a ten-pound eight-ounce baby — me!"

And on I went, covering her long career in the theatre, telling little anecdotes, never mentioning her children again and ending with this:

"One of her last performances was for the BBC television production of *The Singing Detective* as old Mrs. Adams. Fortunately, this too, is preserved on film so now future generations will be able to see her range as an actress — from Phoebe to Mrs. Adams some sixty years later.

"My godfather, Sir Tyrone Guthrie, who was her friend and mentor, gave Mother her start both in England with the Cambridge Festival Theatre Company in 1930 and in Canada in 1956. He also gave our indefatigable mother her motto, 'Rise Above It,' and so she did, whenever life got her down. She certainly has now, she's up there somewhere not waiting in the wings, but waiting for her wings. Cheerio, Mum.'"

I managed to speak, clearly and concisely as though she was listening, but I did choke up at the end.

Susannah had arranged the order of events perfectly. Jack Pinter, one of Mother's Next Stage actors, then played *On A Clear Day You Can See Forever* on his saxophone: Rosie read *A Better Place* by Terrick McHugh, a student of Mother's who had died at a very young age. Next up was Drew Eliot, American actor and family friend. Drew, a student of Mother's in the 1950s at RADA, spoke at length about his admiration and fondness for "Joan White" as he always called her. He had acted with her Off Broadway in New York City, and with myself, long ago at the Berkshire Playhouse. He ended with a reading of Shakespeare's Sonnet Number 30, a favorite of hers.

When to the sessions of sweet silent thought
I summon up remembrance of things past,

Next, an interlude with former student Vannine Parker, singing an Edwardian favorite of Mother's, accompanied by Michael Broadway: *And Her Golden Hair was Hanging Down Her Back.*

Elizabeth Pursey, teacher of speech and dialects at RADA, had worked with Mother throughout her English Theatre School years and into The Next Stage. Elizabeth talked about Teaching at RADA, her friendship with Mother and her love for her.

"It is my privilege to speak of Joan as a teacher/director, this is how I knew her. One day, whilst I was teaching at RADA, Peter

Woodham told me that Joan White was bringing a group of 20 to 30 students for a 6-week workshop based at the Adeline Genée Theatre in East Grinsted and she would like dialect lessons for the six weeks. She requested Cockney, North Country, Irish, Scottish, and Welsh as required for Shaw, O'Casey, Bridie, Priestley and so on. This was February 1970. Joan and I worked together and I thought this would be a one-time happening. Not the yearly event as it turned out to be.

"It was in Seattle that I learned what a unique teacher Joan was. What was it about her that her students loved? To start with, Joan loved life and her students enjoyed being with her, "Learning should be fun, summer schools should be fun, but fun is not enough to arrange and set courses that fulfill university requirements and which connect grades." she would say. Joan was astute and she was lovably odd. These two characteristics surprised her students into self-discovery.

"This quest for giving students the opportunity to love theater never stopped all the time I knew and worked for Joan; 29 years of friendship. And from Seattle in October 1972, Joan wrote, "We have been unanimously approved by the foreign study committee and we are now listed in the university catalog as a permanent part of the drama school".

"But Joan was becoming restless even though she was writing of her work in Seattle in the following terms 'it is a lovely place, flat, job, and security and as I hit 65 yesterday', that was December 3ʳᵈ 1974, 'and have all those grandchildren, six, and two very different, lovely daughters, it behooves me to be relaxed and thank God daily for my good fortune. Late in life maybe, but it's a great compensation for a somewhat stormy past.'

"Her energy was unsurpassed and it came from the fact that she continued to act herself and was constantly putting herself on the line. Oh, she did so much more than talk about theater. 'I'm gregarious', she used to say, 'I love people'. In May 1996 we received a letter to say 'after 10 years and 25 productions we are sad to say goodbye (to The Next Stage). We want to thank you for your loyal support'.

Now dear Joan was a professional, her disciplined realism was highlighted by her trust in a magnificent God, by her trust in people, and by an almost prickly belief that a good idea could be made to work. Joan once ended a letter with "oh if only life was longer and one didn't have to sleep 7 hours in 24". And from her last letter which ended "thank you, thank you". – Thank you, too, dear Joan!"

Jason Mullen was next, to talk about The Next Stage, Mother's last major endeavor. I have quoted Jason's heartwarming speech earlier in this book in Chapter 18. He too opened his remarks with "It's a good house, Joan" and ended with "Rise Above It."

For the finale, what could be better than this read by Paul Scofield.

"The Legacy is a poem, which Joan found in an anthology. She didn't know the author. It was her particular wish that it should be read to you on such an occasion as this."

The Legacy

When I die, give what is left of me to children
If you need to cry, cry for your brothers walking beside you
Put your arms around anyone
And give them what you need to give me
I want to leave you with something
Something better than words or sounds.
Look for me in the people I have known and loved
And if you cannot live without me,
Then let me live on in your eyes, your mind, and your acts of kindness
You can love me most by letting hands touch hands
And letting go of children that need to be free
Love does not die, people do.
 So, when all that is left of me is love, give me away.

The service ended with her favorite, patriotic hymn, *I Vow To Thee My Country* followed by closing prayers led by Reverend Richard Syms.

We left the Church, teary-eyed yet laughing, to Noel Coward's *Don't Put Your Daughter On The Stage, Mrs. Worthington*. We re-gathered at Mother's Club, The Green Room, nearby for warm whiskey and hors d'oeuvres, which in England are now called Starters — but these were Afters!

CURTAIN!

Acknowledgements

There are so many people who have helped me with this book.

For their memories: Chic Silber; Jason Mullen; Isolde O'Neill; Kate Peake; the late Drew Eliot; Lorna Heilbrun; Nicholas Kepros; my daughters Abby Salsbury and Sherrod Bailey, my nieces Sarah Kennedy and Gail Horton, and especially my sister, Susannah Slater. I give thanks to my late mother, Joan White, for all those endless notes, monologues, memories and letters that she wrote and we kept.

For photographs: Jeremy Megrew at the Billy Rose Photography division at New York Public Library of the Performing Arts; Jill and staff at University of Bristol Theatre archives; Arthur Millie at Salisbury Playhouse archives; Kate Maguire for the Berkshire Theatre Archives; Norton Owen at Jacob's Pillow Dance Festival and the Harvard Theatre Collection; Deb Harvey at The Grand Theatre, London, Ont.; Simon Annand for his National Theatre photo of "Bed", Jason Mullen for various Next Stage photos; Abby Salsbury for finding an author photo that I like and to my sister Susannah for digging out more photos of our Mother that I didn't know existed.

For permission to use their words: Alan Strachan for Joan White's obituary; Robert A. Schanke from *Shattered Applause: The Lives of Eva LeGallienne*.

For reading various stages of the manuscript and/or for offering their wisdom: Robert Ashby, David Black, Susan Davies, Tom Detwiler, Elizabeth Diggs, Ron Harrington and Rick Rowsell, Barbara Iuviene, Barney Karpfinger, Sally McCarthy, Emily Arnold McCully, and Dina Harris Walker. Cara Benson for putting the finish on the title. My most recent writing group: Judy Green, Cecele Kraus, Amy White and Cathy Wilkerson. And to the Liz Diggs/Spencertown Academy Memoir group – Zoom on everyone!

For all the technical details of getting the book to press and beyond: Paul Palmer Edwards for the wonderful cover design; Jessika Hazelton and her fabulous crew at Troy Book Makers; Sheafe Walker Esq for legal assistance and teaching me about "due diligence." And to David Carriere and Jason Mullen for helping me get it out there.

And lastly to my husband John Staber, who read every version of the manuscript, copy-edited, and made useful suggestions. He has kept me sane and on target.

Judy White Staber
Old Chatham, New York

CHRONOLOGY 1909 – 1999

1909   Born December 3, Alexandria, Egypt

1909-   Childhood in Carcavelos, Portugal
1918

1919-   Family moved to Azores
1920

1921-   Enrolled at St Helen's School for Girls,
1926   Northwood, Middlesex

1926-   Entered Royal Academy of Dramatic Art,
1929   London

1930-   Cambridge Festival Players - Tyrone Guthrie
1932   director

       Tobias and the Angel (Azorah)

       Festival Players at the Westminster Theatre,
       London

          The Anatomist (Janet) w/Henry Ainley and
          Flora Robson
          The Kingdom of God (Margarita) *Loves Labours*
          Lost (Moth)
          Follow Me (as cast)
          Jonah and the Whale (Euodias)
          Six Characters in Search of an Author (Assistant
          Stage Manager)

1932   *The Melody Maker* (Jerry) w/Charles Hawtrey   FILM

1933   *The Synthetic Virgin* (Eve)   Royalty Theatre

       Marries John Vesey Beanes, playwright

        Clean Hands   Piccadilly Theatre
        Vacant Possession (Angela)   Fortune Theatre
        A Present from Margate (Joan Buckland)   Shaftsbury Theatre

1934   *The Golden Toy* (Madanika)   London Coliseum
        Charlotte's Progress (Charlotte)   Mercury Theatre
        Our Mutual Father (Nurse Caine)   West End London
        Lucky Loser (Alice)   FILM

1935   Beanes marriage annulled

1935	*The Barretts of Wimpole Street* (Bella Hadley)	Piccadilly Theatre
(cont.)	*I'll Leave it to You* (Director)	Bexhill
	Outward Bound (Director)	Bexhill
	Admirals All (Prudence)	FILM
	The Black Eye (Connie Windlestraw)	Shaftsbury Theatre
1936	*Luck of the Devil* (Claudine)	The Arts Theatre
	The Second Bureau (Dorothy)	FILM
	Children to Bless You (Tonie)	Ambassadors & Duke of Yorks
	Housemaster (Button Farringdon)	Apollo Theatre; toured Scotland
	As You Like It (Phoebe) w/ Laurence Olivier	FILM

1937   Marries A.P. Moore Managing Director
The Duke of York's Theatre

	Housemaster continued	Aldwych Theatre
	Susannah and the Elders (Susannah)	London Intl Theatre Club
	Wake Up Famous musical (as cast)	FILM
1938	*Tobias and the Angel* (Sara) w/ Tyrone Guthrie	FILM
	You're the Doctor (Jane) with Googie Withers	FILM
1939	*A Girl Must Live* w/Margaret Lockwood	FILM
	Little Ladyship (Judy Bingley)w/ Lilli Palmer	The Strand Theatre

1939   Susannah Moore born July 12 1939

World War Two begins September 1st, 1939

A.P. Moore enlists in the Army

1943   Joanna Judy Moore born January 3, 1943

1943– 1945	*Junior Miss* (Judy Graves) two year run plus an ENSA tour.	Saville Theatre
1945	*The Cure for Love* (Janey Jenkins)	Westminster Theatre
1946	*GI Brides at Sea*	
	This Desirable Residence	on Tour
	A Phoenix Too Frequent (Doto) w/Paul Scofield	Arts Theatre
	Youth at the Helm (Dorothy Wilson)	FILM

1947   Susannah and Judy enter the Actors Orphanage

	Flat Spin (director and Lady Beatrice)	Her Majesty's Theatre
	Fools Rush In by Kenneth Horne (director)	Worthing
	And Talking of Tightropes (Madame Lola)	FILM
	Tons of Money (Simpson)	FILM

1948	Birmingham Repertory Theatre (Michael Langham)	January – June

Richard III (Duchess of York) with Alan Badel
The Casilis Engagement (Ethel Borridge)
Diary of a Scoundrel (Madame Maniefa)
The Modern Everyman directed by Michael
Langham

1949	Ten Shilling Doll (Leah Barr)	Torch Theatre
	The Happy Man by N. Ginsbury (director)	The New Theatre
	Ten Shilling Doll (Leah)	TV FILM
	The Weaker Sex	TV FILM
	The Rivals (Lucy)	TV FILM
	All Star Performance for RADA The Anatomist	Drury Lane Theatre

Teaches at Royal Academy of Dramatic Arts
1949 through 1955

Salisbury Arts Theatre
September '49 – June '50
Somerset Maugham's The Circle (Lady Kitty)
Chekov's The Proposal
Fry's A Phoenix Too Frequent (Doto)
See How They Run (Penelope Toop)
Sheridan's The Rivals (Mrs Malaprop)
Grundy's A Pair of Spectacles (Mrs Goldfinch)
Aladdin – the Panto (Fairy Rosebud)
Coward's Tonight at 8:30
The Brontes of Haworth (Charlotte)
Caste (Esther Eccles)
Moliere's The Doctor's Joy (Toinette)

1950 Bristol Old Vic
September '50 – April '51
Fry's The Lady's Not for Burning (Margaret
Devize)
Pinero's The Magistrate (Agatha Posket)
Sheridan's The School For Scandal (Mrs.
Candour)
Eliot's The Cocktail Party (Julia Shuttlewaite)
The Merry Wives of Windsor (Mistress Quickly)
Puss in Boots – the Panto (The Empress)

1951	Storks Don't Talk (Gloria) w/Mischa Auer	Comedy Theatre
1952	The Night of Masquerade w/Robert Eddison	Q Theatre

Dundee Repertory Company   Autumn
The Hollow Crown (Infanta of Navarre)

1952	Dundee Repertory Company Autumn *(cont.)*	
(cont.)	*The Queen's Husband* (as director)	
	The Beaver Coat (Frau Wolff)	
	Moore marriage annulled. Children's names changed to "White"	
1953	Maugham's *The Circle* (Lady Kitty)	The Playhouse, Manchester
	The Sun and I w/Robert Eddison	Theatre Royal, Windsor
	A London Actress w/Edward Byrne	Arts Theatre Club, London
1954	*I Capture the Castle* (Miss Marcy)	Aldwych Theatre, London
	Salisbury Arts Theatre	
	Dial M For Murder (as director)	
	For Better for Worse (as director)	
	Spring at Marino (as director*)*	
	Birthday Honors (Beatrice Titherage*)*	
	Cocteau's *Intimate Relations* (Yvonne)	
1955	*The Farmer's Wife* (Thirza Tapper)	TV FILM
	Noah Gives Thanks (Mrs Snapgood) w/John Phillips	TV FILM
	Concurrent Engagements in Cardiff and Salisbury	
	Prince of Wales Theatre, Cardiff as Director	
	Quality Street; Ten Little Indians; Angels in Love.	
	Salisbury Arts Theatre as Director (alternating with Cardiff)	
	The First Year; Present Laughter; Fresh Fields; The Miser; Saloon Bar; The Bespoke Overcoat and *The Respectful Prostitute.*	
	BBC Sunday Night Theatre	
	Yellow Sands (Minnie Masters)	
	The Cure for Love (Janey Jenkins)	
	The Last of the DeMullins (Miss Deanes)	
	Truant in Park Lane (Mrs. Fishwick)	
1956– 1957	Emigrates to Canada	
	*Present Laughter (*as director)	Crest Theatre, Toronto
	Murder at the Vicarage (Miss Marple)	Crest Theatre, Toronto
	Last of the Mohicans (Laura Dodson)	CBC TV FILM

1956–	Trans-Canada Company at The Grand Theatre	London, Ontario
1957	Season (Producer/Director):	
(cont.)	*Dear Charles; The Seven Year Itch; Anniversary Waltz; When We Are Married; Sabrina Fair; Lucky Strike; White Sheep of the Family; The Tender Trap; I Found April; The Happiest Days of Your Life* and *Ten Little Indians.*	

1957–	*Diary of a Scoundrel* (Madame Maniefa)	FOLIO TV FILM
1958	*The Empty Frame* (Madame LaFleche)	FOLIO TV FILM

Susannah emigrates to Canada

Maple Leaf Theatre Company at The Grand Season (Producer/Director):   London, Ontario
Tea and Sympathy; The Reluctant Debutante; The Solid Gold Cadillac; Light Up the Sky; The Spider's Web; Picnic; Bus Stop; The Seven Year Itch and *The Browning Version.*

1958 Marries Robert Paine Grose, Scenic Designer and Director

My Fair Lady (Mrs. Higgins) 9/58 – 9/59   National Company Tour

1959 Judy emigrates to USA
Moves to New York City

1960 *The Citadel* (Mrs. Page)   TV FILM

Berkshire Playhouse 1960 Summer Season (Co-Producer/ Director/ Actor):   Stockbridge, Massachusetts
Two For the Seesaw; Dear Charles (Denise); *Witness For the Prosecution; Misalliance; The Member of the Wedding; Waltz of the Toreadors* (Emily); *The Happiest Days of Your Life; Angel Street; The Gazebo and Dear Miss Phoebe*

1961 Susannah returns to UK with Jim Walker and baby Jamie
The Cocktail Party (Julia)   Charles Playhouse, Boston

Berkshire Playhouse 1961 Summer Season (Co-Producer/ Director/ Actor):   Stockbridge, Massachusetts
Between Seasons; Breath of Spring; Marriage go Round; Susannah and the Elders; Teahouse of the August Moon; Ten Little Indians ((housekeeper); *Arsenic and Old Lace; Invitation to a March; Roar Like a Dove* and *South Pacific.*

| 1961 | Trelawney of the Wells(Mrs. Telfer) | Equity Library |
| (cont.) | | Theatre, NYC |

| 1962 | A Passage To India (Mrs. Turton) | Ambassador Theater, New York |

Berkshire Playhouse 1962 Summer Season
(Co-Producer/ Director/ Actor):
 A Streetcar Named Desire; Send Me No Flowers; You Never Know; Murder at the Vicarage (Miss Marple); *Under the Yum Yum Tree; The King and I; Life With Father; Miss Lucy; The Pleasure of his Company;* and *See How They Run.*

Stockbridge, Massachusetts

| 1963 | *The Invincible Mr. Disraeli* (Mrs. Gladstone) | TV FILM (Hallmark) |

Berkshire Playhouse 1963 Summer Season
(Co-Producer/ Director/ Actor):
 The Grass is Greener; A Shot in the Dark; Lady Audley's Secret; The Cat and the Canary; The Pajama Game; Little Mary Sunshine and *The Corn is Green* (Miss Moffat)

Stockbridge, Massachusetts

| 1964 | Judy marries Colgate Salsbury June 10, 1964 | |

Berkshire Playhouse 1964 Summer Season
(Co-Producer/ Director/ Actor):
 The Time of the Cuckoo; Come Blow Your Horn; The Silver Cord; Journey to Bahia; My Fair Lady (Mrs. Higgins); *As You Like It; Night Must Fall* and *Guys and Dolls.*

Stockbridge, Massachusetts

1965	Yarmouth Playhouse Summer Season	Cape Cod,
	George Washington Slept Here (as director)	Massachusetts
	On A Clear Day ...(Lady Insdale)	Colonial Theatre, Boston
	Major Barbara (Lady Undershaft)	Charles Playhouse, Boston 1966

1966	Divorces Robert Grose	New York City
	Sergeant Musgrave's Dance (Mrs. Hitchcock)	Theatre de Lys, NYC
	Blythe Spirit (Mrs. Bradman)	TV FILM (Hallmark)

| 1967 | *The Importance of Being Ernest* (Lady Bracknell) and *Misalliance* (Mrs Tarleton) *Stephen D.* (Mrs. Dedalus) | Cincinnati, Playhouse- in the Park,OH |
| | *The Importance of Being Ernest* (Lady Bracknell) | 74th Street Theatre NYC Trinity Sq, Providence RI |

1968	*A Madrigal of Shakespeare* (director)	Theatre De Lys, NYC
	Years of the Locust (co-producer w/ Trinity Sq.)	Edinburgh Festival, Scotland
	Nottingham, England	
	King John (Queen Elinor of Aquitaine)	Nottingham Playhouse
	School for Scandal (Mrs. Candour)	
	The Seagull (Paulina)	
1969	University of Washington, Seattle taught Speech and Drama (5 years)	
	A Day in the Death of Joe Egg (Grace)	Seattle Repertory Theatre
1970	*The Miser* (Frosine)	Seattle Repertory Theatre
	The Birthday Party (Meg)	ACT, Seattle
1971	*The Heiress* (Aunt Penniman)	ACT, Seattle
	Hadrian VII (Mrs. Crowe)	ACT, Seattle
1971-1974	English Summer Theatre School under aegis of University of Washington 1975	
	Returns to New York City and continues the school as	
1975-1988	The Joan White English Theatre School (Students perform at Edinburgh Festival every year)	NYC and London
1978	*The Devil's Disciple* by Shaw (Mrs Dudgeon)	Meadowbrook, Rochester MI
1979	*Bedroom Farce* (standby for Delia)	National Tour
1981	*Bedroom Farce* (Delia)	Gryphon Th. ONT
	Just Between Ourselves (Margery)	McCarter Th., NJ
1982	*To Grandmother's House We Go* (standby for Eva Le Gallienne)	Baltimore, MD and Palm Beach, FL
1982-1983	*Alice in Wonderland* (alternate for Le Gallienne)	Virginia Theatre NYC
1983	*Alive to tell the Tale* – Joan White monologue	Lincoln Center
	Returns to London and Chelsea	
1984-1995	The Next Stage Company concurrent with Joan White English Theatre School(Producing plays as showcase for young actors)	
1986	*The Singing Detective* (Mrs. Adams)	BBC-TV Serial

1988	*Bed* (one of The Couple)	National Theatre
	Heinz Baked Bean Commercial	TV
1989	Fry's *One Thing More* (Director)	Whitby Abbey
	One Way Out (Mary)	TV FILM
1990	*Some Lie and Some Die* (Granny Peckham)	TV Series
	Jeeves and Wooster (Old woman) (1st episode)	Granada TV
1992	*Conflict of Interest* (Mrs. Craig)	Kinsey TV Series
1994	*The Wimbledon Poisoner* (Vera Loomis)	BBC-TV Series

1995   Enters Denville Hall, Actors Retirement Home,
Northwood, Middlesex

1999   Joan White dies on June 8th at Denville Hall.